Polish Parishes
of the Diocese of La Crosse
NINETEENTH & TWENTIETH CENTURIES

by REVEREND JANUSZ KOWALSKI, Ph.D.

Point Publications, Inc.
Stevens Point, Wisconsin 2013

Polish Parishes

of the Diocese of La Crosse

NINETEENTH & TWENTIETH CENTURIES

by REVEREND JANUSZ KOWALSKI, Ph.D.

Point Publications, Inc.
Stevens Point, Wisconsin 2013

*"Polish Parishes of the Diocese of La Crosse
Nineteenth & Twentieth Centuries"*
Reverend Janusz Kowalski, Ph.D.

Graphic design: Monika Pawlak

Copyright © 2013 Rev. Janusz Kowalski, Ph.D. All rights reserved.

ISBN 978-0-9837283-5-1

Printed in the United States of America

LA CROSSE

Found by the Author of This Work

Earth has her scenes, where Nature's hand
Has wrought with more than common skill,
Where winding brook, indented land,
Projecting rock, and verdant hill, –
Where ev'ry object, far abroad,
Seems brightened by the smile of God.

"Twere vain, with philosophic eye,
To watch the moving of the soul,
Or ask the throbbing bosom, why
So free the blissful passions roll,
While such fair forms, of heavenly art,
Impress their image on the heart.

There are some spots, where sorrow's tears
Fall bright as drops of pearly dew,
Where, throwing off the weight of years,
Age dreams of youthful days anew;
A hope comes joyous through the gloom,
That long has thickened round the tomb.

Oh! there are sports, where pious thought
Views God, in nobler majesty;
Places, where all is grand, – and naught
Above, beneath the bending sky,
But seems to mirror forth a ray
Of changeless, uncreated day.

And such, La Crosse, thy happy seat,
'Mid tow'ring hill, and shady grove;
Where bounding waters rudely meet,
And blending in fraternal love,
Invite the steamer, in her pride,
To tempt the mighty, rolling tide.

TABLE OF CONTENTS

ACKNOWLEDGEMENTS 13
STUDIES OF POLISH PARISHES IN WISCONSIN 15
    List of English Terms and Abbreviations used in the book 21
    The translations of the patrons of the churches 21
INTRODUCTION 23
CHAPTER I:
CATHOLIC CHURCH AMONG THE POLISH IMMIGRANTS
DURING THE SECOND HALF OF NINETEENTH CENTURY 29
    Diocese of La Crosse Boundary Changes (1868-2000) 35
CHAPTER II:
ORIGIN AND DEVELOPMENT OF POLISH PARISHES IN THE DIOCESE OF LA CROSSE 41
    Polish Parishes during 1868-1905 44
        1. St. Michael the Archangel, North Creek 44
        2. St. Stanislaus, Arcadia 48
        3. St. Boniface, Chetek 51
        4. SS. Peter and Paul, Weyerhaeuser 55
        5. Assumption of the Blessed Virgin Mary, Strickland 58
        6. St. Stanislaus, Superior 62
        7. Most Holy Family, Ashland 64
        8. St. Mary's, Hurley 67
        9. Holy Family, Poniatowski 69
        10. SS. Peter and Paul, Independence 72
        11. St. Hedwig, Poznan 76
        12. Sacred Heart of Jesus, Cassel 81
        13. St. Bartholomew, Mill Creek 84

  14. Holy Cross, La Crosse 87

  15. St. John Cantius, Fairchild 89

  16. St. Lawrence, Grand Rapids (Wisconsin Rapids) 91

  17. Holy Rosary, Sigel 93

  18. Sacred Heart and St. Wenceslaus, Pine Creek 97

  19. Polish Church, Centralia 100

  20. St. Adalbert, Town of McMillan 101

Polish Parishes Included in the Diocese of La Crosse after 1905 103

  1. St. Bronislava, Plover 103

  2. St. Stanislaus Kostka, Stevens Point 107

  3. St. Michael, Wausau 111

  4. St. Michael, Junction City 115

  5. St. Peter, Stevens Point 119

  6. Sacred Heart of Jesus, Polonia 126

  7. St. Casimir, Town of Hull 132

  8. St. Mary of Czestochowa, Stanley 135

  9. Our Lady of Scapular, Fancher (also known as
    the Church of Our Lady of Mount Carmel) 141

  10. St. John the Baptist, Belmont 144

  11. St. Adalbert, Rosholt 147

  12. Immaculate Conception of the Blessed Virgin Mary, Torun 149

  13. St. Stanislaus, Lublin 152

  14. St. Ladislaus, Bevent 154

  15. St. Florian, Hatley 156

  16. St. John the Baptist, Peplin 159

  17. St. Methodius, Pilot Knob 162

CHAPTER III:
DIOCESAN AND RELIGIOUS CLERGY AND NUNS 165

  The Origin and Place of Education and Formation 167

  Female Congregations of Religious Communities in Wisconsin 173

CHAPTER IV:
PLACES OF WORSHIP OUTSIDE OF THE PARISH CHURCH 177
Cemeteries 177
Crosses and Roadside Shrines 178

CHAPTER V:
RELIGIOUS LIFE PARTICIPATION IN THE DIVINE SERVICES AND SACRAMENTAL LIFE........181
Sacramental Baptism..181
Sacrament of the Sick 182
Funerals...182
Participation of the Faithful in Parish Devotions 183
Sacrament of Marriage and Celebration of the Wedding 183
Traditions and the Religious Customs..185

CHAPTER VI:
INSTITUTIONS, ORGANIZATIONS, AND RELIGIOUS ASSOCIATIONS.......................................201
Schools 201
    The Elementary School of St. Michael, North Creek..209
    The Elementary School of St. Stanislaus, Arcadia 210
    The Elementary School of St. Ladislaus, Bevent...210
    The Elementary School of St. Michael, Wausau 211
    The Elementary School of St. Bronislava, Plover..212
    The Elementary School of St. Stanislaus, Stevens Point.....................................214
    The Elementary School of the Holy Family, Poniatowski 215
    The Elementary School of St. Michael, Junction City..216
    The Elementary School of St. Peter, Stevens Point..217
    The Elementary School of the Sacred Heart of Jesus, Polonia..........................219
    The Elementary School of St. Casimir, Town of Hull 221
    The Elementary School of SS. Peter and Paul, Independence 222
    The Elementary School of St. Hedwig, Thorp 223
    The Elementary School of Sacred Heart of Jesus, Cassel...................................224
    The Elementary School of SS. Peter and Paul, Weyerhaeuser...........................225

Organizations and Children's Associations 227
    Association of Scouts of America (Girls and Boys)..227
    Catholic Youth Organization..229
Organizations, Fraternities, and Societies for Adults 229
    Brotherhood of St. Peter 229
    Servers 230
    The Third Order...230
    Ladies Scapular Society..231
    St. Isidore Society...231
    Blessed Virgin Society..232
    The Parish Council of Catholic Women..232
    Altar Society..232
    Third Order of St. Dominic 233
    The Third Order of St. Francis 233
    Holy Name Society 233
    The Marian Sodality 234
    Catholic Order of Foresters..236
    Parish Choir 237
    Knights of Columbus..237
    Rosary Society 238
    Catholic Daughters of America...239
    Parent-Teacher Association 240
    Athletic Association 240
    Press 241

CHAPTER VII:
NON-ROMAN CATHOLIC RELIGIOUS COMMUNITIES
LOCATED IN POLISH COMMUNITIES (DIOCESE OF LA CROSSE) 243
    The Polish National Catholic Church 243
    Polish Orthodox Church...245
    Polish Independent National Church...246

SUMMARY 249

Motives for Immigration 249

Life in Immigration...250

Poles and Changes..250

Clergy..251

Female Religious Congregations 251

Polish Religious Traditional Customs 251

Ethnics Antagonisms...252

Schools...252

Parish Groups, Associations, and Societies..................................252

Polish Press..253

Schism..253

APPENDICES..255

Directory of Clergy in the Diocese of La Crosse

in the Years 1868-1968 and to 2000..255

Interview with Rev. Joseph Rafacz

Genealogy of the Wisconsin Dioceses..267

Diocese of La Crosse 1868-1905 268

Diocese of La Crosse 1905-1946 269

Diocese of La Crosse 1946-Present..270

Local Catholic Wisconsin.. 271

BIBLIOGRAPHY...273

ACKNOWLEDGEMENTS

This book has been many years in the making, and it wouldn't be complete without acknowledging the people who encouraged and assisted me throughout this journey. The aim of this book was to give a general view of Polish settlements in Wisconsin including the culture, traditions, customs, and the influence of religion in their daily lives, as well as the liturgical traditions which these settlers brought with them. Although written first in Polish as my doctoral thesis, I decided to expand on it and update it to include events up to the turn of the 21st century and translate it into English for publication.

This book required extensive research, and the data was not easily located. The archives personnel at the University of Wisconsin Stevens Point, the research personnel at County Historical Societies, library personnel, priests and employees at many parishes who shared their information with me were the people who made this publication possible. I am also indebted to those enthusiastic individuals who so willingly shared memories of traditions and customs at their Polish parish. Some of these are no longer in existence, and this added a personal touch for their parish.

I would like to extend my deep appreciation to those individuals who assisted with arranging appointments, processing, copying, and editing of my book.

STUDIES OF POLISH PARISHES IN WISCONSIN

"Here the church is faced with the challenge of helping their migrants to keep their faith firm even when they are deprived of the cultural support that existed in their country of origin."

— Message of Pope Benedict XVI for:
"The World Day of Migrants and Refugees," 2012

Until almost the end of the seventeenth century, many Polish immigrants came from the East and from the West. Many of them had sought refuge in Poland from religious persecution and various ethnic cleansings. The country was in fact tolerant, and newcomers from other countries called it paradisium haereticorum et Iudeorum.

Poles at that time were rather unwilling to leave their homeland, although there were some who did leave. The first Poles in America stood on its soil in 1608. The movement of the Polish exile, however, intensified during the political weakening of the country and the disappearance of nationhood in 1795. The emigration at that time was mainly political. Among the political immigrants were protagonists who struggled for Polish independence as well as for the United States. Tadeusz Kosciuszko and Casimir Pulaski who died in the Battle of Savannah, Georgia, in 1779 were among the most famous Polish heroes who left their homeland. In the nineteenth century, the emigration of Poles was mostly driven by economic reasons, although the subsequent decline of national liberation uprisings created wave after wave of new political refugees. The United States was among the most attractive countries for Polish economic migrants.

From the seventeenth century, Polish immigrants settled in the area composed of states such as Virginia, Ohio, Pennsylvania, Kentucky, and Tennessee. In 1834, the Polish immigrants were sent to the states of Illinois and Michigan. Many Polish immigrants, despite their great attachment to the old country, actively engaged in the development of their second, new homeland. Their dedication was especially evident during the Civil War in 1861-1863 when the Poles fought for the North. Some Polish settlers also supported the South. At the same time in the old country, a national uprising took place which is known in history as the January Uprising.

A strong influx of Polish immigrants to the United States occurred during the 1870s. Many of them settled in Texas where in 1854 the first Polish settlement named Panna Maria already existed. Subsequent settlements such as Parisville in Michigan and Polonia in Wisconsin competed with Panna Maria over their importance. Immigrants also chose Wisconsin as their permanent place of living. This state truly resembled their previous homeland due to its similar climatic conditions and geographical location. When they arrived in the central part of Wisconsin, Polish immigrants found the land already partially utilized and managed. Huge trees once grew there but were removed by settlers from Germany, Ireland, and Norway who were already ensconced there. That is how the Polish-American settlements and larger centers evolved in Wisconsin. Often they were named after Polish historical cities or were connected with the immigrant's place of origin. In these settlements, churches were built, and whenever possible, new parish communities were established.

It is impossible to talk or write about the history of Polish Emigration to the United States without regard to the Polish parishes. They always were, and remained the most durable and most flexible Polish institutions even when taking into account all of the factors that were aimed against their activities. Therefore, the conclusion that "American Polonia owns its current status to the activity and efficacy of Polish parishes" raises no doubt.[1]

Polish parishes and American Polonia were very integral compo-

---
1 A. Brozek, *Polonia amerykańska 1854-1939*, Warszawa 1977, p. 52

nents of the American Nation.[2] Everywhere when Poles arrived, Polish ethnic parishes grew. The newcomers directed by self-preservation of religion, culture, and language flocked to "their" churches. If they could not find "their" church nearby, they would build a new one. However, many parishes erected by Polish immigrants in the United States lost or began losing their original character. Some ceased to exist physically.

Therefore, the choice of subject for a book by Rev. Janusz Kowalski, Ph.D., is seen as very appropriate. This book is the result of the author's great effort and is very interesting. In undertaking this effort of researching the history of Polish American parishes in the Diocese of La Crosse, Rev. J. Kowalski joined in recent years more and more vivid streams of research on institutional and personalized forms of piety of Polish Emigration. This trend results in a large extent of all kinds of articles (for example published in Polish Diaspora Studies issued by Catholic University of Lublin in Lublin). There are also several books including a book by professor priest John Walkusz[3] and doctor Agatha Rajski,[4] that are both dedicated to Canadian Polonia which recently enjoys more popularity and raises the interest of many researchers even more than the history of Polish Diaspora in the United States of America. However, Polish Diaspora got to be recognized in other publications such as the monograph by Professor Danuta Piątkowska,[5] Reverend Professor Bolesław Kumor,[6] Sister Genevieve Potaczaly,[7] and numerous smaller contributions which were posted in scientific magazines among them the *Polish American Studies* by M. Czerwińska (Issue 28:2007), J. Pietrzykowski (Issue 27:2006), and S. T. Praskiewicz (Issue 27:2006).

---

2   S. Targosz, *Polonia katolicka w Stanach Zjednoczonych w przekroju*, Detroit, Michigan 1943

3   J. Walkusz, *Polonia i parafia Matki Boskiej Częstochowskiej w London, Ontario*, Lublin-Pelplin 2007

4   A. Rajski, *100 years of Polonia in Windsor 1908-2008*, Windsor 2008

5   D. Piątkowska, *Polish Parishes in New York*, New York-Opole 2002

6   B. Kumor, *The History of Polish roman-catholic St. Joseph Church in Norwich, Conn. 1904-1970*, Norwich 1980; also *SS Cyril and Methodius Parish and the Hartford Polonia 1873-1980*. Garret Printing Inc., 1985; also *Saint Stanislaus Bishop and Martyr Parish*, Translated and edited by Rev. Edward P. Gicewicz, CM, Ed.D., New Heaven, Conn. 1987; also, *Saint Michael the Archangel Parish, Derby Connecticut*, Translated and edited by Rev. Edward P. Gicewicz, CM, Ed.D., Derby 1989: also *History of Polish Catholics and Churches in Connecticut* (1870-1986), Kraków 1990; also *Toward Brooklyn's St. Stanislaus Kostka Parish Centennial*, New York 1992; *A Brief History of St. Joseph's Parish, during 75th Anniversary St. Joseph's Church Suffield, Conn.*, Suffield CT 1993, p. 1-12; also *Geographic Derivation of Polish Emigrants from St Joseph in Rockeville, Ct., Demography Statistics and Economics*, Kraków 1994, p. 202-213

7   G. Potaczala, *Polacy na Trójcowie. History of the Holy Trinity Church in Chicago*, bmw 2006

Still today, the publications by Rev. Kruszka[8] have not lost their value. On the contrary, due to the loss of many source materials, they remain a primary source of information.

Therefore, we should enjoy that Rev. J. Kowalski as a new investigator researched the local Poles in exile. The merits of the Catholic Church in support, maintenance, and sometimes even rescue of the national identity of Poles scattered all over the world are enormous and deserve thorough and insightful research reflections. His book presents interesting and widely unknown information (both in Poland and in the United States) regarding the formation of ethnic parishes (Polish) in the state of Wisconsin.

It is a valuable supplement to the information concerning the history of Polish settlement in North America. It fills the lack of studies existing in the literature that discuss the formation of Polish settlement structures in the state of Wisconsin. Actually, this was the only area in which the peasants of Polish descent formed a compact and relatively numerous types of rural settlements.

The author touches on the development process of the different structures of Polish parishes in the Diocese of La Crosse, one of a few (now five), situated in its territory. Adopted by the author, frames are identified with the territorial borders of the Diocese of La Crosse. Chronologically, the author covers a period of over one hundred years starting with the creation of the diocese and ending with the recent changes of its borders. When preparing to write this book, Rev. Janusz Kowalski, Ph.D., performed very arduous but fruitful work. He not only found information for the parishes that were known to have been started by Polish immigrants but obtained facts and information which allowed him to conclude that Poles created some other parishes and towns. The query was difficult because of the lack of pertinent information in the archives of the churches and diocese that described the beginning of Polish parishes. It was necessary, therefore, to collect the scattered scraps of information and reconstruct the events based on them.

Rev. Janusz Kowalski adopted a thematic narrative which is a fair solution. Also, one should appreciate the additional information in-

---

8   W. Kruszka, *A History of the Poles in America to 1908. Part 1-4*, Washington 1993; *Historia polska w Ameryce. Od czasów najdawniejszych aż do najnowszych*, Vol. 1, Milwaukee, Wisconsin 1937

cluded in the annex of the book. This information facilitates the understanding of these events. The illustrative material is very interesting, and it increases the value of the study. The structure of the book adopted by the author, its layout, and detailed solutions are correct. The author did everything to maximally represent all the issues raised by him in this study. Moreover, he confirmed his acquired ability to build a narrative based on traced, tested, and analyzed source materials. The author demonstrated an ability to analyze the material of diverse origin and capacity and to build a narrative based on facts often derived from very meager sources. He found, expanded on, and discussed the vast majority of printed materials that could be obtained in the United States, and therefore his study is innovative and introduces a series of completely unknown information.

The numerous books of jubilee have proven to be especially valuable when writing, despite the small amount of research included in them and lack of the critical objectivity. No doubt, however, most sources of valuable information are parish archives which being public documents in principle guarantee the reliability of their information. The author used printed parish archives, town histories, and ecclesiastical documents published in the special collections of materials, sermons, and pastoral letters. Rev. Kowalski used in his work a very wide range of sources and publications directly linked to the topic of this research. It is worth noting that the vast majority of them are completely unknown in Poland. This author's great merit is to make these primary sources available to Polish and Polish American scholars interested in the past. At this point, appreciation is in order for the fact that Rev. Kowalski assembled such a broad set of sources and studies to complete his research.

In discussing the history of the parishes, Rev. Kowalski did not miss many institutions and organizations working in parishes among them Catholic schools and education. His book because of its scientific value joins the numerous publications of Professor Dorothy Praszałowicz[9] and Professor Andrew Bonusiak[10] about the formation and the structures of

---

9   D. Praszałowicz, *Amerykańska etniczna szkoła parafialna. Studium porównawcze trzech wybranych odmian instytucji*, Wrocław 1986

10   A. Bonusiak, *Szkolnictwo Polskie w Stanach Zjednoczonych Ameryki w latach 1984-2003. Analiza funkcjonalno-instytucjonalna*, Rzeszów 2004

the current state of those parishes and the condition of education. He also recognizes the works of Professor Adam Wałaszek.[11]

While congratulating Rev. Janusz Kowalski, Ph.D., on successful work, I am convinced that his book will bring many readers to appreciate the great contribution of Poles and the Church in the history and development of the United States. Perhaps it will help some find their ethnic roots so that by being proud of their American homeland in which they were born, grew, and worked, they also can feel proud of the contribution of their Polish ancestors who once came to Wisconsin, their new homeland.

Rev. Professor Stanisław Nabywaniec

Rzeszów, 15 of January 2012, Światowy Dzień Migranta i Uchodźcy

---

[11] A. Wałaszek, *Polish Americans*, Western Reserve Historical Society, Cleveland 2002, p. 185-248

LIST OF ENGLISH TERMS AND ABBREVIATIONS USED IN THE BOOK

Some terms and meanings translated from English to Polish:

Bishop	–	biskup
Priest, Father	–	ksiądz
Sister	–	siostra zakonna
Congregation	–	zgromadzenie
Pastor	–	proboszcz
Monsignor	–	prałat
Mother Provincial	–	matka prowincjalna

THE TRANSLATIONS OF THE PATRONS OF THE CHURCHES

St. Mary of Czestochowa	–	Matka Boża Częstochowska
St. Mary of Perpetual Help	–	old translation: Matka Boża od Nieustającej Pomocy; new translation: Najświętsza Maryja Panna od Nieustającej Pomocy
S.S. Cyril and Methodius	–	święci Cyryl i Metody
St. Bartholomew	–	św. Bartłomiej
St. Hedwig	–	św. Jadwiga
St. James	–	św. Jakub
St. John Cantius	–	św. Jan Kanty
St. Casimir	–	św. Kazimierz
St. Paul	–	św. Paweł
St. Stanislaus Kostka	–	św. Stanisław Kostka
St. Wenceslaus	–	św. Wacław
St. Ladislaus	–	św. Władysław
St. Adalbert	–	św. Wojciech
All Saints	–	Wszyscy Święci
St. Michael	–	św. Michał
St. Bronislava	–	św. Bronisława
St. Peter	–	św. Piotr

Sacred Heart of Jesus	–	Najświętsze Serce Pana Jezusa
St. Lawrence	–	św. Wawrzyniec
St. Florian	–	św. Florian
Holy Cross	–	Święty Krzyż
Holy Rosary	–	Różaniec Święty
St. Methodius	–	św. Metody
St. Boniface	–	św. Bonifacy
Assumption of the Blessed Mary	–	Wniebowzięcie Najświętszej Maryi Panny
St. Stanislaus	–	św. Stanisław

INTRODUCTION

"Homeland is all the land and graves. The nations, who lose memory, lose their lives." These words can be read on one of the gravestones at the oldest cemetery in Zakopane, Poland. Apparently, French Marshal Ferdinand Foch expressed himself in these words. The deeper meaning of these words reminds us that our history should never be forgotten. By taking steps in the present, with all the responsibility we look to the future, forming our actions based on the past and experience. These three dimensions of time should always serve people in their actions.

This work is devoted to the history of Polish immigrants settling during the years 1868-2000 in the Diocese of La Crosse (Wisconsin) in the United States of America. It takes into account the religious and ecclesiastical aspects of their lives. The main idea is to explore their settlements, work, family life, moral values, and faith. It is also to show the process of adaptation and integration with the new environment; the creation of parish communities; participation in various organizations, institutions, and associations, both religious and secular; relations with other nations; the status of the clergy; and what goals drove the Poles to choose life in exile and how, in fact, their lives developed from there. The time frame included in the title of the dissertation covers the years from 1868 to 2000. However, occasionally, it steps outside the chronological boundaries in order to represent facts and events more accurately. The earlier chronological boundary represents the year of establishment of the Diocese of La Crosse and the establishment of its first bishop. The later boundary, however, is represented by the last reestablishment of new borders of this diocese. The territorial scope of this study stated in the title covers an area of the Diocese of La Crosse in its historical boundaries, that is, both the area now belonging to the diocese as well as those areas that once were part of the territorial area of the Diocese of La Crosse and now belong to other units of church administration in the local church.

The main sources of information are from parochial and diocesan archives and library collections, and also, special materials from the library of the University of Stevens Point. Most information on the above mentioned issues is only in English. During the search of precious and valuable information, the Historical Societies proved to be very useful. Information previously lacking was found because of their well-archived information on the history of individual counties and cities. In order to objectively present the sometimes distant past, a number of publications and studies by Polish and foreign authors were used.

Many problems were encountered during the search of archives, library materials, and research. The main problem was the complete or almost complete lack of sources of information about Polish parishes. Sources were sought at the Diocese of La Crosse, Diocese of Superior, and Diocese of Green Bay. Virtually, none of the documents pertaining to Polish churches and communities have survived that could be used in this dissertation. Archives were empty due to the principle enforced by the dioceses that what is old is useless and needs to be destroyed to make room for more current materials. There was a lot of contradiction and lack of reliability in the transmission of historical data in the materials that were actually discovered. Fortunately, in recent years, the approach to these types of materials has changed. For several years now, we have seen a slight increase in people's interest in history. Recently, many historians of the Church began searching for residual information and documents.

Personal inquiry was required to obtain information regarding most parishes described in the Diocese of La Crosse. Unfortunately, these parishes did not have documents. Only traces of memories were found that pertained to the history of a particular parish, its formation, and activities. In many cases, the only source of information came from interviews with pastors or administrators.

The County Historical Societies have proven to be a great help in this search. In the archives of these institutions, one could find numerous references to parishes and the employed clergy. Books there contain references to events relating to the construction of the churches, as well as the religious life of the society in that particular county. These references also contain people's names.

Another problem was finding any materials pertaining to churches and villages that no longer exist (a substantial part of this study includes the churches that today no longer exist). These churches and chapels have been demolished or sold or converted to other purposes such as parking lots. The cemetery chapel in the Parish of Saint Michael the Archangel in North Creek is one example.

Parish books which were the primary source of information on some Polish parishes do not have the specified authors and do not include the place of where they were issued. Generally, the state of Wisconsin is entered as a place of publication. Many of them cannot be regarded as an objective source of information. Most of these items are copies of publications prescribed from generation to generation depending on their needs. In these parish books, we may indeed find a great deal of information on the individual parishes; however, we cannot have too much confidence in them especially as relates to specific dates or names of individuals. Usually, they were issued on the occasion of anniversaries of the parish so not much attention was given to important details. Nevertheless, they are important because sometimes they are the only source of information about the parish. Some materials (magazines) were found in which it is impossible to find information about the authors. Some people gave out conflicting information about the same case. This did not help in the study, and sometimes, it constituted a great obstacle. This was true of information regarding the beginnings of settlement in the area of Stevens Point. Often these sources were like stories, and thus, they lacked the character of critical description of the events.

The authors who published in foreign languages, English or German, were not interested in the Polish communities and their lives so the information posted there is very scarce. Of necessity, therefore, this work was based on secondary sources of information of little credibility. Despite such a fragile source of authoritative information, the writing of this work was a necessity. As the years pass, many traces of information that still exist today can be wiped out of the memory or can be irretrievably gone.

Even today, the descendants of Polish immigrants are not able to indicate where in their neighborhood or their city Polish parishes existed. Historical consciousness about the presence of Poles and Polish parishes in the state of Wisconsin is sadly diminishing, and when compared with a standard American Polish community center in Chicago, it is very poor.

In order to achieve the objectives of this study, philosophical, analytical, and retrospective methods were used. The comparative philosophy was used to analyze a variety of historical texts that were available and then attempt to summarize the information contained in them. Application of this method of research forced the following structure of this work which is divided into seven different chapters, each of which deals with a separate issue.

The first chapter entitled "Catholic Church among Polish Immigrants during the Second Half of the Nineteenth Century" discusses the causes of European immigration especially the Polish population in North America. The nineteenth century was a very difficult time for residents of Europe especially for the Poles. They lost their homeland, and their country disappeared from the world's map. The purpose of the chapter is, therefore, to show the motives that guided those who left their families, towns, and villages, and whether or not the conditions which they found in a new place met their expectations; what kind of role a church membership played for them; their devotion to the Catholic faith in their personal and social life; how they referred to the structures and church authorities; how they managed their local parish communities; what motivated them while choosing their place of residence; and what their organizational skills were like in comparison to other ethnic groups that shared the new land with them. The end of the chapter will introduce changes to the boundaries of the Diocese of La Crosse and their impact on the religious life of individuals and parishes.

In the second chapter entitled "Origin and Development of Polish Parishes in the Diocese of La Crosse" the situation of Polish parishes will be presented and discussed in detail. Administrative boundaries of the Diocese of La Crosse, Wisconsin, changed repeatedly. Therefore, the aim of the chapter is to show how these changes affected the spiritual life of Poles living here. The objective is to present the process of emergence and expansion of some parishes and the decline of others. It will also seek to establish the status of the financial resources, personnel, and the number of Polish parishes in the area as well as the motivation which guided the founders of the first Polish parishes in this area. One part is also dedicated to the issue of the language of the liturgy, the appearance of the temples, and the cost borne by their founders.

The third chapter entitled "Diocesan and Religious Clergy and Nuns" is devoted to the origin of the working clergy in the Diocese of La Crosse. The main questions pertaining to the clergy are to determine where they came from; what their education was and where it was acquired; whether there were seminaries for educating priests of Polish immigrants; and the level of their education. Another part of the chapter is dedicated to religious orders operating in the Diocese of La Crosse, and the relationship that prevailed between them and the clergy of the diocese. Relationships between Polish and American clergy will be presented with special focus on church administration in the diocese. The last part of the chapter will be devoted to the work of the clergy in the parishes, the beginnings of pastoral work among the Polish community in America, and the analysis of the motivation which guided the Polish clergy who chose to work in exile.

The fourth chapter, "Places of Worship," is devoted to the analysis of property belonging to the parish. Attention will be given in detail to the legal status of cemeteries, the process of their acquisition, the cost incurred by the parish, the law, and practices in the management of cemeteries and churches, and the applicable rules for funerals. The next part of this chapter will show the importance of cultivating Polish traditions among the immigrants. A section of the chapter will be devoted to roadside crosses and chapels. The author will explore the role they played for the Polish people who tended them, what prayers were used, and whether they played a different role besides their religious significance.

"Religious Life" is the title of the fifth chapter which deals, among other things, with an analysis of the conditions prevailing between the parishioners and priests who were responsible for their spiritual development. The chapter will attempt to answer the following questions: which sacraments were granted most frequently; what requirements needed to be fulfilled by those who asked for them; what did integration with other ethnic groups look like; how frequently did the new immigrants participate in different church celebrations and Masses; and did the customs and traditions brought from their native country help to integrate them with other nationalities, or did they interfere with mutual understanding?

The sixth chapter entitled "Institutions, Organizations, and Religious Associations" will attempt to show the social life of Polish immigrants, their contribution to the American culture, as well as the interests of their individual members. Among other things, this chapter will discuss the education system: what the Catholic schools looked like, what they offered in contrast to public schools, the costs being borne by the parish for the construction of new schools, what conditions prevailed in them, what was the number of students, what language and which courses were taught, who were the teachers, and what was the mission of nuns in parochial schools. Then the discussion will focus on a variety of Polish associations and organizations while exploring their purposes as well as the kind of members who joined them. At the end of the chapter, the goals and tasks of the brotherhoods and groups in the parishes will be explored. This part of the chapter will also examine the role of the local press.

In the last chapter of the work entitled "Non-Roman Catholic Religious Communities Located in Polish Communities (Diocese of La Crosse)" a detailed description of the creation and development of the Polish National Church will be presented. The range and activity of the Polish Orthodox Church will be discussed. The Polish Independent National Church will complete this dissertation.

CHAPTER I

CATHOLIC CHURCH AMONG THE POLISH IMMIGRANTS DURING THE SECOND HALF OF NINETEENTH CENTURY

The organization of the Church and its structure among immigrants in North America was for many the symbol of freedom, the place of prosperity and immense opportunities for energetic and ambitious people. It was alluring to many and appeared as a place of asylum for those who were persecuted on political, racial, or religious principles and for those who fled from famine or military service.[12]

Every year, hundreds of thousands of immigrants arrived in the United States. They came from around the world for work and the hope for a better tomorrow. They came to America in most cases after encouragement by relatives or friends. Also, some of the larger, dynamically developing American companies used their agents to recruit new employees from different countries. These agents often using misleading promises that encouraged people to leave for the United States. In 1920, the U. S. government, at the request of Congress, introduced the official registration of all immigrants coming to America. By 1900, according to statistics, 20 million immigrants arrived in the United States. This happened mostly after 1865 and the Civil War and was the largest number of immigrants who came to America in the history of this country. The reason for the escalation of immigration was that the rapidly developing country was in need of cheap labor. The variable that promoted the emigration to America was the difficult conditions of life,

---

[12] G. B. Tindall, D. E. Shi, *Historia Stanów Zjednoczonych*, Poznań 2002, p. 792

mainly in Europe, because of political persecution. Therefore, many left their countries and came to America to the new "Promised Land." Historical sources indicate that "before 1880 immigrants were mainly of German and Celtic descent, arriving mostly from Northern and Western Europe. However, in the seventies certain signs of change become apparent. The increased portion of immigrants consisted largely from people of Romanesque and Slavic origin, as well as Jews from Eastern Europe and South America. …Among these newcomers were Italians, Hungarians, Czechs, Slovaks, Poles, Serbs, Croats, Slovenians, Russians, Romanians, and Greeks."[13]

Differences between immigrants were substantial in terms of culture, religion, and language. Seafaring became the main means of travel to America. At the beginning, the immigrants would arrive on ships to Canada and from there took trains to the American territory. At a later time, the direct sea route to New York was opened. Immigrants, exhausted after many months of traveling, were frantically looking for a place to live as well as looking for work. They were hired by all sorts of people including representatives of factories, mines, and different production facilities. The type of employment had a significant influence on prosperity and accommodations in their later life.

Most immigrants, including Poles, tried to stay together in national groups working and inhabiting different regions of America. Cohabitation also gave them a sense of security, the opportunity to nurture native traditions and customs, speak their native language, and practice their religion.[14]

Conditions for the newcomers were often appalling. Migrants arriving from Europe lived in harsh conditions (several people in one room). Payment for a night cost about five cents per person. People would be locked up in small rented flats where the spread of disease and epidemics was not uncommon. Many people died without receiving medical care due to the lack of money and insurance.

The reluctance of Americans to accept immigrants became the second obstacle that they encountered. Americans believed that their exis-

---

13   Ibid., p. 793
14   E. Kleban, T. V. Gromada, 'The Polish Americans', *The Polish Review*, Vol. 2:976, no. 3, p. 43

tence was threatened and that the influx of a cheap workforce might aggravate the economic status of their families. Americans, mostly Protestants, often did not understand nor did they want to accept the religious differences of the newcomers most of whom were Roman Catholics.[15] Those who came to America much earlier thought they should occupy higher social positions. The Northern European immigrants who were mostly Irish and fluent in English had more chances to find better employment. In fact, the clergy of Irish origin had a much better chance of achieving a position in the hierarchy of the Catholic Church.

The Poles came to the United States in the three separate periods of time that are closely linked to historical events in Poland.[16]

- Colonial emigration in the years 1608 to the mid-eighteenth century
- Political emigration in the second half of the eighteenth century to 1865
- Economical emigration from 1865 until 1939

Even though not confirmed by historical sources of legendary communications, it is known that Poles also made their way to America during the Middle Ages and also during expeditions in 1492.[17] The first historically documented arrival of the Poles is linked to the second transport of settlers that arrived on the *Mary and Margaret* (ship) on October 1, 1608. The arrival of the Poles was due to the existing demand for professionals capable of processing wood and the production of a variety of other popular products. They lived together with the other expedition participants in the settlement of Jamestown.[18] Polish émigrés from the last of these groups came mostly from lower socioeconomic classes, coming from farms, and not having any education.

It is extremely difficult to figure out how many of these immigrants

---

[15] R. Aubert, P. E. Grunican, J. T. Ellis, 'Kościół w Stanach Zjednoczonych od roku 1850', in: *Historia Kościoła 1848 do czasów współczesnych*, Vol. 5, Warszawa 1985, p. 192

[16] Parish Book, *SS. Peter & Paul Church 1875-1975*, Wisconsin 1975, p. 29

[17] W. Kruszka, *Historja polska w Ameryce*. Od czasów najdawniejszych aż do najnowszych, t. 1, Milwaukee, Wisconsin 1937, p. 15-20, 32-34; W. Słabczyński, *Polscy podróżnicy i odkrywcy*, Warszawa 1988, p. 235-241

[18] L. Pastusiak, *Kościuszko, Pułaski i inni*, Toruń 2003, p. 10-11

came here because of records problems. For example, the U.S. Immigration and Naturalization Service quite frequently changed regulations and laws that applied particularly to the newcomers from Poland.

In times of increased immigration, Poland was under foreign rule. Poles that arrived during these times were frequently identified and classified by the nationality of the partitions where they were from instead of as Poles. Some stated their arrival as only temporary while others immediately opted for permanent residence. There were problems with the identification of arriving Poles perpetrated by American officials who were not familiar with Poles.[19] There were problems on both sides both among immigrants and among the officials who received them. Most of the immigrants arriving in America would travel into the country, or to land they had already heard about, or to an area which was inhabited by some relatives or friends. They sought new places for themselves and their families looking for new and better living conditions. Most of the time, they would choose sites similar to those in which they lived in Poland with a similar climate and terrain. Most of them were planning on going back to their homeland after a few years of work in order to save up enough money to buy land in their country.

According to statistics, in the years 1899 to 1913, about 1.5 million Polish immigrants arrived in America. Among them, 47% came from Galicia, 49% from the Russian sector of partitioned Poland, and only 4% from the Prussian sector. Between 1870 and 1900, most of the arriving men were unmarried and between 14-44 years in age. Statistics show that 90% of the arrivals were engaged in farming before emigrating to America.[20] Most immigrants from the Polish territories came here and settled before the beginning of the Civil War. They came from the Kashubian area and part of West Prussia (Gdańsk, Bydgoszcz, Poznań, and Gniezno). This was one of the largest waves of immigration in America.

One of the states that resembled Poland because of its climate and geographic location was the state of Wisconsin. Therefore, Wisconsin was often chosen as a place of settlement by Polish immigrants because

---

19 H. Znaniecka Lopata, *Polish Americans*, New Jersey 1976, p. 33
20 J. S. Pula, *Polish Americans an ethnic community*, New York 1995, p. 18-19

it reminded them of their abandoned homeland. In the central part of Wisconsin, Poles found the land already partly occupied and managed (after excision of large areas of trees). The arrival of settlers to the area from Germany, Ireland, and Norway contributed largely to this situation. They were already ensconced here when the Poles arrived.

Among many things the Poles brought with them from the "old country" were their cultural values. Among them, the value most deeply rooted in their minds and hearts was their faith. It was their faith that became the main source of strength necessary to survive in the new reality. To create the places for immigrants in different parts of America whether in small groups or larger urban clusters, housing developments were created. However, the most important element in these communities was to start a Polish parish and to build a new church. They always found the resources and land for the establishment of the church.

First, while settling in a new place, Polish immigrants formed a religious commonwealth supervised by a commuting priest. The next step was the actual construction of the new church as well as the rectory and then an application to the bishop for a priest's placement in that particular Polish settlement. The parish church was not only a place of worship, but also a place that enabled the people to cultivate Polish customs and traditions and to share them with each other. Polish immigrants were characterized with a strong faith, devotion to traditions, and patriotism.[21] With the establishment of the parish, strong efforts were made to build schools to enable children of Polish descent to learn their native language and religion. The next step in the organization of society was the establishment of various kinds of associations and organizations. These were secular organizations designed to help the community and to promote the development of a variety of individual interests.

Polish immigrants had many problems with the acceptance of authority, structure, and style of ministry presented by the Catholic Church in America. The American Church, to organize and streamline their own structures, insisted very strongly on the use of the English language in the church and the elimination of the Polish language, traditions, and customs of their homeland. Many times Poles were forced

---

21 Ibid., p. 21

to become members of a parish that was totally foreign to them. They were unable to use their native language and had to participate in Sunday services celebrated in other languages. They tried to form parish communities with the Germans, Italians, and Irish. However, they encountered many problems on this level. Often English speaking parishes were against the creation of other Catholic communities that contained a mostly Polish population.[22]

As a result of this situation, the Polish Catholic National Church was created. Due to the misunderstanding of the ecclesiastical hierarchy and the superficial treatment of immigrating Poles during the years between 1870 and 1924, the number of Polish Catholic National Churches and its members increased enormously. During this time, 1600 Polish National Churches were established including 336 Polish churches, 346 German churches, and 214 Italian churches.[23] The Poles felt abandoned, helpless, and were often treated with disdain. Hence, this was their answer. After some time, the Church hierarchy understood its mistake. Appropriate decisions were taken at the diocesan level. Orders were given that priests in their pastoral work were to use the individual national languages and that they cultivate in the parishes the customs and traditions of immigrants brought from their homeland.

The Polish initiative became very important in this respect. Polish community leaders organized a meeting on October 3, 1873, in Michigan under the leadership of Rev. Joseph Gieryka and Rev. Vincent Barzynski. During this meeting, a new committee of influential people was elected who began to create an organization with the task of defending the Polish in exile. That is how the Union of the Polish Roman Catholic Church was created. Its objectives were to preserve values such as faith and patriotism, promote Polish schools and help young people, as well as to build the spirit of Polish-American cooperation. During this time, many other smaller and larger organizations were established which had similar goals. These efforts aimed at strengthening the faith of their ancestors, the spirit of national unity, and patriotism of the immigrants brought definite results in the future.

---

22   D. S. Buczek, "Polish-Americans and the Roman Catholic Church," *The Polish Review*, Vol. 2:976, No. 3, p. 43

23   J. S. Pula, *Polish Americans an ethnic community*, p. 40

DIOCESE OF LA CROSSE
BOUNDARY CHANGES (1868-2000)

The origin of the Catholic Church in the state of Wisconsin goes back in time to the pontificate of Pope Clement X.[24] A petition from the French Church was submitted to the Pope to appoint a new Diocese of Quebec in Canada. The intent was to extend the work of evangelization and pastoral care in areas which were not under the jurisdiction of the Church at that time. As a result of this action, Pope Clement X, after various consultations, created the Diocese of Quebec on October 1, 1674. This was the beginning of work in the completely new area. The organization of the work of evangelization and pastoral care was supervised by the bishop of the Diocese of Quebec. This situation of legal and administrative control lasted for over one hundred years until 1784 which marked the end of the official jurisdiction of the bishop of Quebec over part of Wisconsin.

With the passing of time, the composition of the population of the diocese changed rather quickly. Besides the local Indian tribes, more and more immigrants were arriving from all over the world but specifically from Europe. Out of concern for the Church in America, Pope Pius VI made a very important decision. He promoted Rev. John Carroll as bishop in order for him to preside over all missions and churches in all provinces in the New Republic of the United States of North America. Rev. John Carroll was the first ordained bishop in the United States.[25] He was ordained in England on August 15, 1790, and in December of that same year, he came to America.

The new bishop did not desire to promote a German or Irish church, but he wanted to concentrate on creating a strong and solid new American Church. The newly arrived immigrants proved to be very helpful in the accomplishment of this task. They realized that the number of new Catholics was enormous, and the future of the new American Church

---

24 Clement X (born on July 13, 1590 and died on July 22, 1676) ruled the Church from 1670 to 1676 and was elected to the Holy See at the age of 79 after a long service in Vatican diplomacy, http://www.ratzingerbendettoxvi.com/clementeX.htm (December 20, 2008).

25 G. E. Fisher, *Dusk is my Dawn*, La Crosse 1969, p. 7

would largely depend on them. During this time, emigrated Catholics resided mostly in Maryland, Kentucky, and Pennsylvania. They constituted a very large religious group of around 35,000 people.[26] They were actually the first wave of settlers from exile.

Another influx of Catholic immigration occurred during the 1850s. Seven hundred eleven thousand immigrants arrived at that time from Ireland, from Germany about 152,000 came, and from France 65,000 settled. At the same time, new areas of missionary and evangelism emerged. The fate of the state of Wisconsin also endured some transformation especially during the War of 1812. Bishop Flaget of the Diocese of Milwaukee which covered a huge area of land in the north of the state toward Lake Superior decided that it was not the right time to take care of the land and its Catholic inhabitants along the Ohio River. Therefore, the Catholics who lived there were completely on their own. The Church hierarchy seeing the enormous spiritual needs of believers and guided by the need to improve pastoral activities directed the request to Rome asking to nominate a new bishop[27] to preside over the vast area of Cincinnati, Ohio, and Michigan which was part of Wisconsin. The request was accepted, and Rev. Edward Fenwick was appointed as the new bishop. He was the first bishop who for the sake of the faithful entrusted to him personally visited Catholics in Wisconsin. However, this state still waited for its own bishop.

President James K. Polk on May, 29, 1848, established Wisconsin as the thirtieth state in America with a population of 250,000 that increased each year. Farming was the primary focus, although on a smaller scale, some industries were being developed. In Wisconsin, there were discoveries and the mining of lead, iron, marble, copper, silver, and precious clay for brick making. There were, however, not enough hands to work the extremely fertile land as well as remove the trees and process them. This situation developed very rapidly, and labor was urgently needed. From 1840-1880 in America, the number of migrant workers coming to the state of Wisconsin as well as the number of immigrants from Europe that settled here increased significantly (a large number of

---

26 R. Aubert, E. Crunican, J. T. Ellis, *Katolicyzm w świecie anglosaskim*, in: L. J. Rogier, R. Aubert, M. D. Knowles, *Historia Kościoła 1848 do czasów współczesnych*, Vol. 5, Warszawa 1985, p. 191
27 Ibid., p. 9

which were Poles). As a result of that, by 1860, the population of the state of Wisconsin escalated to 700,000 people.

In 1866 in Baltimore during the second meeting of the Plenary Synod on the diocesan level, an agreement was reached to create two new dioceses: Green Bay and La Crosse. On the basis of the projects from Baltimore, Pope Pius IX approved and called upon the formation of these new dioceses.[28] In the region of the newly created Diocese of Green Bay, there resided 10,000 Catholics and twenty-five priests. On the other hand, in the Diocese of La Crosse, there were eighteen priests who led over 30,000 Catholics. The boundaries of the diocese show that the Diocese of La Crosse extended from the Wisconsin River on the east side to the Mississippi River to the west. On the south side, it covered a region from the point of where the Wisconsin River emptied into the Mississippi and then extended all the way to Lake Superior on the north.[29]

In June 1868, Rev. Michael Heiss[30] was nominated as the new bishop of the newly established Diocese of La Crosse. He was consecrated on September 6, 1868, at St. John's Cathedral in Milwaukee. The feast of the consecration of the new bishop was attended by three thousand Catholics. Bishop Heiss was consecrated by Bishop Henni who was assisted by other oligarchs: Bishop John Hennessey from the Diocese of Dubuque and Bishop Thomas Grace from the Diocese of St. Paul.[31] The new bishop, of German origin, set a date of the 29th of September to assume his duties in the diocese. After the farewells held in St. Mary's Church and in Saint Francis Seminary, the new bishop embarked on the journey to embrace his duties as the head of the diocesan church in La Crosse.

According to historical sources, it was not the first time that the new

---

28 W. Kruszka, *A History of the Poles in America to 1908, Part 4*, Washington D.C. 1993, p. 93

29 G. E. Fisher, *Dusk is my Dawn*, p. 24; F. Crane, *Catholic History of La Crosse, Wisconsin*, La Crosse 1904, p. 7. In the book: H. H. Heaming, *History of the Catholic Church in Wisconsin*, Milwaukee 1896 p. 757 contains the number of 15 priests working in the Diocese of La Crosse. The author of this development is in favor of the Heaming version which gives the number of 15 priests, because it is the oldest historical development and its author had perhaps the greatest potential to reach the sources.

30 Michael Heiss – The first ordinary of the Diocese of La Crosse in the period from March 3, 1868 to March 14, 1880 when he was appointed coadjutor archbishop of the diocese of cum iure successionis Milwaukee, Bishop of Milwaukee (1881-1890).

31 G. E. Fisher, *Dusk is my Dawn*, p. 24

bishop had been in contact with the area of the new diocese. Seven years earlier, he corresponded in writing with the missionary who worked on the north side in the basin of the Mississippi River and resided in Eau Claire. So his shepherd's mission was launched much earlier. On arrival in La Crosse, the new bishop was surprised by many things. There was a shortage of clergy, as well as a shortage of places to worship, not to mention the small number of Catholic schools, and the poor level of education in existing schools.

The first and the oldest Catholic temple in the seat of the Diocese of La Crosse was a church dedicated to the Virgin Mary in La Crosse. The new bishop noted that it was the only church in town, and it was being attended by five different nationalities. He realized that the needs were great. Under his leadership, the hard work began to improve the functioning of the diocesan church organization and the work of the clergy. Already in 1870, a new church was built and consecrated in La Crosse which was dedicated to St. Joseph. With this new church, a parish community was organized for the people of German origin. Over time, the church became the cathedral of the bishop.

In other places in the diocese, construction had begun on creating new churches and parishes depending on the needs of the people in the region and existing budgets. The bishop supported all of the initiatives pertaining to the creation of new places of worship. He blessed all the new temples, and he dedicated the foundation stones of new churches throughout the diocese. This portion of the diocese developed very well.

The next problem was the creation of new schools. Bishop Heiss realized immediately that Catholic education in this region was very poorly developed. Being an educated man himself, he was acutely aware of the importance of good education. He took the need for improvement of the education system to heart and during his service as a bishop, he supported all actions that lead to the elevation of the level of parochial education in the diocese. When he was transferred to assume the duties of the Archbishop of Milwaukee on May 11, 1880, he left the diocese with twenty-four new schools with a noticeably higher level of general and religious education.[32]

32　H. H. Heaming, *History of the Catholic Church in Wisconsin*, p. 757

Another problem that called for immediate attention was the relatively small number of clergy in the diocese. With time, however, the situation slowly improved. In 1878, there were already forty-seven priests who performed their priestly ministry over 40,000 Catholics.

Special attention should be given to the year 1871 during which Bishop Heiss motivated by his fellow priests decided to visit various Indian reservations. The bishop was emotionally touched and surprised by the Indians' deep faith which he personally experienced during his visit. The opening of the Catholic mission for Indians was the fruitful result of this visit. The bishop appointed several clergy for the missionary work among Indians. These priests came mostly from Saint Francis Seminary in Milwaukee, Wisconsin. Two of them, Rev. Casimir Mogot and Rev. Odorick Derenthal, became over time soul specialists and Indian advocates as they worked for the bishops of the Dioceses of La Crosse, Green Bay, and Superior.[33] After twelve years of priestly ministry in the Diocese of La Crosse, Bishop M. Heiss left a very large legacy: a well-functioning Indian Mission in the northern part of the diocese, an impressive number of new churches that had increased from forty-seven to one hundred one, and the number of schools increased from two to fifty-nine.[34] After Bishop Heiss left, the administrative duties over the diocese were assumed by Rev. Henryk Kampschroer.

In the summer of 1881 less than a year later, Rev. Kilian Flasch was nominated as the new bishop of the Diocese of La Crosse. He was consecrated on August 24, 1881. He was also of German descent. For ten years, he satisfied his episcopal ministry serving the faithful with great commitment and sacrifice. He died on September 3, 1891. On December 14, 1891, the Diocese of La Crosse received news that a new bishop, Rev. James Schwebach, was appointed. His consecration took place on February 25, 1892. The diocese needed a strong shepherd because of the increasing number of challenges and also the increasing number of Catholics who needed spiritual direction. Catholics accounted for 80,000 of the faithful in 1898; however, in the year 1900, this number increased drastically to over 97,000.

---

33 Ibid., p. 33
34 F. Crane, *Catholic History of La Crosse, Wisconsin*, p. 7

Bishop Alexander J. Mc Gavick[35] became the successor of Bishop Schwebach. He was nominated to the office of the Ordinary of the Diocese of La Crosse on November 21, 1921. He performed his duties and held the episcopal ministry for twenty-seven years until 1948.

In 1948, Rev. John P. Treacy became the new bishop of the Diocese of La Crosse and served this office until 1964. In 1965, Rev. Frederick W. Freking became the new bishop of the diocese. After him, Rev. John J. Paul became the Ordinary Bishop from 1983 until 1994. He was an Auxiliary Bishop prior to this appointment from 1977 to 1983 in this diocese. In 1994, Bishop John Paul was replaced by Rev. Raymond Leo Burke who held this position until 2003.

Over the time of nearly one hundred years of the existence of the diocese, many new things evolved and changed in the actual work of this institution. Bishops were changing, as were the conditions of pastoral care, and also the needs and expectations of the faithful. One of the most important events which influenced the work of the diocese was the change in its territorial boundaries that occurred twice during its history. Those changes were influenced by the formation of new dioceses. In 1905, the new Diocese of Superior was created which was cut out partially from the Green Bay and La Crosse Dioceses.[36] The Diocese of La Crosse was then severely truncated losing the counties of St. Croix, Polk, Burnett, Douglas, Bayfield, Ashland, Iron, Washburn, Barron, Rusk, Sawyer, Price, Taylor, Vilas, Oneida, and Lincoln. It gained, however, the counties of Grant, Iowa, La Fayette, and part of Marathon County. The creation of the Diocese of Madison during 1946 influenced yet another change to the borders of the Diocese of La Crosse and reduction of its territory.[37] As a consequence of this change, the counties of Pierce, Dunn, Chippewa, Pepin, Buffalo, Eau Claire, Clark, Jackson, Trempealeau, La Crosse, Vernon, Crawford, Richland, Monroe, Clark, Juneau, Adams, Wood, Portage, and Marathon[38] remained within its diocesan territory.

---

35 Alexander J. Mc Gavick was nominated Bishop for the Diocese of Chicago February 3, 1899. Compare this information with *Chicago Tribune*, February 4, 1899.
36 Gerald E. Fisher, *257 Things you should know about the Diocese of La Crosse*, 1993, p. 42.
37 Ibid., p. 62
38 G. E. Fisher, *Dusk is my Dawn*, p. 124

CHAPTER II

ORIGIN AND DEVELOPMENT OF POLISH PARISHES IN THE DIOCESE OF LA CROSSE

It had been a long-lived custom and tradition that those who were emigrating to America always participated in the Holy Mass at their home parish. They asked for a special blessing for their journey as well as good care for their families they were leaving behind. Before the actual trip, families would very carefully gather information about those who had already settled in America. The purpose of that was to stay in touch with friends and family. This also enabled the new immigrants to quickly contact their friends and family shortly after arrival. It gave them some sense of safety and security and the possibility of a much easier assimilation into the new promised land.

The first months in the foreign country were not easy. Polish immigrants had to learn new laws, and new, sometimes not very well understood traditions, and customs of people who lived there. The lack of knowledge of English presented a huge problem. The Poles had to start learning everything and learn it fast If they were going to be of any help to their families at home. The traditions and strong faith[39] brought from the homeland served as a buffer for all the stress related to the whole process of immigration. However, the colliding of two totally different worlds was very difficult for the new arrivals.

Polish immigrants that were arriving in America would bring with them just the basic items for daily use. In this situation, the prospect of

---
39 T. Polzin, *The Polish Americans Whence and Whither*, Pulaski, Wisconsin 1973, p. 143-146

rapid earnings and the return to the homeland receded into the background. Finding a job to support their families became one of the most important tasks for immigrants. The next step was to pay back the debt assumed for the purchase of farms, agricultural equipment, or the opening of their own businesses. Polish immigrants tried to live close to each other. Life among people who used the same language gave them a sense of security, strength, mutual aid to each other, and the possibility of practicing their own traditions and faith.[40]

Faith in God was from the very beginning the fundamental element of everyday life for Polish people. It helped them function in this foreign and often hostile environment. Unfortunately, the practicing of one's faith in one's native language was not always possible. Quite frequently, Polish immigrants coexisted closely with other ethnic groups forming neighborhoods as well as religious communities. Together, they organized their religious lives. By common effort, they would build places of worship where there would be room for all the faithful, regardless of their origin or native language.

The Catholic Church administration was quite open to the newcomers; however, it was not totally prepared and did not know how to satisfy their religious needs or how to organize them into one religious commonwealth. All that had to be learned. The Church helped to create new parishes, build churches, and build new schools. There were many stumbles and mistakes during the process of developing faith communities. Frequent prejudice, lack of understanding from the Church, and ignorance toward certain ethnic groups led to multiple disputes and conflicts. The formation of the Polish National Catholic Church can serve as an example of the struggle to gain religious independence. During this undertaking, Polish immigrants were supported by Polish clergy who arrived with them to serve and deliver their priestly ministry on the foreign soil.

By the year 1932, there were 800 Polish Roman Catholic parishes and around 1,000 clergy.[41] The priests who came to America were inspired by different reasons. Most of them made the decision based on

---

40   D. Kolinski, "The origin and early development of Polish settlements in central Wisconsin," in: *Polish American Studies*, Vol. 51, No. 1, Spring 1994, p. 33
41   www.pchswi.org/archives/polish_heritage/soroka/soroka_pages_52 (September 19, 2008)

the needs of their parishioners. Some were trying to escape political persecution on the part of occupants of Poland. At times, bishops by writing reviews for emigrating priests often did not give the true motivations of their trips in order to dismiss the uncomfortable or disobedient priests from their parishes.

During the time of the development of the new American Church and the increased level of education of the new generation of Poles, male religious orders and female religious convents were making a permanent mark on the history of Polish communities. Those two institutions had a great influence on the Christians' consciousness and identity of the Catholic immigrants. They were also pioneers in preaching the Gospel in this new territory.

Regardless of numerous difficulties, Poles were able to find common ground and face their struggles especially when it came to practicing their religion. The dynamically growing Polish communities were building churches and forming parishes. In the beginning, however, that process took place in large metropolitan areas such as New York, Detroit, Chicago, and Milwaukee. After that, it expanded into smaller cities and towns. Quite frequently, Mass was celebrated in private homes due to the need of the clergy to travel in order to provide the religious ministry to as many of their countrymen as possible. Later, when the Polish communities became well organized, churches and rectories were built, and the Poles would ask the bishop for their own priest. This was not easy and required a great deal of work and commitment. Regardless, Polish immigrants would undertake these tasks joyfully and praised God for his many blessings and his grace in the new homeland.

POLISH PARISHES DURING 1868-1905

1. St. Michael the Archangel, North Creek

Church of St. Michael the Archangel, North Creek 1873
Source: Parish Book St. Michael Archangel, *North Creek, Wisconsin 1988*

The first new church dedicated to St. Michael is located four miles north of Arcadia in Trempealeau County in the state of Wisconsin. It is situated on the hill and divided by a flowing stream on the north side.[42]

Due to a complete partition of Poland, many Polish immigrants had settled there. This wave of immigration started in the winter of 1862-1863. Those who came during that time arrived from Pomerania, the Province of Poznan, and all of them spoke only Polish.[43] They settled and started a new life by building homes and forming smaller and larger communities. Polish settlers were very hard workers whose faith was engraved in their hearts; therefore, they were also very generous donors to the church. Because of their generosity, the Church of St. Michael's was established.

The idea for the formation of this church came from three priests who visited this area between 1870 and 1872: Rev. Mislewicz, Rev. Bartkiewicz, and Rev. Szulak.[44] All three of them were missionaries who traveled to various Polish communities and settlements in the state of Wisconsin. They delivered pastoral care, Holy Sacraments, and provided spiritual guidance for families that actively participated in the celebrated liturgy. As time went on, the number of Catholics increased significantly, and the need for more places of worship became even more

---

42 Parish Book, *Parish of St. Michael the Archangel* 1873-1988, Wisconsin 1988, p. 17.
43 F. Curtiss-Wedge, *History of Trempealeau County Wisconsin*, 1917, p. 150-152.
44 No first names for Mislewicz, Bartkiewicz, Szulak are given not due to inaccuracies in the author of this study but with the lack of source text. This problem will be repeated later in the book.

urgent. The residents of North Creek petitioned the bishop of La Crosse regarding a new church. They received the bishop's permission to build the church and form a new parish community on July 12, 1872.[45]

The land for the construction of this church was donated by three families: Anton and Dorothea Sobotta, 3.57 acres; Alexander and Frances Bautch, 1.80 acres; and Albert and Josephine Bucht, 1.50 acres.[46] Before the construction of the church, the missionaries in order to support this effort celebrated Masses and preached the Gospel in the household of the Stachowski Family.

From the very beginning, the construction of the church occurred at a fast pace. Therefore, it was finished within a year (1873). Two years later, on October 6, 1875, the church was consecrated by Bishop M. Heiss of the Diocese of La Crosse.[47] The Parish of St. Michael in North Creek became a close neighbor of SS. Peter and Paul Church in Independence which was built and consecrated one day later.[48]

The capacity of the new church was 150 people. After a few years, in 1896 due to the increasing number of faithful, it was enlarged to accommodate all who came to worship in St. Michael's every day. The addition to the church measured 25 square feet. In 1910, Peter J. Pierzina donated part of his land to the parish to start a new cemetery.

Rev. Hieronymus Klimecki[49] became the first permanent pastor of the Parish of St. Michael on March 27, 1876. Until that time, this church was regarded as a mission, and pastoral care was provided by a priest who traveled from Pine Creek.[50] From May 10, 1882, until March 18, 1883, Rev. D. Mayer became the successor of pastor Klimecki. In 1883, a new pastor Rev. A. Warnagris assumed the du-

---

45 Only in the Book, *Parish of St. Michael the Archangel 1873-1988*, p. 18, is a reference to the establishment of the parish in 1872 while another year of the foundation of this parish is 1875 and is given by another three sources. These three sources are W. Kruszka, *History of the Poles in America, Part 4*, p. 97; H. H. Heaming, *History of the Catholic Church in Wisconsin* p. 841 in J. L. Hauck, *Catholic Church in Trempealeau County*, in: F. Curtiss-Wedge, *History of Trempealeau County Wisconsin* 1917, Chicago-Winona 1917 p. 845

46 Parish Book, *Parish of St. Michael the Archangel* 1873-1988, p. 18

47 W. Kruszka, *A History of the Poles. Part 4*, p. 97

48 Ibid., p. 97

49 F. Curtiss-Wedge, *History of Trempealeau County*, p. 845. In the book: H.H. Heaming, *History of the Catholic Church in Wisconsin*, p. 841, was given a different version of events from the start work by the first parish priest Rev. H. Klimecki. The first day of his ministry in the parish was according to this author March 8, 1876.

50 Ibid., p. 845

ties in St. Michael's and served the parish until 1886.[51] Rev. Joseph Tomaszewski came for less than one year. After his departure, the parish was left without a permanent pastor until 1887. During that time, all Sunday Masses were celebrated by Rev. Roman L. Guzowski[52] from La Crosse. Rev. Dutkiewicz[53] attended the pastor's duties during 1887-1890. His successor Rev. Anzelm Kroll was consecrated in 1890 and arrived in the parish that same year. Upon his arrival, he had a house built for the nuns who helped with the many organizational and housekeeping duties in the parish. Rev. August Babinski who resided in Independence served at the parish for one year (1892). He was replaced by Rev. Konstanty Frydrychowicz who ran the parish from 1893 until 1896. Rev. Alexander Siwiec[54] served in the Parish of St. Michael's during 1896-1900. After that, he received a new position and moved to Milwaukee and became a permanent pastor there. History then repeated itself; St. Michael's was left without its own priest.

During this pastoral vacancy, care for the parishioners was provided by several priests including Rev. A. Gara from Independence and Rev. Joseph Miller (1900-1901). Church authorities then sent Rev. Francis Kroll[55] who remained in the parish just a few months. At the end of 1901, Rev. Francis Jachimiak performed the pastoral duties. In 1902, Rev. Lugsiorski[56] arrived in the Parish of St. Michael and provided pastoral care again only for a few months. Rev. A. Gara also worked in the parish for a very short time. The next priest Rev. James Korzyk, who came in 1902, celebrated Masses only for a few weeks. Rev. F. Jachi-

---

51 Ibid., p. 845. Here is different selection of time and persons in the parish of St. Michael in the years 1885-1886 while Rev. Tomaszewski was the pastor.

52 Parish Book, *Parish of St. Michael the Archangel 1873-1988*, p. 22 gives the name of the pastor as Rev. Roman L. Guzowski, while in H.H. Heaming, *History of The Catholic Church in Wisconsin*, p. 841 in given the same first name but the last name is Gurowski.

53 There is a lack of the name of Rev. Dutkiewicz, as well as his name is spelled differently as Dutkiewic and compares with H. H. Heaming, *History of the Catholic Church in Wisconsin*, p. 841

54 Ibid., p. 841-842

55 There is a difference in the name of the priest, Parish Book: *Parish of St. Michael the Archangel*, p. 20, gives Rev. Francis Kroll, and in: W. Kruszka, *A History of the Poles. Part 4*, p. 98 Rev. F. Król.

56 In the case where the author of the above gives only the last name without a first name it means that the sources he used did not contain this information. In the history of the church in the Diocese of La Crosse such cases appear very often. Sometimes it is possible to supplement data from other sources (which is also the author of the above studies made very often). However in many cases this issue is hopeless. Hence the names of many priests and other people must remain on this paper incomplete. Another problem that has already been partially presented in the footnotes is given by various sources indicating different spellings of names or the names of places (Americanized or Latinized Polish first and last names).

miak[57] returned after a while to serve the parish but had to resign due to serious health issues. In 1904, Rev. N. Naturki worked in the parish but also only temporarily. As a result of all these changes, the parish ceased to exist as an administrative institution and was integrated with SS. Peter and Paul Parish in Independence.

The Parish of St. Michael gained its independence again in 1905 when Rev. Ignatius Orlik was appointed as a permanent pastor and cared for the parish for four years. During that time, the community was struck by a tragedy. During one of the severe thunderstorms, the school building was completely destroyed by fire. This caused some tension and disputes in the community. Some parishioners wanted to rebuild the school; some wanted to change its location closer to Arcadia. Because of this event, sixty farmers left St. Michael's Church and started to build a new church dedicated to St. Stanislaus[58] in Arcadia.

St. Michael the Archangel Church, North Creek 1988
Source: Parish Book St. Michael the Archangel Church

At this time, St. Michael's was still undergoing changes of pastors. Rev. John Rajski served the church from 1909 until 1913. In 1910, the parish population grew to 120 families. The next pastor Rev. Ladislaus Mcisz[59] worked there from 1913 until 1919. During the same year, pastoral ministry was assumed by Rev. Joseph Andrzejewski.[60] In 1920, a huge fire destroyed the church completely. The new church was built quickly during the same year. Rev. Stephen Miezkowski became the new pastor, and his successor Rev. Stanley Symczak served the parish during 1929-1938.

When Rev. Francis Pielarski worked in the parish (1938-1942), a

---

57 W. Kruszka, *A History of the Poles. Part 4*, p. 98

58 F. Curtiss-Wedge, *History of Trempealeau County, Wisconsin*, p. 845-846

59 The difference in the last name of the priest in Parish Book, of the *Parish of St. Michael the Archangel*, p. 20 provides Rev. Mcisz while F. Curtiss-Wedge, *History of Trempealeau County*, p. 845 provides Micisz.

60 Parish Book, *Parish of St. Michael the Archangel*, p. 20

new rectory was built. Unfortunately, Rev. Pielarski was transferred to a different parish, and his duties were taken over by Rev. John Krasowski who provided pastoral care to the parish until 1944. After him, diocesan authorities were sending different priests. Among them were Rev. Roman Papiernik (1944-1945), Rev. Edward Roskos (1945-1952), Rev. Jerome Kamla (1952-1957), Rev. Suleka (1957-1960), and Rev. James Ennis (1960-1961). Finally, Rev. Francis Disher remained in the parish for ten years bringing a sense of stability to St. Michael's.

For only three months in 1971, the church was cared for by Rev. James Chaffer. However, his successor Rev. Chester Moczarny was appointed as St. Michael's official administrator in 1986 and performed his duties until 1988. He came originally from St. Stanislaus Parish. Over time, St. Michael's Church ceased to be an independent institution and became a mission of SS. Peter and Paul Parish in Independence led by Rev. James Binkowski who was the permanent pastor of this community.

2. St. Stanislaus, Arcadia

Toward the end of 1909, forty families of Polish descent decided to prepare a construction plan for a new church. Until that decision was made, all of the families attended St. Michael the Archangel Church in North Creek.[61] The preparation work took until July 8, 1910, when the organizational committee announced among their Polish comrades that permission for the construction of a church and formation of the new parish was granted by Bishop James Schwebach.[62] One of the most important aspects that the bishop considered while making this decision was the increasing number of faithful in that region. There were enough to get permission to create a new parish. The construction committee wanted to build a church that was centrally located and accessible to all but also to build a new school and facilities in Arcadia. Bishop James Schwebach became the president of the construction committee which

---

61   F. Curtiss-Wedge, *History of Trempealeau County Wisconsin*, p. 850
62   J. L. Hauck, *Catholic Church in Trempealeau County*, in: F. Curtiss-Wedge, *History of Trempealeau County Wisconsin*, 1917, p. 850

also included Rev. John Rayski as the vice president, John Soppa as the secretary, and the treasurer Mike Sobatta. The decision to construct a new church was a much better solution for the residents of Arcadia than their earlier missionary affiliation with the Parish of St. Michael the Archangel in North Creek.[63]

Church of St. Stanislaus, Arcadia
Source: Holy Family Parish, Arcadia

In late summer of 1910, the construction committee signed a contract to build the new church. Jack G. Schneider prepared building plans and also became the project contractor. The parcel for the construction was purchased from John C. Gaveney for the amount of $700.[64] The construction plans stated that the church was to be built mainly of brick in neo-Gothic style with a seating capacity of 360 people. Toward the end of the same year, the shell of the church was completed. The finishing work on the inside of the church continued. On May 14, 1911, during the ceremony of consecration of the church bells, the first worship took place. An impressive ceremony of the dedication of the church to St. Stanislaus took place on July 4, 1911, during the anniversary of the independence of the United States.[65] The dedication was celebrated by Bishop James Schwebach with a large group of other priests. Pastors came from neighboring churches: Rev. John Rayski, Rev. J. L. Hauch, Rev. Andrew Gara, and Rev. Kulig.[66] A year later in 1912, the parishioners constructed a new rectory with eight rooms inside. The cost of this project was $2,500.

During 1909 and 1912, Rev. John Rayski the pastor of St. Michael's Parish in North Creek supported the building project of the new church and assumed administrative duties there for one year. The parish registry

---

63   Parish Book, *St. Stanislaus Parish*, Wisconsin 1961, p. 5
64   F. Curtiss-Wedge, *History of Trempealeau County Wisconsin*, p. 850
65   J. L. Hauck, *Catholic Church in Trempealeau County*, p. 850
66   Parish Book, *St. Stanislaus Parish*, p. 6

showed that ninety families belonged to the parish at that time.[67] Rev. Ignatius Orlik became the first permanent pastor of St. Stanislaus Parish in 1912. He attended to the parish needs until 1914. He supported the purchase of new Stations of the Cross which were blessed and consecrated in February of 1912. The cost of this purchase was $670. His successor Rev. Francis Barszczak arrived in Arcadia in 1914 and served the parish until 1919.

In September of 1915, a new parish school was opened and was run by nuns from the Congregation of St. Joseph from Stevens Point in Portage County.[68] Both Polish and English languages were taught in all grades. Religious training was very important and was taught only in the Polish language. The school had two rooms accommodating four grades in each room.

Rev. James Korczyk took over the management of the church in March of 1919 until the end of November of the same year.[69] Rev. Francis Pudlo arrived in the parish in November and attended to the pastoral duties for one year. For the next two years from 1920 until 1922, the church was managed by Rev. Lucien J. Kufel. A newly appointed pastor Rev. Joseph Andrzejewski came in September of 1922 and remained in the parish for 45 years.

During this time, the church was completely renovated. A new organ was installed in the choir loft, and the parish school expanded by adding on four new classrooms to accommodate the increasing number of students. In the meantime in 1942, the church was struck by lightning and was completely consumed by fire. It was a difficult time for the parishioners. The old armory became the temporary facility for all liturgical needs until a new church could be built. The estimated cost of a new church was $300,000. It was supposed to have a larger seating capacity of 650 people. Before it was completely finished, the liturgical ceremonies were celebrated in its basement. When the church was finished, it was consecrated by Ordinary Bishop John P. Treacy on May 16,

---

67   J. L. Hauck, *Catholic Church in Trempealeau County*, p. 850

68   F. Curtiss-Wedge, *History of Trempealeau County Wisconsin*, p. 850

69   http://holyfam.com/St.%20Stanislaus%20History.hmt (January 3, 2012). The site does not mention Rev. Franciszek Pudlo holding the pastoral ministry of the parish. It only mentions the one year assignment of Rev. James Korczyk to November 1920 and his successor, Rev. Lucien J. Kufel from September 1920 to 1922.

1948.[70] In 1961, a new altar and balustrade were built. A new grotto of Our Lady of Lourdes located in the front of the church was also opened for use by all the faithful.

After 45 years of service to the church, Rev. Kufel retired and left the parish. The parish underwent a period where its pastors again changed frequently. A new pastor was appointed on June 15, 1967. The pastoral office was assumed by Rev. Roman J. Papiernik who worked there for two years. In 1969, the parish got yet another new pastor Rev. Edward Sobczyk who in 1974 was transferred to a different parish. During the five years that he held the pastoral office, a Parish Council was created to effectively help the pastor in the management of the parish. After the pastor's departure from the parish, the Church of St. Stanislaus did not have a permanent pastor for three more months until March 1974 when Rev. James Halmann became consecrated into the pastoral service. Pastor Halmann improved the celebration of the liturgy. During his work as a pastor, a new lector's function was introduced as well as the distribution of Holy Communion by lay people in unusual circumstances.[71] Also in 1979, a new rectory was built for the amount of $60,000. Rev. Halmann held the pastoral office until 1982 and then was assigned to a new parish. His position was taken over by Rev. Chester Moczarny.

Holy Family Church, Arcadia 2012
Source: Author's Collection

3. St. Boniface, Chetek

The mission dedicated to St. Boniface was established by Rev. Joseph Dole seventeen or maybe eighteen years before its official registra-

---

70 Parish Book, *St. Stanislaus Parish*, p. 7
71 Ibid., p. 8

tion in 1889. Twenty Polish families belonged to this mission.[72] The first foundation of this church began with just a few Catholic families that met on a regular basis at the house of John Kleve. Rev. J. Dole traveled from Our Lady of Lourdes Parish in Dobie[73] and visited those families. In the spring of 1884,[74] Rev. J. Dole and a few people from the families that resided in Chetek purchased a wooden, six-year-old school building as well as the land that came with it. The old school building was renovated and adapted for liturgical purposes. This project called for an investment of $650. According to the parochial archives, it took the parish fourteen years to pay back this debt. The main reason for such a lengthy period of repaying this money was the relatively small number of parishioners at that time. St. Boniface Church was officially registered in the state of Wisconsin on October 18, 1884, by Bishop Kilian C. Flasch in the city of La Crosse. On August 22, 1889,[75] it was registered in Barron County.

Church of St. Boniface, Chetak 1889
Source: Parish Book St. Boniface, *Chetak 1984*

Regardless of the fact that a railway ran through Chetek, travel was not easy. It became a common practice to host the commuting priests overnight. In 1901, the community of Chetek voted during one of their meetings that Mass would be celebrated in their church six times per year. The old church bell was sold for $1.75, and a new one was purchased for $40.50.

Parochial archives state that during that year, seven children were baptized in the parish. A small annotation from 1908 mentions two funerals that took place. There were twenty-six people who received the

---

72   H. H. Heaming, *History of the Catholic Church in Wisconsin*, p. 836. There is little surviving specific information concerning the establishment of the mission parish, closure or of the clergy working in the mission.

73   Parish Book, *Saint Boniface Chetek*, Chicago 1984, p. 4

74   http://www.rootsweb.ancestry.com/-wibarron/communities/chetekhist.htm. Here is mentioned that the land was purchased along with the adjacent buildings in 1880.

75   Parish Book, *Saint Boniface Chetek*, Chicago 1984, p. 4

sacrament of Confirmation in 1905.[76] Preparation for the sacrament of Holy Communion is mentioned in notes from 1916 stating that there were forty-one people who received the sacrament.

The new rectory was finished in 1914. The pastor of this parish appointed in the fall of 1912 was Rev. Ladislaus Nowacki who commuted also to Barron and Cameron to deliver his services to the faithful. The parish grew very fast, and the need for a larger house of worship became evident. Rev. Damian Kvitek organized a gathering in 1939 with all the residents, and all agreed on the plan to build a new church. In the month of March 1946, the amount of money collected toward the project equaled $16,000. After Bishop Albert G. Meyer accepted the plan of the new church, the preparations for the construction started. Two years later in the spring of 1948, the actual building process began. This was a brick church with a seating capacity for 300 people. The whole project cost $69,637. The parishioners collected a total of $39,637. So the difference of $30,000 had to be mortgaged through First National Bank of Minneapolis. The new church building was fully put to use in 1949. The old school building which had served as a place to worship was moved, and its purpose was changed. In 1946, the number of registered parish families was 146; however, by the year 1983, it had almost doubled to 289.

Church of St. Boniface, Chetak 2012
Source: Author's Collection

TABLE 1: Pastoral Registry for St. Boniface Parish, Chetek

Rev. Joseph Dole	1880–1900
Rev. J. J. Miller & Rev. A. D. Miller	1900–1902
Rev. Henry Glaser	1902–1903
Rev. R. A. Heinzman	1903–1904

---

76 Ibid., p. 5

TABLE 1: Pastoral Registry for St. Boniface Parish, Chetek

Rev. Francis Ritka	1904–1906
Rev. Francis Olfen	1906–1907
Rev. E. Kostorz & Rev. McCarthy	1907–1908
Rev. F. Malicki	1908–1909
Rev. T. Dugnay, Rev. A. F. Norwicki, Rev. Joseph Olech	1909–1910
Rev. J. Gratya, Rev. J. A. Pilon, Rev. A. Jaydyewski	1910–1912
Rev. Ladislaus Nowacki	1912–1915
Rev. Anthony Nauza	1915–1916
Rev. Damian Kwitek	1916–1917
Rev. Adalbert Janda, Rev. Thomas Vopatek	1917–1918
Rev. Czril Zenisek	1918–1919
Rev. W. Tabenski	1919–1922*
Rev. Konwinski	1922–1923
Rev. Norbert Lukes, Rev. Vitus Haman	1923–1924
Rev. Maurus Vachout	1924–1928
Rev. Damian Kvitek	1928–1930
Rev. Anthony Vouza	1930–1932
Rev. Maurus Vachout	1932–1934
Rev. Damian Kvitek	1934–1944
Rev. Anselm Fleisig	1944–1946
Rev. Raphael Kubat	1946–1953
Rev. W. Michalicki	1953–1962
Rev. Gerard E. Mach	1962–1965
Rev. Norbert Groene	1965–1971**
Rev. James Griffin	1971–1972
Rev. Marion Schuetz	1972–1976
Rev. Peter L. Makk	1976–1978
Rev. Richard R. Verberg	1979
Rev. Norbert Vest	Oct.1979
Rev. Joseph McCormack	1980–1982
Rev. James J. Kraker	1982–1984

TABLE 1: Pastoral Registry for St. Boniface Parish, Chetek	
Rev. Jack Regh	1984–1993
Served by interim priest	June 1993–94
Rev. Michael Tupa	1994–1996
Rev. Gerard Willger	1996

* www.rootsweb.ancestry.com/-wibarron/communities/chetekhist.htm. The arrival date of Rev. W. Tabencki to the parish is given as February 1918

** Parish Book, *Saint Boniface Chetek*, Chicago 1984, p. 5

4. SS. Peter and Paul, Weyerhaeuser

Before a Catholic parish was founded in the town of Weyerhaeuser, spiritual care was provided for its residents, mostly Poles, by different commuting priests. They celebrated Eucharist in the private households of Leopold Kassela and Paul Frenchick and granted the sacraments of baptism and marriage.[77] Between the years 1891 and 1896, fifty Polish families resided in Weyerhaeuser. The representatives of the Polish immigrants that resided in this part of Wisconsin turned to the bishop of the Diocese of La Crosse to ask for permission to build a new Catholic church in this region. After the bishop granted his permission, preparatory work started at a fast pace. The owner of the wood and lumber yard company, Fredrick Weyerhaeuser, donated twelve acres of land as well as some of the wood for the construction of the church. Rev. Konstanty Frydrychowicz was the initiator of this project. He was the one who first went into the forest to start the excision of trees. When all the preparations were completed, Rev. K. Frydrychowicz

Church of SS. Peter & Paul, Weyerhaeuser 1898

Source: Jubilee 2000 Christ yesterday, today and forever, *Diocese of Superior*, Olan Mills 2000

---

[77] *People of Rusk County, Wisconsin*, Rusk County Historical Society, History of Rusk County Wisconsin, Rusk County Historical Society 1983, p. 54

left town and was replaced by Rev. Korczyk who commuted 95 miles from the town of Poznan. All parishioners actively participated in the construction of the church. Residents who did not belong to this parish and those who lived close by also supported the formation of the new church either by donations of money or wood or by sharing their talents.

The church was finished and put to use in 1896.[78] During Rev. Jacob Gara's work at the parish, the inside of the church was completely finished. A rectory was built in 1906 for use by the priest.

The parish school had two levels. The first one included students from 1st to 4th grade and the second one was for students from 5th to 8th grade. Children who attended the public school would come for religion classes on Saturday morning taught by nuns. Unfortunately, Bishop George Hammes closed the school on May 10, 1967.[79]

Church of SS. Peter & Paul, Weyerhaeuser 2012
Source: Author's Collection

As time went by, the small wooden church became too small and insufficient for the continuously increasing number of parishioners. Because of this growth in 1943, a church building fund was established reaching $1300 at year-end. In 1948, the building fund had reached $40,000 with the commitment of a new pledge for an additional $25,000 over the next five years. The construction of a new church started on April 24, 1951. Bishop Albert G. Meyer consecrated the foundation and the cornerstone of the new church on Sunday, July 8, 1951. The church was completed in May 1952.[80]

---

78 W. Kruszka, *A History of the Poles. Part 4*, p. 107

79 *People of Rusk County, Wisconsin*, Rusk County Historical Society, History of Rusk County Wisconsin, Rusk County Historical Society 1983, p. 54. However, in the *Diocese of Superior, Our Journey through Faith a History of the Diocese of Superior*, Ireland 2005, p. 157 is a discrepancy stating that the school was closed in 1968.

80 *Diocese of Superior, Jubilee 2000, Christ yesterday, today & forever*, Olan Mills 2000, p. 4

Rev. William Olszewski[81] came in 1953 and remained until 1968. During his pastoral service, a new rectory was built. The old one was renovated for use as a convent by the sisters of the Congregation of Handmaids from the town of Ladysmith.

From the very beginning, it was a Polish church where the native language was used. This situation remained until 1970 when Rev. Wladyslaw Kowalski took over the pastoral office and only spoke English.

TABLE 2: Pastoral Registry for SS. Peter & Paul Parish, Weyerhaeuser

Rev. Konstanty Frydrychowicz	?–1897
Rev. J. W. Korczyk	1897–1899
Rev. James W. Gara	1899–1900
Rev. T. Lugowski	1900–1901
Rev. J. W. Korczyk	1901–1902
Rev. A. Babinski	1902–1903
Rev. A. M. Wuchter	1903–1905
Rev. F. A. Retka	1905–1907
Rev. E. Kostorz	1907–1908
Rev. Thomas. F. Malecki	1908–1909
Rev. John Barca	1909–1910
Rev. Konstanty Frydrychowicz	1910–1911
Rev. A. E. Nowicki	1911–1913
Rev. Thomas F. Malecki	1913–1915
Rev. L. S. Nowacki	1915–1916
Rev. Stanley Topolski	1916–1942
Rev. Henry Gozanski	1942–1953
Rev. William Olszewski	1953–1968
Rev. Robert Szyma	1968–1970*
Rev. Wladyslaw Kowalski	1970–1983
Rev. Charles Murphy	1983–1984

---

81 Ibid., p 7

TABLE 2: Pastoral Registry for SS. Peter & Paul Parish, Weyerhaeuser

Rev. Albert Verdegan	1984–1990
Rev. James Horath	1991–1992
Rev. John R. Long	1992–1998

* Parish Book, *The Blue Hills Catholic Cluster, St. Mary – Bruce, SS. Peter & Paul – Weyerhaeuser, Assumption of the Virgin Mary – Strickland*, Wisconsin 1993, p. 1

5. Assumption of the Blessed Virgin Mary, Strickland

The town of Strickland in the state of Wisconsin resembles small Polish towns because of its location and scenery. One can find there huge forests, a number of rivers, streams, and lakes, as well as fertile soil for farming. All of these qualities were important to the Polish settlers. They arrived here by train or by a wagon drawn by two horses, settled here, and worked very hard.[82] The land that they purchased was mostly covered with big trees so a great deal of effort was required to prepare it for farming. Polish settlers also worked in the local sawmill where they earned about 75 cents per day. The very beginning of the Polish settlement in this region was extremely difficult and stressful. However, their strong faith in God's Providence and the protection of our Lady (which is deeply rooted in Polish tradition) and their determination and optimism helped them to survive the most difficult times.

Church of the Assumption of the BVM, Strickland 1898
Source: Jubilee 2000, Christ yesterday, today, & forever, *Diocese of Superior*, Olan Mills 2000

In 1890, Rev. Konstanty Frydrychowicz came to Strickland from Pennsylvania and became the spiritual advisor and caretaker for the Polish community. He made his decision to leave Pennsylvania based

---

82 *Diocese of Superior, Jubilee 2000, Christ yesterday, today & forever*, Olan Mills 2000, p. 1

on an advertisement in the local newspaper which informed him of the great, fertile soil in northern Wisconsin that was available for purchase. First liturgical celebrations took place in private households. The houses and a small wooden chapel built on the property of the Olechowski[83] Family had a special meaning for the Poles.

Driven by their strong faith and ambition, Polish residents desired to build their own church. During the harvest of the trees on their new land, they gathered timber not just to build their own homes but also to accumulate enough material for a new church. On March 28, 1895, the Chippewa Logging Company which was owned by Frederick Weyerhaeuser sold to the Polish community five acres of land for the amount of $1.00. It was a symbolic amount to provide a starting point for the new church. The remaining fifteen acres were purchased on July 30, 1900, in order to enlarge the new church property. This task was accomplished with the help and encouragement from Bishop James Schwebach of the Diocese of La Crosse.[84] Available records indicate that the church was possibly built in 1895 or 1896. Today, the verification of the correct date is almost impossible. The church was named and devoted to the Assumption of the Blessed Virgin Mary. Rev. K. Frydrychowicz, who lived in Strickland with his parents, left the town in July of 1897. From that time, the parish assumed the role of a mission which was managed by a pastor from SS. Peter and Paul Parish in Weyerhaeuser.

During the time when the pastoral office was held by Rev. James Gara,[85] the church was completed. After that project was concluded, parishioners faced the problem of repaying the mortgage on the church. Existing parochial documents indicate that to accomplish that goal, the parishioners organized several different picnics. During the first picnic on August 15, 1914, they raised $18.00. On November 4, 1916, the earned amount was $45.09, and in June of 1920, the profit from the picnic amounted to $199.32.[86]

---

83 *People of Rusk County, Wisconsin*, Rusk County Historical Society, History of Rusk County Wisconsin, Rusk County Historical Society 1983, p. 43

84 Ibid., p. 43

85 W. Kruszka, *A History of the Poles. Part 4*, p. 108

86 *Diocese of Superior, Jubilee 2000, Christ yesterday, today, & forever*, p. 5

According to the parish registry, between 1920 and 1925 there were ninety Polish families in the parish. Unfortunately, calamity did not spare this young parish community. On Sunday, July 17, 1923, the vestry caught fire. The fire spread to the roof, and eventually the whole church burned to the ground. This event took place when the pastoral office was held by a commuting priest Rev. Stanley Topolski. The church was poorly insured. Instead of a celebration of the twenty-fifth anniversary of the parish, the parishioners had to struggle with this tragedy. In a short time, a decision was made to rebuild the church. After such a big loss, the parishioners celebrated all Catholic worship services at Halas Dance Hall & Saloon. On July 4, 1924, the first attempts were made toward the construction of a new church.[87] In the beginning during the planning of the church, parishioners wondered if this church should have a basement. Most of the work at the construction site was performed by the parishioners. A full day's wage was $2.50. When working with their horses, a full day's wage was $5.00. Each family was expected to donate at least $25.00 toward this project. The church was finished in 1925 at the final cost of $5,452.16. The number of families at that time reached eighty families. The church was consecrated in August 1925 during the feast of Mary, Mother of God.

Church of the Assumption
of the Blessed Virgin Mary, Strickland 2012
Source: Author's Collection

In 1929, a community of the Holy Rosary was established. It included thirty members, and its spiritual director was Rev. Stanley Topolski. Rev. Topolski served as a pastor for the parish in Weyerhaeuser and for the mission in Strickland for twenty-six years. In 1954, sisters from the Order of St. Francis started religion lessons which took place every Sunday in the church. During the same year, Rev. William Olszewski renovated the main entrance of the church and in 1960 installed a new

---

87 *People of Rusk County, Wisconsin*, Rusk County Historical Society, History of Rusk County Wisconsin, Rusk County Historical Society 1983, p. 43

heating system. In 1959,[88] the mission of the Assumption of the Blessed Virgin Mary in Strickland became integrated with the Parish of St. Peter in Cameron. Rev. Robert Szyma became the new pastor for both of those communities. In 1984, the parishes in Weyerhaeuser, Bruce, and Flambeau were consolidated into one parish which was managed by Sister Martha Kormandy.[89]

TABLE 3: Pastor Registry for the Assumption of the Blessed Virgin Mary Parish, Strickland

Rev. Konstanty Frydrychowicz	?–1897
Rev. J. W. Korczyk	1897–1899
Rev. James W. Gara	1899–1900
Rev. T. Lugowski	1900–1901
Rev. J. W. Korczyk	1901–1902
Rev. A. Babinski	1902–1903
Rev. A. M. Wuchter	1903–1905
Rev. F. A. Retka	1905–1907
Rev. E. Kostorz	1907–1908
Rev. T. F. Malecki	1908–1909
Rev. K. Frydrychowicz	1909–1911
Rev. A. E. Nowicki	1911–1913
Rev. Thomas F. Malecki	1913–1915
Rev. L. S. Nowacki	1915–1916
Rev. Stanley Topolski	1916–1939
Rev. John Nawa	1939–1942
Rev. Henry Gozanski	1942–1953
Rev. Wiliam Olszewski	1953–1959
Rev. Alphonse Zoltowski	1959–1960
Rev. Norbert West	1960–1964
Rev. Alphonse Zoltowski	1964–1969

---

88 Ibid., p. 45. Here occurs another date year 1969 as the time of the combining of these two parishes and not as is mentioned in the book *Diocese of Superior, Jubilee 2000, Christ yesterday, today, & forever*, p. 7, the year was 1959.

89 *Diocese of Superior, Jubilee 2000, Christ yesterday, today, & forever*, p. 7

TABLE 3: Pastor Registry for the Assumption of the Blessed Virgin Mary Parish, Strickland

Rev. Robert Szyma	1969–1970
Rev. Wladyslaw Kowalski	1970–1983
Rev. Charles Murphy	1983–1984
Rev. Albert Verdegan	1984–1990
Rev. Robert O'Connell	1990–1991
Rev. James Horath	1991–1992
Rev. John R. Long	1992–1998
Rev. Lewis E. Burden, Jr.	1998–

6. St. Stanislaus, Superior

The city of Superior is located on a picturesque lakeshore with the same name. During the beginning of the 1890s, a group of Polish Catholics from Superior gathered for worship in private households. These Catholics held in their hearts a desire to build a church, but their financial abilities were very limited. This situation lasted for ten years. When the community grew in numbers,[90] they decided to undertake the actions toward the construction of a new church. A Polish parish was established there on May 27, 1899,[91] by Rev. Korczyk. Bishop Schwebach appointed Rev. Korczyk to coordinate and to supervise the construction. Also, he obliged him to visit this developing parish every month to as-

Church of St. Stanislaus, Superior
Source: Diocese of Superior

---

90 "Beautiful new $50.000 Church is community center for Poles," in: *The Superior News Tribune*, April 29, 1917, p. 1

91 www.ipgs.us/parishhistories/ststaislaussuperiorwi.html (January 9, 2012) and here is information that the parish was established May 18, 1901.

sure the proper and uninterrupted process of all the work involved in this project. The people adopted St. Stanislaus, Bishop and Martyr as the patron of their new, developing parish.[92] First, the people built a small wooden church for the amount of $2,500. Actually, this amount was the cost for ten parcels for the church grounds. All other work was done by volunteers. The church had two levels. The upper level was to serve all the liturgical needs, and the lower level was for the needs of a new parochial school. During the construction of the church, the parishioners attended neighboring St. Joseph Parish. Rev. Korczyk was the pastor and the executor of the construction project until 1901. Under his competent and caring eye, a new rectory was also built. On November 14, 1901, the church was consecrated and put into use.[93] The whole project cost $10,000.[94]

In 1901, Rev. August Babinski was appointed the new pastor and served the parish until his death in 1911. During his time in office, the lower level of the church was improved for the purpose of providing religion classes for the students. One lay teacher and sisters from the Order of St. Francis in Milwaukee were hired to teach until 1909. In 1906, a new convent was built, and sisters from the Order of St. Joseph from Stevens Point replaced the Franciscan Sisters.

The successor of Rev. August Babinski, Rev. A. Gawenda[95] became the next builder in the Parish of St. Stanislaus. During one of the meetings of the parish community, people voted to build a new, bigger church. The parish had grown, and now one hundred families attended the church on a regular basis. Soon the old church was sold for the sum of $1,000, and all efforts concentrated on the new building project. On November 17, 1915, the cornerstone for the new church was blessed by Rev. A. A. Jazdzewski and Rev. Schultz. Each parishioner was obligated to contribute $50 toward this project. In a relatively short time, the new and larger church was built. It had two levels. Its length was 145 feet, width – 66 feet, and a height of 30 feet. It was able to accom-

---

92 W. Kruszka, *A History of the Poles. Part 4*, p. 111
93 L. S. Nowacki, "St. Stanislaus Congregation Superior" in: *Catholic Herald Citizen*, September 5, 1953, p. 4
94 W. Kruszka, *A History of Poles, Part 4*, p. 111
95 www.ipgs.us/parishhistories/ststaislaussuperiorwi.html (January 9, 2012). Information here states the successor of Rev. Babinski was Rev. Anthony Borucki followed by Rev. A. Gawenda.

modate 600 people. The consecration of the church took place on May 21, 1916, and was celebrated by Rev. J. M. Koudelka. A new organ, valued at $3,000, was installed[96] and was consecrated on April 23, 1917. Windows for this church, the baptismal fountain, and the confessionals were a part of the financial donations of parishioners, organizations, and associations that functioned within the parish.

In 1916, Rev. L. S. Nowacki became the new pastor of St. Stanislaus Parish. He served the church for many years until October 1, 1968. Between 1968 and 1970, two priests worked at the parish: Rev. Brendan Kunda and Rev. Alphonse Gostomski. In 1970, Rev. William Cary became the newly appointed pastor and served the parish until May 5, 1975. During the same year, the Parish of St. Stanislaus was integrated with the Parish of SS. Cyril and Methodius. The last Mass was celebrated at St. Stanislaus on January 3, 1982. The church was demolished that very same year.

Many organizations and institutions existed during the operation of the parish which included Pulaski's Organization (founded in 1902), Sacred Heart (founded in 1911 by Rev. Borucki with approximately 60 women and young girls), the Community of St. Joseph (founded in 1892 uniting 80 members), Community of the Holy Rosary (founded in 1907), and the Community of SS. Peter and Paul (founded in 1900), and the Community of Unity.[97]

7. Most Holy Family, Ashland

The Most Holy Family Church in Ashland is one of the oldest Polish parishes in the diocese. Its beginning occurred on September 14, 1899.[98] The very first Catholic parish in Ashland was founded in 1874[99] by the Irish immigrants and was dedicated to St. Agnes. During the years 1886-1888, spiritual care was provided for the twenty-one Poles

---

96 "Beautiful new $50,000 Church is community center for Poles," p. 1
97 Ibid., p. 1
98 Parish Book, *Holy Family Parish*, Ashland, Wisconsin 1954, p. 6
99 *Diocese of Superior Our Journey through Faith, A History of the Diocese of Superior*, Ireland 2005, p. 80. Information states that Dr. Edwin Ellis offered three plots for the building of the church on June 21, 1873.

in Ashland by Rev. Anastasius Czek.[100] After that, liturgical services and sacraments were provided by Rev. Damian Koziolek who commuted to Ashland from time to time.[101] He traveled from the Parish of St. Xavier in Superior. The Polish immigrants rented the St. Agnes Church from the Irish for the amount of $200 per year in order to have a place to practice their faith. This amount covered rent, religion lessons for their children, electricity, heat, and the use of liturgical garments and sacred vessels. In the meantime, the number of Polish families grew, and naturally, they started thinking about building their own church. For the sum of $2,300, they purchased eight parcels toward this investment.[102] Along with the construction of the church, the Polish residents planned to build a new school as well. The importance of education became more and more evident among the Polish settlers. The school that their children currently attended was quite a distance away. The construction committee of the church and school was selected on October 1, 1899. By the end of the same year, the committee had already collected several thousand dollars toward the new church. The representatives of the committee traveled to the diocese to obtain permission for the construction of a new church. Among the delegates were Charles Masloiowski, August Gierszewski, and Boleslaw Pipke.[103] The result of this mission was that permission was granted by the bishop.

The church was built in a relatively short time. The handiwork was started in the middle of 1891 and was finished on September 28, 1902, when Bishop Schwebach consecrated the church.[104] The church was 128

Church of the Most Holy Family, Ashland
Source: Diocese of Superior

---

100   WI History Records Survey 1936, Church Records by Box 226 Folder 11 County of Ashland
101   www.ampoleagle.com/default.asp?sourceid=&smenu (January 8, 2009)
102   W. Kruszka, *A History of the Poles. Part 4*, p. 109
103   WI History Records Survey 1936, Church Records by Box 226 Folder 11 County of Ashland
104   W. Kruszka, *A History of the Poles. Part 4*, p. 110

feet long and 54 feet wide. The lower level was 11 feet high. The whole project cost $20,000. In 1900, 180 families belonged to the Parish of the Most Holy Family. Some Lithuanian and Slovakian families attended the church. The school was also finished and opened in January 1901 with a construction cost of $4,300. However, it had only four grades. It was attended by 240 students and the sisters from the Order of Saint Francis were in charge of education.

The first pastor of the Most Holy Family Parish Rev. Damian Koziolek was replaced by Rev. Methodius Kielar in 1911. He provided pastoral care to the parish until March of the same year. The next pastor Rev. Rembert Stanowski concentrated his effort on paying off the mortgage. During his days in the parish office, the debt decreased significantly. He implemented monthly envelopes for each family to be able to donate toward this effort. He worked in the parish until 1918, and his successor Rev. Wenceslaus Krzycki worked there only until October of the same year. Rev. Cyril Miter came to the parish and performed pastoral duties during 1918-1926. The parish was able to pay off its debt, and the pastor could finally focus on the spiritual needs of his parishioners. He eventually was transferred to Pulaski, Wisconsin, and replaced by Rev. Canute Lolinski. In August of 1932, Rev. Canute was moved to Cleveland, Ohio, to St. Stanislaus Parish, and for two consecutive years pastoral care in the Most Holy Family Parish was attended by Rev. Stanley Jaworski. The next change came about on the last Sunday of July 1934 when Rev. Rembert Stanowski for the second time was assigned as pastor at the parish.[105] The population of the parish during the period from 1920 to 1930 decreased to 735 people and only 90 students still attended the school.

TABLE 4: Pastoral Registry of the Most Holy Family Parish, Ashland

Rev. Ladislaus Siekaniec, OFM	1949–1955
Rev. Casmir Wisniewski	1955–1959

---

105   I was unable to determine the dates which could place the time of the parish priests during their pastoral ministry in the parish of the Holy Family and also failed to determine the names of the priests. This is due to the lack of the source materials and poor historiography of the Diocese of La Crosse until 1905. Little information about the clergy working in the Northern part of the Diocese of La Crosse can be found among others such as in: L. J. Siekaniec, "The Poles of Ashland, Wisconsin," 1884-1888, *Polish American Studies*, Orchard Lake, Michigan, January-June 1949, p. 14-17.

TABLE 4: Pastoral Registry of the Most Holy Family Parish, Ashland

Rev. Humbert Korgie	1959–1977
Rev. Isidore Langheim	1977–1982
Rev. Arthur Fuldauer	1982–1985
Rev. Cyril Wagner	1985–1986
Rev. Vermon Olmer	1986–1990

8. St. Mary's, Hurley

As Polish immigrants established themselves in Hurley in Iron County their thoughts turned to their faith. Because faith was such an integral part of their lives, it was important to have religious services, and the first Holy Mass was celebrated in St. Mary's on November 1, 1885. The parish was founded by Rev. Crysostom Verwyst a priest who visited this area serving the Catholics who lived there. Bishop Flasch appointed Rev. Gilbert Nuonno as the new pastor for the parish. He served this parish faithfully until his death in 1908 after a short illness. As pastor, he guided a diverse parish consisting of Poles, Irish, Germans, and Italians in a town which was quite wild. These new Polish settlers had a goal to have a church of their own, and this was accomplished in just one year. A request was submitted to Bishop Kilian Flasch of the Diocese of La Crosse for permission to erect a church. The building committee consisting of J. H. Carroll, Thomas Kielty, D. P. Mc Niel, and John Hoye drew up construction plans for a church in the spring of 1886. The first Holy Mass was celebrated in the renamed church St. Mary of the Seven Dolores on August 15, 1886.[106]

Church of St. Mary, Hurley around 1895
Source: H. H. Heuming, History of Catholic Church in Wisconsin

---

106 www.stmaryshurley.org/history.htm

During Rev. Nuonno's ministry in 1890, land was purchased north of the church where a school was constructed. Although originally sisters from New York were to staff the school, they found the area too far from their motherhouse. The Franciscan Sisters were contacted and agreed to come to northern Wisconsin and take over the administration of the school which had 120 pupils in attendance. They taught the usual subjects and instructed the children in their faith. A rectory was built east of the church in 1894 which served as the pastor's residence until its replacement in 1955.

In 1905, St. Mary's was transferred to the newly created Diocese of Superior. At that time, St. Mary's Parish had grown to 400 families. The year 1906 was an exciting time for the parishioners. On July 15, 1906, a cornerstone was consecrated for the construction of a new church. The red sandstone church was finished quickly, was opened to the parishioners, and consecrated by the bishop in 1907. Rev. John Klopp became the new pastor of the parish on January 16, 1908, and served for twenty years.

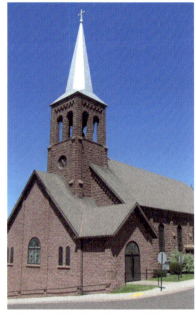

Church of St. Mary, Hurley 2012
Source: Author's Collection

In November 1927, a new pastor Rev. Peter Meyer[107] arrived at the parish. He performed his duties until October 2, 1946. Over the years, improvements continued which included additions to the church, enlarging the cemetery area, electricity, and a new heating system was installed. In 1934, a new pipe organ was purchased, and beautiful music emanated from it during church services.

The Parish Council in 1936 reached a decision to erect a new parish school. The depressed economy resulted in a period of time passing before the actual construction could begin. However by 1940, Rev. Meyer had enough funds ($30,000) which along with parish member

---

107   A. Cirilli, "St. Mary History, long, colorful-with long tenured priests," in: *The centennial Jubilee 1886-1986 St. Mary of the Seven Dolores Catholic Parish, Hurley, Wisconsin*, 1986, p. 6

assessments allowed for the school construction to begin. In 1941, the parochial school was completed.[108]

By 1948, Rev. Meyer had accumulated funds for the construction of a house for the nuns. This brick structure consisted of twenty-three rooms including bedrooms, living areas, and a chapel. Upon completion, it was blessed in February 1949.[109]

His successor Rev. Michael Prock worked in the parish until August 1965 after he asked to be transferred to a different parish. Rev. Henry Gozanski the new pastor after one year of service also requested a transfer to a different parish in July 1967. During the same year, Rev. Robert Schipper arrived in Hurley and worked for the parish until May 28, 1970.

TABLE 5: Pastoral Registry of St. Mary's Parish, Hurley from 1966-2000

Rev. Henry Gozanski	1966–1967
Rev. Robert Schipper	1967–1970
Rev. Vincent Bromley	May 1970–July 1970
Rev. Clarence Ludwig	July 1970–1980
Rev. Joseph Willger	1980–1986
Rev. Vincent Lynch	1986–1992
Rev. Hugh Briody	Jul 1992–Dec 1993
Rev. Robert E. O'Connell	Dec 1993–

9. HOLY FAMILY, PONIATOWSKI

At the end of 1875 and the beginning of 1876, a large group of Polish immigrants traveled from Milwaukee to the town of Poniatowski in

---

[108] A. Cirilli, *Diamond Jubilee 1961 of St. Mary's Church,* Wisconsin 1961, p. 2. I mentioned this church as an example, because in many other cities churches shared the same fate – a few ethnic groups and a common goal: to own the church and to establish the parish. So it was in the towns: Mellen, Jennings, Glenwood, Price County, Oneida, Stanley, Fond du Lac, Sheboygan, Fox River, Montello, Neshkoro, Red Granite, Kilbourn, Merrill, Angelica, Shawano, Lancy, Almond, Wautoma, Spalding, Three Lakes, and Pelican Lake. There are no names listed for the churches. These places are given only as examples of existing groups of Polish immigrants in different parts of the state of Wisconsin in the Diocese of La Crosse and the Diocese of Superior. Look in: W. Kruszka, *A History of the Poles,* p. 108-112.

[109] www.stmaryshurley.org/history.htm

the state of Wisconsin.[110] Upon their arrival, they started the hard work of building their own households and their future. They found a very fertile soil suitable for farming. They also worked at the local lumber company cutting trees as well as worked in the town's paper factory.

From the very beginning, priests were closely connected with the immigrants in Poniatowski. They commuted from Stevens Point and Arcadia to attend to the spiritual needs of the immigrants. They celebrated the Holy Mass and delivered sacraments in private households. Among those who served the immigrants in Poniatowski were Rev. W. Bukowski from Stevens Point and Rev. Klimecki from Arcadia. To fulfill all the needs of the immigrants in Poniatowski,[111] this service was just not sufficient.

People in Poniatowski saw their future in a unity that would always emerge from their faith, religion, and church. Therefore, quickly after settling, they made a decision about the creation of a new church. It was to be an independent Polish religious commonwealth. In 1878, the local administration of the Polish faith community made the decision to start the process for the creation of a new church. Twenty acres of land were donated by the Rietbrock family for this building project. The construction work took less than one year. In this short period of time due to the effort of all the parishioners, a new wooden church was erected and devoted to St. Joseph. Soon after that, the parish house was finished and put to use in 1879. In the meantime, a lot of effort was directed toward finding a priest who would like to provide spiritual and liturgical services to this new, developing community.

Rev. John Maczynski[112] from the Order of St. Francis became a pastor in this new parish in 1883.[113] He worked there for two years. The next pastor Rev. August Rogulski had to commute to Poniatowski from time to time to deliver Catholic services. On September 22, 1886, Rev. Andrew Gara arrived at the parish. He attended to all pastoral duties during the next twelve years. During this time, the development of his parish community expanded. Therefore, the decision for the creation

---

110 Parish Book, *Holy Family Church, Poniatowski, Wisconsin*, 1977, p. 5
111 W. Kruszka, *A History of the Poles. Part 4*, p. 98
112 Here is the different last name: H. H. Heaming, *History of the Catholic Church in Wisconsin*, p. 849, the last name is Rev. J. Maczynski while W. Kruszka, *A History of the Poles. Part 4*, p. 99, he gives the last name as Rev. Jan Mączyński.
113 Parish Book, *Holy Family Church*, p. 5

of a new church was made swiftly, and on July 20, 1888, Bishop Kilian Flasch of the Diocese of La Crosse gave his permission to start this project. He also renamed the church and dedicated it to the Holy Family.[114] Rev. Gara left the parish in 1898,[115] and the next priest Rev. Konstanty Frydrychowicz started his service in 1899. During his ministry, the Holy Family Parish in Poniatowski was closed. The church and the pastor were suspended, and Rev. Frydrychowicz was forced out of the parish. Parishioners closed the church in February 1901. After about four months, the parish sprang back to life under the management of Rev. Joseph Biela.

Church of the Holy Family, Poniatowski 1918
Source: *Parish Book* Holy Family Church, *Poniatowski 1977*

During Easter of 1902, Rev. Joseph Miller assumed the pastoral duties in this parish. He was of German descent and had a nationalistic attitude. The year 1905 brought new changes for the parish community. A new pastor Rev. Ignatius Modarski who came to replace Rev. Miller[116] resigned from this office in 1905 and left Poniatowski. In 1909, Rev. Florian A Kupka became the new pastor and served the ninety-five families who actively participated in the parish.[117] He was involved in all aspects of his work and renovated the church and the rectory. Cooperation between him and

Church of the Holy Family, Poniatowski 2012
Source: Author's Collection

---

114 W. Kruszka, *A History of the Poles. Part 4*, p. 99
115 Parish Book, *Holy Family Church*, p. 6
116 Ibid., p. 7
117 L. Marchetti, *History of Marathon County Wisconsin and representative Citizens,* 1913, p. 561

the parish community was very good. Rev. Kupka worked in this parish until his retirement after thirty-two years of service. Rev. Maximilian Kluczykowki became the successor of Rev. Kupka in 1941. In 1948, he was replaced by Rev. Stanislaus Lapinski. On June 9, 1952, Rev. Edward Rokosz came to the parish. He served the church for a very short time until August 17, 1952, when he retired. He was replaced by Rev. Richard J. Herman. His replacement Rev. Thomas Langer came in 1975 and served until 1979 when he requested a leave from the diocese. The next change at the parish was the arrival of Rev. Lloyd Geissler who remained at the parish until his retirement (the date of which is uncertain). After he retired, various priests including Rev. Al Sloviak, Rev. Steven Gross, Capuchins from the monastery in Marathon, and Deacon LeRoy Knauf handled the needs of the parish.

10. SS. Peter and Paul, Independence

While talking about the Polish immigrants, it is impossible not to mention the family of Albert Butach. The family arrived on a ship in Quebec, Canada, in the 1850s. From Quebec, they took a train and arrived in Watertown where they lived for one year. After that, they moved to New Lisbon where they engaged in farming. In May 1863, the family moved to North Creek near the city of Arcadia. At the end of 1869 and the beginning of 1870, they moved again to the settlement of Burns.[118] At that time, these were the outskirts of the newly developing city of Independence. Also in this area, a fairly strong Polish community was growing. Following the example of the early Polish settlers, new immigrants were

Church of SS. Peter & Paul, Independence 1875
Source: Parish Book SS. Peter & Paul, *Independence 1975*

---

118 Parish Book, *SS. Peter & Paul Church, 100 years in the Lord service 1875-1975*, Wisconsin 1975, p. 30

arriving here. New residents were trying to connect their daily lives with their religious duties. So the idea of building a new church and creating a Polish parish came very soon.

The beginning of this parish was similar to other Polish parishes in Wisconsin. Priests were commuting there to celebrate the liturgy in private homes. When the Polish community grew to sixty families, ten acres of land were purchased for the future construction of the church.[119] This project progressed quickly, and the construction of the main church building was finished in the fall of 1875. On October 7, 1875, Bishop of La Crosse Michael Heiss[120] consecrated the church and named it SS. Peter and Paul Parish.

During this same time period, the construction of the rectory was finished as well. Since the beginning of this parish, ten pastors and twenty-five vicars worked there. The first priest that served this parish was Rev. Hieronymus Klimecki. He also at the same time served the Church of St. Michael in North Creek. With time, this particular church became one of the largest churches in the Diocese of La Crosse.

Rev. Klimecki remained at SS. Peter and Paul Parish until May 10, 1882,[121] at which time he resigned. Over the next ten months, the parish did not have a permanent priest. Spiritual, sacramental, and liturgical care was provided to this community by Rev. Dominik Majer.[122] After that, a permanent pastor was appointed. Rev. A. Warnagris[123] attended to his pastoral duties at the church until November 30, 1885, and then was replaced by Rev. Raphael Tomaszewski who constructed the parish school in 1887. It was a brick building that cost the parish $3,000.[124] In September of 1887, Bishop M. Heiss came to Independence to bless the new school. Sisters from the Order of St. Felician were hired to manage the school and provide education for the children. Soon, three

---

119 To compare the information included in the Parish Book, *SS. Peter & Paul* information here says that 10 acres of the land was purchased for the church while in F. Curtiss-Wedge, *History of Trempealeau County Wisconsin*, p. 846, gives information that 10 acres of land for the church was donated Geo. H. Markham.

120 Ibid., p. 31

121 H. H. Heaming, *History of the Catholic Church in Wisconsin*, p. 820

122 W. Kruszka, *A History of the Poles. Part 4*, p. 96

123 The source lacks the first name and only indicates the last name and the first initial.

124 J. L. Hauck, *Catholic Church in Trempealeau County*, in: F. Curtiss-Wedge, *History of Trempealeau County Wisconsin* 1917, p. 847

sisters had arrived to work with 115 Polish students. The old rectory was renovated and adopted for the needs of the sisters.[125] That triggered a new idea regarding the construction of a new rectory. In March of 1888, Rev. Tomaszewski was transferred to a different parish, and Rev. R. L. Guzowski took his place.[126]

His successor Rev. Anselm Kroll worked in the parish for only eight months from February 20, 1890, until September 3rd of the same year.[127] After his departure from SS. Peter and Paul, the parish remained without a pastor for seven months. The vacancy in the parish ended along with the nomination of Rev. August Babinski as the new pastor. He arrived at the parish on September 2, 1890.[128] During his first year as a pastor along with the parishioners, the decision was made to build a new church. The construction plans described a church built from brick and stone to be 131 feet long and 56 feet wide. The work started in 1895, and in the fall of 1896, the project was finished. The cost of this new church building was $25,000. On October 28, 1896,[129] Bishop James Schwebach came to Independence and consecrated the new church.[130] Along with the construction of

Church of SS. Peter & Paul, Independence 2012
Source: Author's Collection

---

125 W. Kruszka, *A History of the Poles. Part 4*, p. 96
126 The source lacks the first name and only indicates the last name and the first initial.
127 H. H. Heaming, *History of the Catholic Church in Wisconsin*, p. 821
128 F. Curtiss-Wedge, *History of Trempealeau County Wisconsin*, p. 847
129 Ibid., p. 847. Here is a date October 3, 1896 when the church was dedicated.
130 W. Kruszka, *A History of the Poles. Part 4*, p. 96.

the church, a sisters' house was built as well. Rev. Babinski in 1905 was transferred to a new Polish parish in Superior. He had contributed greatly to the formation and creation of religious and spiritual life of his parishioners.

Rev. Andrew Gara became the new pastor in Independence where he continued his service for twenty-one years. While he held the pastoral post, the parish had purchased a new organ in 1902 for $1,600. His pastoral work and influence helped to create a new church and parish community dedicated to St. Stanislaus in Arcadia. The parish community in Independence grew to 300 families which amounted to 1,600 faithful. Therefore, an extension of the church was built in 1908.

One of the biggest events in the parish was the arrival of a new vicar in 1917. His name was Rev. James Brzezinski.[131] Parochial archives state that in 1917 the number of families reached 425 which amounted to 2,100 believers. The parochial school in 1917 provided education for 225 students. Teaching duties were fulfilled by one lay teacher who also served as an organist and four sisters[132] who came from Stevens Point. The next vicar Rev. Joseph Andrzejewski fulfilled his religious duties in this church for thirteen months.

In 1919, a new vicar arrived. Rev. Stephen Mieczkowski served the church for only two months. In September 1922, a new pastor Rev. Lucien J. Kufel was nominated. He performed his pastoral duties and served his parishioners until September 1, 1961. His successor Rev. Edmund Klimecki worked in Independence from 1961 to 1968. He supervised, with his competent eye, the construction of the new school which was finished in 1968. He then left the parish and was replaced by Rev. Chester Moczarny who attended to the needs of the faithful people of the parish until 1971. In that same year, Rev. Herbert Zoromski became the new pastor of SS. Peter and Paul Parish.

---

131 F. Curtiss-Wedge, *History of Trempealeau County Wisconsin*, p. 847, on April 7, 1917 Rev. James Berczezinski arrived as assistant and here his last name is changed.

132 J. L. Hauck, *Catholic Church in Trempealeau County*, in: F. Curtiss-Wedge, *History of Trempealeau County Wisconsin*, 1917 p. 847.

TABLE 6: Pastoral Registry of All Pastors and Vicars in SS. Peter and Paul Parish, Independence from 1875–1971

PASTORS	VICARS
Rev. Hieronymus Klimecki 1875–1883	
Rev. A. Warnagiris 1883–1885	
Rev. Dominic Majer 1885	
Rev. Raphael Tomaszewski 1885–1888	Rev. J. Brzezinski Rev. Joseph Andrzejewski Rev. Stephen P. Mieczkowski
Rev. R. L. Guzowski 1888–1890	
Rev. Anselm A. Kroll 1890	
Rev. August Babinski 1890–1901	
Rev. Andrew W. Gara 1901–1922	
Rev. Lucien J. Kufel 1922–1961	Rev. Al Glinski Rev. Max Kluczykowski Rev. Edward J. Roskos Rev. Francis A. Piekarski Rev. Methodius Dobrzlewski O.F.M. Rev. Eugene Zynda Rev. Francis Przybylski Rev. Edwin P. Klimeszewski Rev. Constant Chilicki Rev. John J. Krakowski Rev. Ernest Kaim Rev. Edwin J. Stanek Rev. Augustn Sulik Rev. Edward Masalewicz

More detailed information regarding the vicars' work is unavailable. It was only possible to establish who served as a pastor during their time of service.

11. St. Hedwig, Poznan

A parish community in the town of Poznan, with a postal address in Thorp, was located north of Clark County and founded in 1891.[133] The history of Polish immigrants to this territory starts in 1885. Just like

---

[133] WI History Records Survey (Series 1953) 1936-42 Inventory of Church Records by County Box 229 Folder 12 County Clark, p. 1. Information states that the parish was established in 1890 by the Rev. Konstantin Frydrichowicz from Mill Creek, Portage County.

other nationalities, the Poles came here in search of work and of a better future. Polish settlers came here encouraged by the promise of well paid jobs waiting for them, and the promise of new land with fertile soil that was suitable for farming. Encouraged by the promises from the government as well as from the owners of various factories, they traveled deep into the country to find the perfect place to settle.

The first Polish person Valentin Malecki arrived here in 1888. He came into this territory with the purpose of purchasing farm land. Once he had accomplished that, he returned to the northern part of Michigan where he lived and worked.[134] When he returned to the town of Poznan to settle permanently, he encouraged many Poles to also start their new life there. In June of 1891, the number of Polish immigrants included twenty-five families.[135] All agreed that their goal should be the construction of a small, modest church just for the needs of their community.

Church of St. Hedwig, Poznan 1906
Source: www.usgennet.org/usa/wi/county/clark/webbbs/records/index.cgi?read=3812

During one of the first meetings of the construction committee, people decided that all of the Polish families who wanted to have their own church must donate some wood and timber for the purpose of this construction. Significant excitement among the Polish families sped up the construction process, and the church was finished quickly. Help also came from two Polish gentlemen, Plotrowicz and Slupecki, who worked in Milwaukee. They donated ten acres of land to the church in June 1891.[136]

The church was finished in September 1891, and on September 27th, Rev. Konstanty Frydrychowicz blessed the church.[137] He also named and

---

134   Parish Book, *St. Hedwig's Church Congregation 1891-1966*, Wisconsin 1966, p. 18-19
135   W. Kruszka, *A History of the Poles. Part 4*, p. 105
136   F. Curtiss-Wedge, *History of Trempealeau County Wisconsin*, p. 736
137   Parish Book, *St. Hedwig's Church Congregation*, p. 19. In the book F. Curtiss-Wedge, *History of Trempealeau County Wisconsin*, p. 738. Information states that the church was dedicated by Bishop James Schwebach in September 27, 1891.

dedicated it to St. Hedwig, even though all parishioners and their priest preferred a different name, the Parish of All Saints. Bishop Schwebach nominated Rev. Frydrychowicz as the first administrator of the newly created pastoral outpost. Rev. Frydrychowicz commuted here from Mill Creek. This small mission community grew dynamically.

The first sacrament of Baptism was granted in the new church on the day of its consecration, September 27, 1891. Two months later on November 25, 1891, the first sacrament of marriage was celebrated.

In 1893, Rev. Frydrychowicz was transferred by the bishop to a Polish church in North Creek. He was replaced by Rev. Francis Jachminiak who became the new administrator of this small mission. He celebrated Holy Mass two times per month.

The next change came about in March 1896 when Rev. Frydrychowicz returned to the mission.[138] Rev. Jachminiak left the parish, and Rev. Frydrychowicz worked there for another year. He was transferred again on September 2, 1897, to western Wisconsin. The position of the new pastor at St. Hedwig was assumed by Rev. James Korczyk[139] who resided in Thorp from September 1897 until February 1900. The administrative custody for St. Hedwig mission was provided by the pastor of St. Bernard Parish in Thorp. During the time that Rev. Korczyk worked with the mission, the church building was completely renovated. The new bell was installed in the church's tower, and three new altars were erected inside the church. Also on June 16, 1898, the new rectory building was finished. Unfortunately, it was built about two miles (3.2 km) from the church.

On February 9, 1900, the bishop of La Crosse appointed a new pastor for St. Bernard's Church in Thorp. The new pastor Rev. Joseph Biela spent only fifteen months in the parish and then resigned from the position. He was followed by Rev. Ignatius Orlik from Buffalo, New York. While he was there, the functioning of the church was reorganized. He organized the first meeting of the Parish Council in June 1901 during which the basic principles for the management of the parish were defined. Also during this meeting, parishioners agreed that the pastor's

---

138   W. Kruszka, *A History of the Poles. Part 4*, p. 105
139   H. H. Heaming, *History of the Catholic Church in Wisconsin*, p. 850

earnings should be $700. The involvement and hard work of the new pastor were quite fruitful for the entire congregation.

During subsequent meetings, parishioners adopted a plan to build a new church. This decision was influenced by the growth of the Polish population. In 1904, the foundation for the new church was consecrated, and construction work began soon after that.

In September of 1905, Rev. Orlik was transferred to a different parish, and his duties were assumed by Rev. Xavier Pudlo. The number of parishioners continued to rise to 370 families.[140] According to available resources, in 1905,[141] 400 Polish families belonged to the congregation. It soon became the largest Polish congregation in the Diocese of La Crosse. For this reason, the church had to be enlarged. However, the people decided that they would rather invest in a new, larger church. A short amount of time passed from that decision until October 17, 1906, when the church was finished. It was built with brick walls and could hold 1,200 people. The basement was 12 feet (around 4 meters) high and was built to host classrooms for its future students. The interior of this new church was quite rich as far as its furnishings ranging from wooden sculptures of the saints to fourteen extremely beautiful stained glass windows. The windows were donated by families within the parish, and they were expensive. The cost of one window was $2,000. New pews and a modern heating system were installed in the new church. The total cost incurred was $30,000.[142] The consecration of the church was celebrated by Bishop James Schwebach.

During this time, the Parish Council introduced a $10 charge for

Church of St. Hedwig, Poznan 2012
Source: Author's Collection

---

140 *Thorp Courier*, Taylor County, Wisconsin, August 19, 1906. A discrepancy exists between sources as to the number of families in the parish at this time.
141 W. Kruszka, *A History of the Poles. Part 4*, p. 106
142 www.usgennet.org/usa/wi/county/webbbs/records/index.cgi (February 1, 2009)

two seats closest to the presbytery and $8 for two seats in the middle of the church. As the seats were closer to the exit of the church, the rate was reduced an additional $2. Parishioners began to argue about their rents especially if guests from the city arrived in church and sat in seats paid for by parishioners. With the passage of time, this practice was abandoned. The finishing and decorative changes were brought to an end in 1907.[143]

On April 17, 1914, the congregation of St. Hedwig received a second priest. The Vicar Rev. Bronislaus Szymczak arrived at the parish but stayed there only for three months. Toward the end of Rev. X. Pudlo's service in 1914, three new church bells were purchased. Soon, electricity was also installed in the church. The congregation grew to 525 families. Father's next initiative was the construction of the new parish school. However, the Parish Council and most of the parishioners were against this idea. Rev. X. Pudlo baffled by his parishioners' attitude sent his resignation to the bishop on January 3, 1916. However, the bishop did not accept his resignation. Rev. Pudlo became very discouraged and sent another complaint to the bishop. It would not be until three years later that his petition was finally accepted. In 1918, Rev. Pudlo supervised the process of the enlargement of the north side of the parish cemetery. On November 3, 1919, after fourteen years of service at St. Hedwig Parish, Rev. Pudlo was transferred to Arcadia.

At the end of 1919, Rev. James Korczyk came to the parish, but on October 25, 1920, he received a new assignment and moved to a Polish parish in La Crosse. For a short time, Rev. Lucien Kuffel worked for the parish. In November 1920, Rev. Francis Kulig became a pastor at St. Hedwig in Poznan. After twenty years in 1940, a change in the pastoral office took place when an assistant pastor Rev. Roman Papierniak joined the congregation. In 1941, another assistant priest Rev. Ted Szczerbicki joined Pastor Rev. Kulig and worked with him until June 1, 1942. Rev. Sigismund Lengowski replaced Rev. Szczerbicki. Pastor Kulig died on August 13, 1942.[144]

The new nomination to the pastoral office honored Rev. Francis Piekarski who served the parish for sixteen years. In 1945, he requested

---

[143] N. J. Le Page, "Hands Foundation gives gift to Thorp Museum," *Marshfield News-Herald*, January 31, 2009, p. 1.

[144] Parish Book, *St. Hedwig's Church Congregation*, p. 22

that a vicar be appointed to provide additional help for the parish. Rev. Raymond Rucki received this assignment and stayed until July 1, 1947. He was followed by Rev. Ernest Kaim who attended to his duties until August 9, 1950. In the meantime, the Parish Council led by the pastor made a decision to build a new school to serve the children and teens in the parish. This project was finished in 1949, but happiness was short lived for the building was destroyed by fire in February 1950. Thanks to quick restoration, the school was fully functioning again in the summer of the same year. In 1950, a new vicar was sent to help the pastor. Rev. Joseph Walejewski served the parish for one year until July 2, 1951. Other vicars who worked at the parish included Rev. Herbert Zoromski, (who transferred to St. Therese Parish in Rothschild), Rev. Edward Masalewicz, Rev. Meyer, and Rev. Chilicki. A new pastor Rev. Francis Disher along with new vicar Rev. George Becker assumed their duties on June 3, 1959. Pastor Disher received a new pastoral office in 1961, and Poznan got a newly appointed pastor Rev. Edward Masalewicz on June 8, 1961. He held the office until 1968. During this time, there were several vicars that worked with him. Among them were Rev. Donald Halaska (1961-1963), Rev. Roy L. Mish (1963-1967), and Rev. William Matzek in 1967. A change in the pastoral office occurred again, and Rev. John Puerner worked there. In January 1974, the two parishes of St. Hedwig and St. Bernard joined together.

12. Sacred Heart of Jesus, Cassel

The two towns of Cassel and Marathon are located close to each other in an area southeast from the town of Poniatowski. The town of Cassel was founded on November 12, 1891.[145] The first Polish settlers arrived at the beginning of 1875. They tried hard to settle and organize in this new environment.[146] After ten years when they grew in number, they decided to build their own church. Thirty Polish families sent a petition to the bishop of La Crosse regarding their idea. Bishop Kilian Casper Flasch

---

145 L. Marchetti, *History of Marathon County Wisconsin...*, Chicago 1913, p. 575
146 Parish Book, *Sacred Heart of Jesus Christ Cassel, Wisconsin*, 1986, p. 8

responded positively to this request and granted a permit to start the preliminary work and to organize everything needed for the construction and creation of the parish. The bishop also directed that the new church be called Sacred Heart of Jesus. The church was built in 1886.[147] This was a wooden church. The four acres of land for the church were donated by Carla and Frances Lepak. In 1905, it was reconstructed into an all brick wall church. Another reconstruction followed in 1908.[148]

Church of the Sacred Heart of Jesus, Cassel
Source: Parish Book Sacred Heart of Jesus

The newly created parish at first served as a mission and did not have a permanent leader. All liturgical needs were attended to by Pastor Andrew Gara who commuted from Poniatowski.[149] He also served other small churches in the region: the Most Holy Family Parish in Poniatowski, the Holy Trinity Parish also in Poniatowski, and the Holy Savior Parish in Athens.[150]

The first sacrament of marriage was celebrated in this church on January 18, 1887, when Frances Adamski and Charles Lepak were married. The first sacrament of Baptism was administered to Sophie Joswiak[151] on May 5, 1887. The new rectory was built in 1901,[152] and then in 1949, it was renovated and modernized. This small but very dynamic congregation also built their own new school in 1910.[153] Rev. Theofilus Wojak became the first permanently residing pastor.

The Felician Sisters managed and taught at the school. Their residence was attached to the school. The sisters had the use of a small garden, small chicken farm, and the hay loft. These were donated to them

---

147   *Town of Cassel Centennial 1891-1991, Wisconsin*, 1991, p. 38
148   Ibid., p. 38
149   W. Kruszka, *A History of the Poles. Part 4*, p. 100
150   Ibid., p. 100
151   Parish Book, *Sacred Heart of Jesus Cassel Wisconsin*, p. 4
152   A.G. Straub, Assisted by Joe Szymanski, *The History of Marathon, Wisconsin 1857-1957*, Marathon, Wisconsin 1957, p. 19 states that in 1902 the rectory was built in Cassel.
153   *Town of Cassel Centennial 1891-1991*, p. 38

by the parishioners.[154] Until the year 1930, the main language taught in school was Polish.

In 1936, the parish celebrated its golden anniversary (fifty years of existence), and in 1961, seventy-five years of its dedication to the Lord were commemorated. One year earlier in 1960 during one of the parish meetings, people voted in favor of building a newer church. The collection of money started right away. This collection process was rather slow, and only $1,586.10 was collected.

Church of the Sacred Heart of Jesus, Cassel 2012
Source: Author's Collection

In 1963, Bishop John Patrick Treacy presented a plan aimed at closing the church. He justified his decision with an argument that there were other smaller churches in this region: St. Mary's Parish in Marathon, St. John's Parish in Edgar, and St. Patrick's Parish in Halder that could handle those parishioners. All the parishioners were outraged with such a plan. They created a Parish Council which immediately intervened to the bishop and asked to preserve the parish at its current status. Permission was granted, and this fact motivated the parishioners to take better care of their congregation and their parish. Their motivation was reflected by a collection of $11,138.88 by December 1968.

During that same year in June, a newly nominated pastor Rev. Joseph Rafacz came to manage the parish. The first issue that he attended to was the creation of a Parish Advisory Council which served as a supportive arm for the project of building the new church. Representatives of the Parish Advisory Council had a series of meetings with Bishop Frederick William Freking,[155] The members of the Advisory Council introduced the building plans to the bishop, and he allowed for the preliminary work to begin under one condition: the congregation was to

---

154 Ibid., p. 39

155 Frederick William Freking – Ordinary Bishop of the Diocese of La Crosse from December 30, 1964 to May 10, 1983. Before that he was Bishop of the Diocese of Salina, Kansas. Born on August 11, 1913, in Heron Lake, Minnesota, and ordained on July 31, 1931, in Winona, Minnesota. Retired in 1983 and died on November 28, 1998.

collect $50,000 before any work was done. This condition was met by organizing a special dinner for all the parishioners and other interested parties at the cost of $25.00 per plate. The Advisory Council that supported the pastor introduced plans for the new church building with special regard to the internal structure of the new temple which was to be made out of steel. Choosing a qualified and experienced firm that could be entrusted with the whole building was the next step.

The Butler Company was chosen, and in the fall of 1961, the process of building the new church began. The plans called for a church that would accommodate 240 people. In addition, the plan was to include a large dining area with a kitchen, bathrooms, and a maintenance room with a new furnace to heat the church. In 1969, the vestry was finished; the presbytery was decorated with a huge cross; and the tabernacle was placed in the church. During the Christmas Vigil, Rev. J. Rafacz organized a solemn procession whereby the Blessed Sacrament was transferred from the old church to the new one. Officially, the church was consecrated by Bishop Frederick W. Freking of the Diocese of La Crosse[156] on June 5, 1970. The entire project was completed, and the congregation had no debt. After the Holy Mass of Thanksgiving, all parishioners were invited to dinner. The first marriage was celebrated in the new church on May 17, 1970, when Bonnie Wadzinski and Hay Heindl tied the knot.

The future of small parishes like Sacred Heart of Jesus in Cassel during that period relied on integration with other small parishes. Another factor determined their fate: the small number of priests and the small number of seminarians.[157] In 1970, the school in Cassel was closed due to the small number of students and the departure of the sisters.

13. St. Bartholomew, Mill Creek

The first traces of Polish settlers in the Mill Creek area were seen in the 1860s. Because of an advertisement in a Chicago newspaper that informed people of the possibility of procuring good land, this region

---

156 Parish Book, *Sacred Heart of Jesus Cassel Wisconsin*, p. 11
157 Ibid., p. 11

became very popular among new Polish settlers. Though small at the beginning, this settlement community started growing rapidly, and eventually the population reached forty-five families. Some of the residents attended Holy Mass and other worship services in Stevens Point which was located about five miles from Mill Creek. Others wanted to have their own church in their own town.[158] In a short time, the community of Mill Creek came to a decision to build a new church and received the blessing and permission of the bishop. In 1883, construction was started and completed that same year after spending $3,000.[159]

Church of St. Bartholomew, Mill Creek around 1895

Source: H.H. Heaming, History of the Catholic Church in Wisconsin

At the beginning, the parish in Mill Creek was a mission and was served by priests from Junction City. One of the commuting priests Rev. August Krogulski[160] would come to lead the community in prayer once a month. His successor in Junction City Rev. Babinski also would visit the mission once a month until August 1890. For a period of one year, Rev. T. O. Lugowski substituted for him. Starting in 1891, the mission developed dynamically, and in 1892, ninety families[161] settled there. The parishioners then decided during one of their meetings to send a delegation of the community to Bishop Schwebach with a request for a permanent pastor for the parish. The bishop sent Rev. Konstanty Frydrychowicz[162] who celebrated Holy Mass in Mill Creek three times per month. On the last Sunday of each month, he would travel to the church in Poznan in Clark County. In 1893, the bishop appointed a new

---

158 W. Kruszka, *A History of the Poles. Part 4*, p. 24-25
159 H. H. Heaming, *History of the Catholic Church in Wisconsin,* p. 834
160 D. Kolinski, *The Origin*, p. 35
161 W. Kruszka, *A History of the Poles. Part 4*, p. 25
162 Rev. Konstanty Fredrychowicz name is spelled as Frydrychowicz in the parishes of SS. Peter and Paul, Weyerhauser, Assumption of the BVM in Strickland, Holy Family in Poniatowski, and St. Hedwig in Poznan.

pastor Rev. Francis Jachimiak.[163] During his stay at the parish, he built a new school which was opened in 1900 and was attended by thirty-five students. In that same year, there were 150 families in the parish. In 1903, Rev. Jachimiak assumed a new position in the Church of Blessed Virgin Mary in Texas, and Rev. Frydrychowicz returned to Mill Creek. After a few months, he left the parish and was replaced by Rev. T. Lugowski (1903-1909). Rev. August Fortysiak served in Mill Creek from 1909 to1916 and built a new neo-Gothic brick and stone church for the amount of $9,000. The bells were moved from the old church to the new one. The new temple was consecrated by Bishop J. J. Fox from the Diocese of Green Bay on November 21, 1910. During the subsequent years, the pastoral office in Mill Creek was held by Rev. M. Klosowki, Rev. Stan Lipinski (1916-1921), and Rev. Leo Jankowski (1921-1928). As administrators, Rev. W. Pruc, Rev. F. A. Nowak, and Rev. S. Lapinski worked in Mill Creek until 1928.[164]

Church of St. Bartholomew, Mill Creek 2012
Source: Author's Collection

During the administration of the parish by Rev. Pruc, several important repairs and renovations were done. The rectory was in need of extensive repair so the construction of a new one began. However, the work progressed slowly, and three of his successors: Rev. A. Nowak, Rev. S. Lapinski, and Rev. Ignatius Grad (1929-1931) had to temporarily live in Stevens Point. March 30, 1931,[165] the church was destroyed by fire while Rev. Ignatius Grad was at the Mill Creek parish. The cause of this fire was the inattention and carelessness of the custodian who wanted to warm up the church for the cleaning women. People were able to salvage the Blessed Sacrament, some benches, and a few furniture pieces. Although the walls of the church remained

---

163   H. H. Heaming, *History of the Catholic Church in Wisconsin*, p. 835

164   www.pchswi.org/archives/church/st_bart. html (August 20, 2008), p. 6

165   www.pchswi.org/archives/church/religionPChtm (July 16, 2008), p. 10 gives a different date as to the fire of the church (1932).

intact, the whole inside of the building was destroyed. The next pastor Rev. P. J. Novitski (1931-1934) after receiving $20,000 from the insurance of the church organized a Renovation Committee. Because of the insurance money, the church was quickly rebuilt and then consecrated by Bishop Paul Rhode from Green Bay on the December 13, 1931. Other pastors who serviced the church in Mill Creek included Rev. Victor Hoppa (1934-1938), Rev. Bernard Hoppa (1938-1947), Rev. Joseph Shulist (1947), Rev. F. S. Szymczak (1948-1962), Rev. Peter Rombalski (1962-1969), Rev. Stanley Chilicki (1969-1973), Rev. James Shafer (1973), Rev. Raymond Rucki (1973-1981), and since 1981, Rev. John Mauel.[166]

14. Holy Cross, La Crosse

Holy Cross Church, La Crosse 1885
Source: F. Crane, The Catholic History of La Crosse *1904*

A group of Polish immigrants who settled in the city of La Crosse (the seat of the diocese) with joint efforts built a new church and established the foundation of the Parish of Holy Cross. Bishop K. Flasch consecrated the church on September 13, 1885. He was assisted by the following priests: Rev. Schwebach, Rev. Wiedmann, Rev. Obermueller, Rev. Fitzpatric, Rev. Blaschke, Rev. Byzewski, and Rev. Harrier. During the consecration ceremony, the school in the lower level of the church received its blessing as well. The congregation had eighty-five families,[167] and seventy-two students attended the school.

---

166   www.pcswi.org/archives/st_bart.html (August 20, 2008), p. 6
167   F. Crane, *The Catholic History of La Crosse*, p. 18

Rev. John A. Blaschke became the first pastor of Holy Cross. He also served as a pastor in St. Wenceslaus Parish. He attended to his pastoral duties at Holy Cross until 1887.[168] During that same year, a new rectory was finished and occupied.[169] The following priests were the subsequent pastors at Holy Cross: Rev. R. L. Guzowski for a little less than one year; Rev. Louis Kaluza (January 1888-September 1888); Rev. Stanislaus Baranowski served the church during the second half of 1888 until June 1890; and Rev. Joseph Horbaczewski was in the office for a very short time from June 1890 to March 1891. The next pastor Rev. John Prucha held the pastoral office from April 1891 until July 1892. During the same year, the number of parishioners grew to ninety-five families. For only two months from July to September 1892, Rev. Joseph Miller served as pastor at Holy Cross.

Another change in the parish occurred when Rev. Anselm Kroll came to the pastoral office in 1892. He worked for the parish for ten years until the time of his death. Ninety-six students attended the parish elementary school which was run by two sisters from the Order of St. Francis, St. Margaret, and St. Bernadette.[170] The parish population was recorded as 125 families. In 1897, the first permanently residing pastor Rev. John Blaschke came to the parish. During the next year (1898), the unfinished church was destroyed by a strong wind storm. A new school with four new classrooms opened in 1915. On October 20, 1920, Rev. J. M. Korczyk came to the parish and served the congregation for twenty years until his death on December 5, 1940. The whole church was renovated during the same year. From 1940 to 1952, Rev. Stanley Andrzejewski served as pastor at Holy Cross and was replaced by Rev. Nicholas Beschta. In 1956, the population of the parish was 370 families, and the number of students in the school grew to 175 children.[171] The church was demolished, and the parish closed in 1960.

---

168   H. H. Heaming, *History of the Catholic Church in Wisconsin*, p. 762.
169   Parish Book, *Our Stewardship Program, Holy Cross Parish, La Crosse*, p. 3
170   H. H. Heaming, *History of the Catholic Church in Wisconsin*, p. 763
171   Parish Book, *Our Stewardship Program, Holy Cross Parish, La Crosse*, p. 3

15. St. John Cantius, Fairchild

In 1883, the owner of a great estate in Fairchild, M. C. Foster sold a portion of his land to another resident of Fairchild named Hines. In 1886, Mr. Hines donated two acres of this for a church in order to encourage residents to stay in Fairchild and to attract newcomers to settle in this area. Settlers were needed because of the founding of the great pulp mill which employed 260 men and needed more manpower. In 1887 through the efforts of Rev. August Babinski, a wooden church was built for thirty-eight Polish families and was named St. John Cantius. On October 27th of the same year, the church was consecrated by Bishop Kilian Flasch of the Diocese of La Crosse. The total cost of building the church was $2,000. Originally, the church was a mission church to which priests commuted by train from La Crosse.[172] The parish was located in the county of Eau Claire.[173]

Church of St. John Cantius, Fairchild 1950
Source: Parish Book, St. John Cantius 1887-Centennial-1987

The church was built with a heating system fueled by wood and coal and had to be tended to by an individual. Later in 1942, this system was converted to oil and used until 1956 when it was replaced by LP gas which was much more efficient. Originally, lighting for the church was provided by gasoline lanterns, but in 1926 electricity was installed. Over the years, many changes took place: new altars, a remodeled sacristy, and metal siding to replace the wood siding.

Parish books show that the first Baptism in the Church of St. John Cantius took place on December 11, 1887. The child who was baptized was named Elizabeth Melka. The first wedding took place on May 1, 1890. Rev. August Babinski blessed the couple: Rosalie Kubacki and Martin Szule.

---

172   Parish Book, *St. John Cantius 1887-Centennial-1987*, Wisconsin 1987, p. 6. It notes that the clergy traveled from North Creek, near Arcadia once a month.
173   W. Kruszka, *A History of the Poles. Part 4*, p. 107

Church of St. John Cantius, Fairchild 2012
Source: Author's Collection

In 1924, nuns arrived at the parish for one month each year. They taught children religion. The teaching of religion in such a way lasted until 1954. Also, in 1954, the parish purchased a garage across the street from the church and remodeled it into a parish hall which was used for religious instruction, parish fund-raisers, funeral breakfasts, wedding receptions, and many other special celebrations. One year later in 1956, the parish newsletter was published addressing the current business of the parish and the deanery. In that same year, the parish consisted of eighty-one families.[174]

TABLE 7: Pastoral Registry of St. John Cantius Parish, Fairchild

Rev. August Babinski	1887–1889
Rev. Anselm Kroll	1889–1920 – the status of parish mission
Rev. Francis Brzostowicz	1921–1925
Rev. Stephen Mieczkowski	1925–1929
Rev. S. F. Szymczak	1929–1938 – the status of parish mission
Rev. Francis Piekarski	1938–1941
Rev. August Ausman	1941–1943 – the status of parish mission
Rev. Ralph J. Geissler	1943–1945
Rev. Joseph Brake	1945–1948
Rev. Claire Cooney	1948–1950
Rev. Carl A. Wohlmuth	1950–1952
Rev. Andrew Bofenkamp	1959–1959
Rev. Matthew Molinaro	1959–1969
Rev. Rudolph Urbic	1969–1973
Rev. David Ziegelmaier	1973–1980
Rev. John V. Cassidy	1980–1985
Rev. James J. Lesczynski	1985–

---

174   Parish Book, *St. John Cantius 1887-Centennial-1987*, Wisconsin 1987, p. 8

16. St. Lawrence, Grand Rapids (Wisconsin Rapids)

The city of Grand Rapids is located on the beautiful Wisconsin River. Already in 1890, fifteen Polish families resided there.[175] The Poles wanted to have their own Polish church. The temporary spiritual leader of this community who commuted to Grand Rapids from Junction City was Rev. Joseph J. Miller. In the years 1899 to1900, he visited the Polish immigrants in Grand Rapids several times. At one meeting, it was decided to collect money and take on the work of building their temple. On December 31, 1899, a collection was taken, and the total amount received was $925.00. With this money at the beginning of 1900, they bought eight plots for the construction of a new church. The next step was to name the church, and the decision was made to name it St. Lawrence. This happened because one of the residents of Grand Rapids Wawrzyniec (Lawrence) Klepien offered the most money for the construction of the church.[176] As an expression of his contribution, a token of one dollar, people selected St. Lawrence to be the patron. Providing care over the faithful in Grand Rapids was first taken by Rev. J. Gara from Junction City, then Rev. Stanislaw Elbert from Plover, and Rev. James Korczyk from Pine Creek. Rev. James Korczyk was appointed by Bishop Schwebach of La Crosse for this newly created position of pastor of the new church and parish.[177]

Church of St. Lawrence, Wisconsin Rapids 1904
Source: http://www.flickr.com/photos/mcmillanlibrary/page5/

In the meantime, the parish held a meeting concerning the construction of the church. During this meeting, people wondered if they should combine the construction of a new church with a new school and rectory. During the meeting held on May 28, 1903, the decision

---

[175] Parish Book, *History of St. Lawrence Parish*, 2004, p. 2. Information indicates that there were about 33 Polish families who arrived in this area.
[176] W. Kruszka, *A History of the Poles. Part 4*, p. 103
[177] G. O. Jones, *History of Wood County Wisconsin*, Minneapolis, 1923, p. 121

was made to combine the projects of building a new church and school. A few weeks later in July 1903, the contract was signed for construction of a new church and school for a total cost of $11,700. The community of Grand Rapids grew during this period from fifty-two to 200 families. While construction was taking place, parishioners attended Saints Peter and Paul Church for their services.[178] The construction work continued. On September 13, 1903, the cornerstone was blessed, and on March 12, 1904, the first Mass was celebrated presided by Rev. James Korczyk. The church was built of red brick with beautiful decorations. An electrical system was installed in the church and school as was a steam heating system and plumbing. On the ground floor were three classrooms and three rooms for the nuns. The liturgical area in the church was located above these rooms. The parish had about 130 families, and the school had about 114 students.

Church of St. Lawrence, Wisconsin Rapids 2012
Source: Author's Collection

In 1908, the parsonage was built for the pastor. Another building was built for parish functions in 1909.[179] Also in that same year, Rev. J. Korzyk was appointed to the position of professor at St. Francis Seminary, and Rev. Theofilus Wojak became his successor.[180] In August 1910, the Felician Sisters arrived at the school and replaced the Franciscan Sisters. They worked in the parish until 1971. On May 8, 1914, the church and the school were completely destroyed by fire, but soon the vigorous work of reconstruction began. In October 1915, construction was completed on the new structure of the church. At the same time, parishioners attended the nearby Church of Saints Peter and Paul like they had done in the past.[181] The name of the town was changed in 1920 from Grand Rapids to Wisconsin Rapids.

---

178   Ibid., p. 121
179   www.scls.lib.wi.us/mcm/taylor/album_pt3.html (February 10, 2009)
180   G. O. Jones, *History of Wood County Wisconsin,* Minneapolis 1923, p. 121
181   Ibid., p. 122

On May 31, 1931, during a parish meeting, it was decided to build a larger church. This decision was dictated by the growing number of parishioners. Soon work began, and on August 16, 1931, the cornerstone was laid. A year later on the opposite side of the road, the new church was opened for use. On June 12, 1932, the new church was consecrated by Bishop Alexander J. Mc Gavick who assisted Rev. S. P. Mieczkowski.

On April 30, 1950, the newly built rectory was opened. The old parsonage was modernized and renovated for use by the nuns. In 1971, the nuns left the school, and the school continued its work with lay teachers. Later, the need to build a new parochial school became evident. Construction was completed on July 1, 1975. The old school building was then demolished.

TABLE 8: Pastoral Registry of St. Lawrence Parish, Grand Rapids

Rev. Florian Marmurowicz	1945–1956
Rev. Chester Zielinski	1956–1969
Rev. Raymond Rucki	1969–1974
Rev. Aloysius Wozniak	1974–1978
Rev. Richard Tomsyck	1978–1982
Rev. Joseph Bilgrienn	1982–1988
Rev. John Hogan	1989–

17. Holy Rosary, Sigel

Holy Rosary Parish in Sigel is one of the oldest Polish parishes in the area. The first Polish settlers went to the church in nearby Grand Rapids (Wisconsin Rapids) which was dedicated to Saints Peter and Paul. They attended there until 1881.[182] On November 21, 1881, an agreement was made to sell five acres of land for the church. The contract was between the owners Anna and Joseph Jagodzinski and Bishop Kilian Flasch of the Diocese of La Crosse. At the same time, the bishop appointed Rev. Klemecki pastor from Independence with the responsibil-

---

182 G. O. Jones, *History of Wood County Wisconsin,* Minneapolis 1923, p. 122

ity for the preparation, creation, and construction of the parish church. The price for the land was set at $25. After purchasing the property, it was decided that three acres would be used for the church and the remaining two acres for the parish cemetery.[183]

The parish originated with Polish settlers who were mainly farmers or who worked in the forest felling trees and transporting them from the forest. Even before construction of the temple, this area was covered by special pastoral care whereby once a month a priest came to Sigel from North Creek (Arcadia). The priest commuted by train to Grand Rapids with the last portion overland by horseback or carriage.

Church of the Holy Rosary, Sigel
Source: Parish Book Sto Lat Wiary Holy Rosary

The first church was built in the summer of 1882 and was built of wood. The building had two levels: an upper which was used for liturgical services and the lower which held the school. In 1883, Mass in the church was celebrated in Sigel twice a month.[184] On the other two Sundays, the residents of Sigel participated in the liturgy at Saints Peter and Paul Church in Centralia.[185] The parish at that time consisted of one hundred families.

The parochial school in Sigel began its operation in 1883. Students attended grades one through four. The number of students attending the school grew to between fifty and sixty young people.[186] The school was managed by lay teachers. In 1913, the parish school was closed.

When Rev. Klemecki was transferred to another parish, his successor was Rev. D. Majer of Pine Creek who only stayed for one year. Starting in 1883 and then for the next five years, the parish priest in

---

183   www.holyrosarysigel.com (August 19, 2008)
184   W. Kruszka, *A History of Poles, Part 4,* p. 104
185   In the present time this is the new name Wisconsin Rapids.
186   On the web site www.holyrosarysigel.com the number of students is 50-60, but in the W. Kruszka, *A History of the Poles. Part 4,* p. 100-103 stated the number at 100 students.

Sigel was Rev. A. Krogulski. In October 1888, Rev. A. Van Sever was appointed pastor. He commuted from Rudolph. The next summer, a new priest was appointed, Rev. A. Babinski. He commuted to Sigel from Junction City. Over the next fifteen years, pastoral care was exercised by the parish priests commuting from Junction City. They were Rev. Theodore Lugowski (1890-1895), Rev. J. J. Miller (1895-1900), Rev. J. Gara (1900 until June 1904), and Rev. J. Korczyk until 1908.

For the first two years, the priest from North Creek commuted to this church after a priest commuted from Rudolph for one year. Over the next twenty years, the pastoral ministry in Sigel was offered by the priest from Junction City. Then the situation was changed. Over the next six years, the pastor from Sigel commuted to the mission churches in City Point and Spaulding, to St. Lawrence (for twelve years), and to Vesper for thirty-five years. The priests working in Sigel since 1909 were Rev. J. Rayski, Rev. Ignatius Orlik, and from August 1910, Rev. Theoplius Wojak, Rev. L. Kufel, Rev. Francis Kulig, Rev. J. J. Robiecki, Rev. C. Ciszewski, and Rev. C. W. Gille served there.

Church of the Holy Rosary, Sigel 2012
Source: Author's Collection

The current Church of the Holy Rosary was built in Sigel in 1901 for the sum of $4,625. The old church building was used for social gatherings. The construction of the new temple was supervised by Rev. Jakob Gara. Three wooden altars were made in Stevens Point for this church, and many of the furnishings were donated by the parishioners. A two story rectory was constructed on the north side of the church during 1908. Also in 1908 on the night before Thanksgiving, a tornado caused damage to part of the church and repairs were made immediately. Lightning struck the church in 1926 during Mass and destroyed the floor in the sacristy and started a fire.

In 1937, electricity was installed in the church. This church was a mission church for seventy-six years. Through the 1940s and 1950s, the church was run by the pastor and two trustees: Henry Schroedel and Fabin Krekowski. In the same years, the school sisters of SS. Peter and Paul in Wisconsin Rapids taught religion for two weeks every year. The youth were taught Monday through Friday from 9:00 AM to 3:00 PM.

The furnace room for the church was built in 1947, and the oil furnace was installed much to the relief of the furnace tenders. In 1948, the church was struck by lightning again. The damage was that the plaster was cracked on the walls. The back room for the kitchen and stairs were built onto the hall in 1950. The life of this church rapidly changed. In 1957, this mission parish was changed to a regular parish with a resident pastor Rev. Edmund Klimek.[187]

The first Parish Council was formed in 1970. Eight years later in 1978, the hall which was used for gatherings was torn down, and a new parish center received approval for construction in 1980 for the sum of $120,000.[188]

Because of the lack of resident priests the rectory deteriorated and was sold to Frank Jagodzinski in 1993 and torn down.

TABLE 9: Pastoral Registry at Holy Rosary Church, Sigel

Rev. Peter F. Rombalski	1953–1957
Rev. Edmund J. Klimek	1958–1961
Rev. George Stashek	1961–1966
Rev. Raymond J. Pedretti	1966–1968
Rev. Joseph Martinson	1968–1974
Rev. Joseph M. Irvin	1975–1977
Rev. Aloysius Wozniak	1977–1978
Rev. Richard S. Tomsyck	1978–1980
Rev. Francis M. Mancl	1980–1983
Rev. Richard A. Wisnewski	1983–1985
Rev. Richard J. Hermann	1986–1997
Rev. Chester J. Osowski	1997–2000

---

187   www.holyrosarysigel.com (February 11, 2009)
188   Parish Book, *Sto Lat Wiary 1881-1981*, Wisconsin Rapids 1981, p. 26-27

18. Sacred Heart and St. Wenceslaus, Pine Creek

The third oldest church and one of the oldest Polish pastoral centers in Wisconsin is the Church of Sacred Heart and St. Wenceslaus in Pine Creek. The first traces of Polish settlement in this area date back to 1857.[189] The parish is the third oldest Polish speaking parish formed in Wisconsin and the tenth oldest in the United States.[190] It was canonically organized on February 7, 1864. Land for the church (ten acres) was given by Pawel and Antonina Libera. A wooden church was built there, and it was given a double title by the Polish and Czech immigrants. To celebrate St. Wenceslaus the patron of Bohemia, the church was named after that patron.[191] The title of the Sacred Heart of Jesus was added when Polish families became the majority when their number increased to 170 families. This temple was a mission parish, and a priest commuted from Pine Creek for liturgical services.

Church of the Sacred Heart, Pine Creek 2012
Source: Author's Collection

Rev. Florentine Zadziorski became the permanent priest for the parish in 1866. He served very faithfully until 1868. His successor was Rev. Wenglikowski who worked until 1871.[192] The next two years, Rev. Joseph Musielewicz performed the functions of pastor. He was replaced by Rev. E. Bratkiewicz who lived in Pine Creek until 1874. The next year, Rev. Adolf Snigorski arrived at the parish.[193] During his stay, the church was built in the style of Doric architecture which became one

---

189   In the book J. L. Hauck, *Catholic Church in Trempealeau County*, in: F. Curtiss-Wedge, *History of Trempealeau County Wisconsin*, 1917, p. 838 is given different date of arrival of the first Polish settlement in this area. The years found in this book are 1862-1863.

190   P. Libera, "Polish settlers in Winona Studies, *Polish-American Studies*, Vol. 15:1958, p. 1

191   E. Curtiss-Wedge, *History of Trempealeau County Wisconsin,* 1917, p. 838

192   Absence of the name in the source.

193   W. Kruszka, *A History of Poles, Part 4,* p. 95

of the most beautiful temples in the country. The church's dimensions were 44 feet wide (about 14 m) and 125 feet long (about 41 m), and the cost of construction was $18,000.

The dedication of the church was on November 21, 1875. At that time, 130 Polish families and ten immigrant families from Bohemia belonged to the parish. In 1878, the pastor of Pine Creek Rev. A. Snigorski[194] returned to Poland. His successors were Rev. Wawrzyniec Spryszynski and Rev. Henryk Cichocki. In the same year (1878), the new priest Rev. Dominik Majer arrived from Chicago. He remained there for another six years until 1884. In 1882, a fire in the rectory destroyed it completely. Rev. Cichocki was replaced as a parish priest by Rev. Rafal Tomaszewski who held the pastoral ministry in the parish until 1887. After him, Rev. Roman Guzowski came to Pine Creek, and he remained there until 1889.[195] Once again the pastor in Pine Creek was Rev. Rafal Tomaszewski, and after him in 1891 until 1895, Rev. R. Guzowski returned to Pine Creek. During the second term of Rev. R. Guzowski, the parish school was built with a brick exterior for a total amount of $2,200.[196] Also purchased for the church was a new altar for the sum of $520 and a new pulpit for $160. In 1896, the school had an enrollment of seventy-five students.

From 1895 to 1898, the pastor of Pine Creek was Rev. T. Lugowski who was replaced by Rev. Jacob W. Gara (1898-1901). While Rev. Gara was responsible for the pastoral care of Pine Creek, a new organ was purchased for the church, and renovation of the school building and parsonage occurred. The parish consisted of 190 families, and in the school, Franciscan Sisters were teaching over one hundred students. In 1901, the successor to Rev. Jacob Gara was Rev. J. M. Korczyk.[197] Rev. J. M. Korczyk worked in the parish from 1901 to 1904 and then was replaced by a prior priest Rev. Jacob Gara.

---

194 In the book by J. L. Hauck, *Catholic Church in Trempealeau County*, in: F. Curtiss-Wedge, *History of Trempealeau County Wisconsin*, 1917, p. 838 a slightly different last name of this priest is given, Father A. Singoski. But in the book of H. H. Heaming, *History of the Catholic Church in Wisconsin*, p. 844, the last name of the same priest is spelled A. Snigorski.

195 H. H. Heaming, *History of Catholic Church in Wisconsin*, p. 844

196 In the book by W. Kruszka, *A History of Poles, Part 4*, p. 95, author mentioned the sum of $2,200.00 but in the book of J. L. Hauck, *Catholic Church in Trempealeau County*, p. 838 the amount listed was $3,000.00.

197 In the book W. Kruszka, *A History of Poles, Part 4*, p. 95 a different last name of the priest was Korczyk, and in the book of J. L. Hauck, *Catholic Church in Trempealeau County*, p. 839, the last name was J. M. Koresyk.

There were a number of parish associations including the Catholic Order of Foresters, the Sacred Heart Society, the St. Joseph Society, the Holy Rosary, Ladies Foresters Union, and for the school children, the Association of the Infant Jesus.

In 1906, the rectory was rebuilt and restored to its splendor for a total sum $7,000. Three years later in 1909, an extension was added to the school building. Two hundred students were enrolled. The parish celebrated its 50th anniversary in 1912 during which time there were 170 families in the parish.

The school was moved to the eastern side of the church in 1961. A new building was erected on land donated by Joe and Dorothy Kujak. This building was used as a school and also as a house for the sisters. The Congregation of Franciscan Sisters taught in the school. In school the Congregation of Franciscan Sisters taught but in the years 1949-1976 the ministry of the congregation engaged the Sisters of the Congregation of St. Joseph. The school was closed in 1976 due to decreased enrollment. In 1984, the church was completely renovated. Three years later, the parish celebrated its 125th anniversary and was comprised of 140 families.

TABLE 10: Pastoral Registry of Sacred Heart & St. Wenceslaus Parish, Pine Creek

Rev. Florentine Zadziorski	1866–1868
Rev. T. Wenglikowski	1868–1871
Rev. P. Musielewicz	1871–1873
Rev. Erasmus Bratkiewicz	1873–1874
Rev. Adolphus Snigorski	1874–1878
Rev. D. Mayer	1878–1884
Rev. R. Tomaszewski	1885–1887
Rev. Roman Guzowski	1887–1889
Rev. R. Tomaszewski	1889–1890
Rev. Roman Guzowski	1890–1895
Rev. T. Lugowski	1895–1898
Rev. Andrew Gara	1898–1901
Rev. James Korczyk	1901–1904

TABLE 10: Pastoral Registry of Sacred Heart & St. Wenceslaus Parish, Pine Creek

Rev. Jacob Gara	1904–1937
Rev. Charles Achtelik	1938–1942
Rev. Francis Piekarski	1942–1943
Rev. Francis Brzostowicz	1943–1948
Rev. Florian Marmurowicz	1948–1949
Rev. Stanley Krakowiecki	1949–1959
Rev. A. J. Sulik	1959–1969
Rev. Matthew Malinaro	1969–1971
Rev. Edwin Stanek	1971–1982
Rev. John Beckfelt	1982–1988
Rev. Raymond Pedretti	1988–1994
Rev. Thomas Finucan	1994–1996
Rev. Robert Polcyn	1996–

19. Polish Church, Centralia

This Polish parish in Centralia became a mission parish that was established on the Wisconsin River near Sigel and was founded in 1900. Rev. James W. Gara commuted to this parish from Junction City. [198] Additional information about this church, its name and title, and its subsequent fate unfortunately could not be traced due to lack of both sources and publications. Also erased is the memory of the church among the modern inhabitants of Centralia. It should be noted that in 1920 Centralia was located on the west bank of the Wisconsin River, and Grand Rapids was built on the eastern bank of that river. After 1920, one name for both villages was accepted, and it was called Wisconsin Rapids. [199]

---

198 W. Kruszka, *A History of the Poles. Part 4,* p. 104
199 www.mcmillanlibrary.org/history/shorthistory.html (January 29, 2012)

20. St. Adalbert, Town of McMillan

The beginning of the parish of St. Adalbert Church starts early in the 20th century. The idea of having a church began in July 1903. Before 1906, Masses were said at the home of Adalbert Mrozinski for the four Polish families that had settled in the area. After that time, steps were taken, and land for the new church was donated by Adalbert Mrozinski. An additional 2.4 acres of his farmland were given for the parish cemetery. A committee was established, and the participants were A. Mrozinski, Joseph Mallich, John Schwabe, and Anton Belinski. In 1904, construction began and leadership was taken by A. Mrozinski because of his extensive skill as a carpenter. The church was completed in May 1906. The liturgy was moved from a home to the church. However, the church became a mission church without a permanent priest. The first priest who commuted to this church was Rev. Theophilus Wojak the pastor from Sacred Heart in Cassel. His pastoral care was offered until 1907.[200] Rev. T. Wojak was succeeded by Rev. John Raicki and Rev. Francis Czyzewski. These two priests each worked two years. The subsequent priests were Rev. Joseph Miller and Rev. J. Karcz. They remained in the parish for only one year each.[201] From 1914 to 1920, Rev. F. Kulig offered his priestly ministry to the church.

In 1920, the church burned down caused by a fire of an unknown origin.[202] The number of families in the congregation was growing, and

Church of St. Adalbert, McMillan
Source: Record Herald Newspaper

---

200   *Record Herald Newspaper*, Wausau, Wisconsin, March 26, 1954
201   *Record Herald Newspaper*, Wausau, Wisconsin, January 1, 1967
202   *Record Herald Newspaper*, Wausau, Wisconsin, March 26, 1954 stated that the fire occurred in 1920. However in *Times-Review, La Crosse Diocesan Newspaper,* September 17, 1970 p. 8 it states that the fire was in 1921.

after this huge loss, the community decided to rebuild the church out of bricks instead of wood. Because the old church was insured, the insurance proceeds were used for the new construction. Labor during the building of the church was donated by parishioners. Masses were again said in the home of A. Mrozcinski during the construction of the new church. In 1921, the church was completed and dedicated. The first priest to celebrate Mass in this church was Rev. Francis Brzostowicz. He continued his ministry as a pastor there until 1928. He was replaced by Rev. Max Kluczykowski who remained in the parish for another fourteen years. Rev. Kluczykowski was transferred to Poniatowski, and a new pastor Rev. S. S. Szymanski came from Mill Creek in 1942 and remained in the parish until 1948. During this year, a decision was made to eliminate the celebration of the liturgy in the Polish language.

The parish became a mission of the Church of St. Joseph in Stratford[203] whose pastor at that time was Rev. Anthony Fisher. In 1963, St. Adalbert became independent of St. Joseph under the leadership of Rev. Nelles. The parishioners within a three mile radius of the church were given a choice of staying with St. Adalbert or going to St. Joseph.[204] In 1970, Most Rev. F. W. Freking, Bishop of La Crosse, announced the dissolution of the Parish of St. Adalbert effective immediately. The mission parish would be consolidated with St. Joseph in Stratford.[205] The Church of St. Adalbert continued to be used as a "chapel of ease" for special occasions. A few years later, the church was torn down, and the material from the church was sold to Mr. Ed Robers who used it to construct a home.

---

203 www.stjosephstratford.org/church-history.html (July 18, 2012)
204 *Stratford Centennial Book 1891-1991*, Stratford, Wisconsin, p. 90
205 *Times-Review Diocesan Newspaper*, September 17, 1970, p. 8

POLISH PARISHES INCLUDED IN THE DIOCESE OF LA CROSSE AFTER 1905

1. St. Bronislava, Plover

In the 1880s, the city of Plover which was located in the county of Portage a few kilometers south of Stevens Point became a very special place for Polish immigrants. Settlement of Polish immigrants in this area was a very dynamic process. At the beginning of 1896, eighty Polish families took a petition to Bishop Sebastian Messmer of the Diocese of Green Bay for permission to build a church.[206] On October 12th of the same year, the bishop excited the Polish settlers of Plover when he sent his delegates in the persons of priests Rev. Xavier Kasperski and Rev. Jan Zielinski the pastor of St. Peter Church in Stevens Point. Most Plover residents of Polish descent were willing to attend the first meeting regarding the creation of the parish and establishment of a church building committee. Following the interviews, there was a preliminary decision made to establish a new Polish parish in Plover. The pastor of the new parish was Rev. X. Kasperski who was a great patriot and zealous priest. The newly formed parish chose as its patron St. Bronislava.

Church of St. Bronislava, Plover
Source: Portage County Historical Society & University of Wisconsin; Stevens Point University Archives

The language used in the pastoral ministry was Polish. It was the language understandable to all parishioners. Only the Liturgy of the Eucharist was celebrated in Latin. The newly founded Parish of St. Bronislava became a special place for Rev. Kasperski. At the same time, he became an administrator of three other newly founded parishes. On a temporary basis, the pastor celebrated sacraments and the celebration

---

[206] M. J. Goc, *Native Realm,* 1902, p. 41. While in the Stevens Point area the Genealogical Society on the page of the history of St. Bronislava Parish-Plover, Wisconsin from January 29, 2012, the number of Polish families is 60.

of Masses only on the first and third Sunday of each month.[207] On the other Sundays, parishioners were required to participate in Mass at the nearby church in Stevens Point.

Historical sources indicate that the builders of St. Bronislava were Frank Lila, John Gleszczynski, and Leo Worzalla. In one year in order to fulfill the promise made to the bishop, they completed the construction of the lower church. They then completed the construction of the sacristy and a 23 meter high bell tower (large for those times). The bell weighed 250 kilos and first sounded during the Easter season in 1897. After completing the first part of the work, worship services were celebrated in the church. Rev. Kurzejka was appointed the next pastor of the parish in August of 1897. On December 10, 1897, Bishop Messmer performed the dedication of the new church. Two years later, Frank Lila bought a new altar for the church. This altar was blessed by Rev. John Pociecha who had become pastor of the Parish of St. Bronislava. In March 1900, Rev. John Pociecha became very seriously ill and could no longer fulfill his duties as pastor. For this reason, the bishop of the diocese appointed a new pastor Rev. Stanislaw Elbert. The new pastor also served his ministry in the adjacent towns of Friendship, Pilot Knob, and Plainfield. Rev. Elbert decided to build a new rectory, and work began very vigorously. Completion occurred on October 16, 1900, and nine days later, the pastor moved into the new parsonage.

On June 23, 1903, the bishop moved Rev. Elbert to Wausau and in his place appointed Rev. Michael Klosowski. Rev. Klosowski served as pastor for the next thirteen years. In 1905, the churches in Pilot Knob and Friendship were transferred to the Diocese of La Crosse. This change positively affected the pastor's workload and improved his ability to be involved in the pastoral work in fewer parishes. During this time, the congregation of Plover began to talk of the need to construct a school. The first plans were submitted already in 1905 by Rev. Klosowski, but it was not until 1907 that a positive vote was received for its construction.[208]

In June 1908, the parish school was completed and within the year

---

207   W. Kruszka, *A History of the Poles. Part 4*, p. 23
208   www.stbrons.com/history.htm (January 9, 2009)

consecrated by Bishop Rhode.[209] This school had a room in which sixty students were taught. The lessons were conducted in both Polish and English. The school was led by lay teachers until 1918. In 1919, two sisters from the Congregation of St. Joseph began teaching in the local school.[210]

On August 8, 1910, during a strong storm, lightning struck the wooden church. Within minutes, fire engulfed the entire church building, and within a short time, it was consumed by fire. Only the Blessed Sacrament survived the fire.[211] The pastor and parishioners did not give up because of this tragedy that touched them. Very quickly, a joint decision was made to rebuild the temple. The foundation stone was laid on June 21, 1911, by Rev. P. Lochman, and less than five months later on November 20th, construction was completely finished on the new church. A day later on November 21st, Bishop Joseph John Fox celebrated the dedication of the church.[212] On the bell tower beside the church were hung two new bells. They were given the names of St. Catherine and St. Joseph.[213] The year 1914 brought another blow to the parish when a raging storm destroyed the roof of the church. The destroyed roof was quickly repaired at a cost of $384.

Church of St. Bronislava, Plover 2012
Source: Author's Collection

After August 1911, the parish in Plainfield received their own pastor. This meant that Rev. Klosowski would be able to celebrate Masses and devotions every Sunday at St. Bronislava. In 1915, Rev. Klosowski was reassigned to another parish and was replaced by Rev. Peter Borowski who was required to split his time between Plainfield and Plover.

---

209   Paul Peter Rohde, the pastor of St. Michael Archangel in Chicago, the first Roman Catholic Bishop in America of the Polish origin; (Auxiliary Bishop of the Archdiocese of Chicago 1908-1915); transferred to the Diocese of Green Bay in Wisconsin as the main bishop of this diocese for the years 1915-1945.

210   Parish Book, *St. Bronislava/Centennial History 1896-1996*, Wisconsin 1996, p. 57

211   www.stbrons.com/history.htm (January 9, 2009)

212   Joseph John Fox – the main bishop of the Diocese Green Bay since May 27, 1904 until November 7, 1914.

213   Parish Book, *St. Bronislava/Centennial History 1896-1996*, Wisconsin 1996, p. 57

This pastoral ministry was held by him until April 1921. Between 1921 and 1923, the four priests serving briefly at this parish were Rev. Leo Jankowski, Rev. Raymond Lonneck, Rev. Leopold N. Blum, and Rev. Andrew Florysia. In 1923, Rev. Stanislaus Lapinski came to the Parish of St. Bronislava. His ministry in the parish continued until 1932. On Sunday, February 9, 1932, while parishioners were faithfully praying in church, news that the school was on fire was reported to them.

The successor to Rev. Lapinski in 1932 was Rev. Ladislaus Polaczyk who lived in the Parish of St. Bronislava until 1944. In 1936 while he was pastor, a fire occurred in the school which was caused by a faulty heating system. The school was a total loss. Although valued at $6,000, only $2,000 was covered by insurance.

Rev. Polaczyk's successors in turn were Rev. Boleslaus J. Walejko and Rev. John B. Gruna. In 1947, the Parish of St. Bronislava received another new pastor Rev. Stephen Mieczkowski who worked in the parish until 1952. For a short period of time, the pastor of St. Bronislava was Rev. Peter Rombalski. In 1953, the bishop of the diocese appointed the next pastor Rev. Francis Przybylski. He remained in this parish for the next twenty-five years.[214] Rev. Charles Rasmussen was appointed co-pastor in 1979 and on August 31, 1979, Rev. Charles Hiebl joined him as co-pastor at St. Bronislava. He became pastor on June 9, 1983, and remained until 1985 when he was replaced by Rev. James Logan. In 1993, the newly appointed pastor in Plover was Rev. Patrick Umberger.

The last service in the Polish language at the Parish of St. Bronislava was celebrated in 1957. It was not the only change in the years of 1950 to 1960. Initially, a small parish in 1950 with a population of 125 families had grown over time to an enormous size in 1983 of a population of 1,200 families.[215] For this reason, in 1991 Bishop Raymond Leo Burke of the Diocese of La Crosse[216] along with the parish committee decided to build a new, larger church. For seven years, the committee discussed what to do with the empty building and for what purpose or function it

---

214 Parish Book, *St. Bronislava/Centennial History 1896-1996,* Wisconsin 1996, p. 34
215 Ibid., p. 58
216 Raymond Leo Burke – Bishop of Diocese of La Crosse December 10, 1994 until December 2, 2003 when he was appointed the Archbishop of St. Louis.

could be used. These discussions, however, contributed nothing. At the beginning of May 1998, in the parish bulletin appeared information that the church would be demolished.[217] A further need was identified in the parish – a new school building. Its construction was completed in 1994, and ninety-one students began their studies in it. Initially education was only offered for the primary grades up to the third grade. Two years later (in 1998), one class was added extending the student body to four grades.

TABLE 11: Pastoral Registry for St. Bronislava Parish, Plover

Rev. David Gilles	1973
Rev. Robert Streveler	1973–1979
Rev. Charles Rasmussen	1979–1982*
Rev. Charles Hiebl	1979–1985

* Parish Book, *St. Bronislava/Centennial History 1896-1996*, Wisconsin 1996, p. 53-54

2. St. Stanislaus Kostka, Stevens Point

Church of St. Stanislaus, Stevens Point 1950

Source: Portage County Historical Society & University of Wisconsin Stevens Point University Archives

In the early 20th century the Church of St. Peter in Stevens Point had become too small. A large number of Polish settlers had come to Stevens Point because of opportunities available to them. As a result, the Bishop of the Diocese of Green Bay Joseph Fox decided to create another parish in the city and to build a new temple. In 1915, the newly nominated Bishop of the Diocese of Green Bay Paul Rohde continued the work of the prior bishop and took the first step to create a new parish. For the price of $5,000, the square was bought at the intersection of Fremont Street, High Street, and Stanley Street. A year later, the church was built, and the patron of this church was chosen as St. Stanislaus Kostka. The total cost of construction was $30,000, and

---

217 Edward Dusza, *Kalendarz polonijny 2010*, Stevens Point 2010, p. 53

the number of parishioners enrolled in this church was 250 families.[218] A large group of volunteers worked on the construction thus significantly reducing its cost.

The generosity and commitment of the parishioners in creation of the new parish was enormous. Thus, rapid changes followed in both the external appearance of the church and also in its internal design. Many Polish families were benefactors of the church. Among them were Frank Trzebiatowski, Sr. and John J. Bukolt. Both of them among others bought the bell for the church. The second bell was purchased by Steven Martenki. The altar for the new church was purchased by the Frank Trzebiatowski, Sr. Family.[219] This spirit of giving did not die with the completion of the church. According to the local newspaper of Stevens Point, Bishop of the Diocese of Green Bay Paul P. Rohde thanked all the parishioners for their great input of labor in the construction of the church. He included this praise on August 8, 1917, when he dedicated the cornerstone. Acknowledgement was made to the bishop in the Polish language since this parish consisted of mainly Polish immigrants and their American born children. The dedication of the church was performed on August 11, 1918.

The first pastor of St. Stanislaus was Rev. Anton Malkowski. He came from Poland and soon was accepted into the Diocese of Green Bay. He worked on the pastoral level at St. Peter's in Stevens Point and then at parishes in Crivitz and Junction City. He also worked as a chaplain at St. Michael's Hospital in Stevens Point. Another initiative was to build a parsonage. Construction was completed in 1922.[220] In 1929, the church was equipped with a new pipe organ which was purchased at a cost of $7,000 from M. P. Meller Company, and also new stained glass windows were installed.[221] At the same time, the house for the nuns was built in which ten sisters dwelled. Soon at the age of forty-four due to cancer, Rev. Malkowski died. He was succeeded by Rev. Francis Nowak who was born

---

218   E. McGlachlin, *A Standard History of Portage County Wisconsin*, Chicago and New York, 1919, p. 190, But in www.pchswi.org/archives/church.religionpc.htm is information that the cost of the church building was $32,000 and that 600 families belonged to the parish.

219   Parish Book, *St. Stanislaus Catholic Church, 75th Anniversary*, Wisconsin, 1992, p. 9

220   Parish Book, *St. Stanislaus Catholic Church, 75th Anniversary*, Wisconsin, 1992, p. 9. This information states the rectory was finished in 1922 and this is different from: www.pchswi.org/archives/church/religionPC.htm which states the rectory and school were finished in 1925.

221   Parish Book, *St. Stanislaus Catholic Church, 75th Anniversary*, Wisconsin 1992, p. 12

in Green Bay, Wisconsin. After completion of the rectory, the construction of the school was finished in 1925. The nuns from the Congregation of St. Joseph were invited to work in the school and to educate the children. Bishop Rohde gave them a very special blessing for this mission and also allowed them $25,000 to build a monastery. Another change occurred in the position of pastor in 1937. The new parish priest was Rev. Hubert Woyak. Less than a year later, he was replaced by Rev. Leo Bartosz. He also did not remain long in the parish. Another year brought another change. The new pastor was Rev. Leo Trojanowski. He remained in the parish from 1938 to 1958. In 1945, some of the parishes from Portage County passed administratively to the Diocese of La Crosse.[222]

Church of St. Stanislaus, Stevens Point 2012
Source: Author's Collection

On August 19, 1951, Bishop John Treacy blessed the new school building which had a cost exceeding $300,000. Another pastor in the Parish of St. Stanislaus was Rev. Joseph Cysewski who worked there from June 1958 to June 1959. He was replaced by Rev. Francis Piekarski. From 1963 to 1964, the school under the title St. Stanislaus Kostka had an enrollment of 757 students.

In 1963, the pastor and the Parish Council made the decision to renovate the church by increasing the size of the sacristy and the main nave. A new addition on the front of the church to include steps was built in 1974. One year later, Rev. F. Piekarski retired, but he remained in the parish as a resident. Nominated as his successor Rev. Vaughn Rockman became the new pastor. He worked in this parish until 1981. The next pastors were Rev. Dennis Lynch in 1982 and then Rev. J. Thomas Finucan. After him, Rev. Donald Przybylski came to the parish.

---

222   Ibid., p. 11

TABLE 12: Pastoral Registry at St. Stanislaus Kostka Parish, Stevens Point

Rev. Anthony Malkowski	1916–1924
Rev. Francis A. Nowak	1925–1938
Rev. Hubert Woyak	1937–1938
Rev. Leo Bartosz	1938–1939
Rev. Leo Trojanowski	1938–1958
Rev. Thaddeus Koszarek	1939–1943
Rev. Casimir Krauklis	1944–1945
Rev. Augustine Sulik	1945–1947
Rev. Stanley Chilijki	1947–1952
Rev. Joseph Henseler	1952–1953
Rev. Richard Tomsyck	1953
Rev. Hilary Simmons	1953–1956
Rev. Aloysius Wozniak	1956–1958
Rev. Richard Wisnewski	1956–1958
Rev. Norman Seneki	1958–1961
Rev. Joseph Cysewski	1958–1959
Rev. James Bertrand	1958–1959
Rev. Francis Piekarski	1959–1975
Rev. Joseph Miller	1959–1964
Rev. George Passehl	1961–1962
Rev. John Puerner	1962–1971
Rev. Robert Greatorex	1964–1965
Rev. William Jablonske	1967–1968
Rev. William Matzek	1971–1974
Rev. Rex Zimmerman	1971–1972
Rev. Dennis Bouche	1973–1974
Rev. James Leszczynski	1974–1975
Rev. Vaughn Brockman	1975–1981
Rev. Dennis Lynch	1975–1982
Rev. Robert Pedretti	1975–1976

TABLE 12: Pastoral Registry at St. Stanislaus Kostka Parish, Stevens Point

Rev. Charles Rasmussen	1977–1978
Rev. Thomas Finucan	1981–1986
Rev. Mark Pierce	1983–1987
Rev. Donald Przybylski	1986–

3. St. Michael, Wausau

In the late 1860s in the eastern part of Wausau on the left bank of the Wisconsin River, a group of Polish immigrants settled. After developing the area, the Polish settlers found their way directly to the Church of St. Mary a parish which was founded by immigrants from Germany. Poles rented the church in order to practice their faith. The pastor of this church was Rev. T. J. Richard. He made sure he could find a priest who could speak the native language of this group of Poles. The liturgical worship in the rented temple took place every four weeks, and the rite was celebrated in the Polish language. The Masses and devotions were celebrated there until the construction of their own church.[223] The priest, a native of Poland, Rev. John Zavistowski served as a pastor for Polish immigrants beginning in 1869.[224] From the very beginning, the Poles from Wausau had the intention to build their own church and wanted to have their own Polish parish.

Church of St. Michael, Wausau 1887
Source: http://www.stmichaelwausau.org/History.htm

---

223 L. Marchetti, *History of Marathon County Wisconsin,* Chicago 1913, p. 357
224 W. Kruszka, *History of the Poles, Part 4,* p. 101

This was due to continuing disagreements and conflicts of the ethnic religious background between immigrants from Germany, Ireland, and Poland. A group of Poles made a petition to the bishop of the diocese to begin the preparation for the construction of a church and the creation of the parish.

Bishop Frederick Catzer[225] of the Diocese of Green Bay agreed to organize a Polish parish in Wausau. He confirmed his decision instantly by sending a Polish priest Rev. Lucas Pescinski who resided in the Town of Hull. This priest bought six plots in the city for the construction of the church and took over the supervision of its construction. The work started, and in 1888 the lower portion of the church was completed and was offered for use. Immediately Masses and devotions were celebrated. The priest who celebrated was Rev. Viktor Lebecki. After another two years, the building of the temple as a whole was completed, and it was dedicated by Bishop Frederick Catzer.[226] At the very beginning, help was offered to the Parish of St. Michael by two priests: Rev. Leopold Garus who commuted from the Church of the Holy Family in Poniatowski and Rev. Lucas Pescinski.[227] In 1889, the first officially appointed pastor to St. Michael's in Wausau was Rev. Konstanty Marszalkowski.[228] Unfortunately, his pastoral ministry lasted only two months. He was succeeded by Rev. Wojciech Pelczar who worked there from 1890 to 1891. Rev. W. Pelczar died as a pastor in Wausau, and he was buried in the local cemetery. Another Polish pastor at St. Michael's in 1891 was Rev. Viktor Lebecki. His successor was Rev. Leopold Garus who worked in the years 1892 to1894. Rev. Theophil Malkowski took over the parish after a four months absence of a pastor, and he served his parish ministry in the years 1894 to1895.

On December 26, 1894, as a result of fire, the church completely burned down.[229] There still remained a huge debt that was incurred in

---

225 Frederick Francis Xavior Catzer – The Bishop of the Diocese of Green Bay since July 13, 1886 until January 30, 1891; Archbishop of Milwaukee (1891-1903).

226 Parish Book, *Church of St. Michael, Wisconsin 1887-1977,* Wisconsin 1977, p. 6

227 H. H. Heaming, *History of the Catholic Church in Wisconsin,* Milwaukee 1895, 1896, p. 752

228 L. Marchetti, *History of Marathon County, Wisconsin,* p. 357. Information here mentions the first resident pastor was Father Lievietzki, and his successor was Father T. Malkowski. This information is contradictory with information which is in the parish book of St. Michael 1877-1987, p. 6, which states that the first resident pastor was Father Konstanty Marszalkowski.

229 W. Kruszka, *History of the Poles, Part 4,* p. 101

its construction. Rev. Malkowski made the immediate decision that as soon as possible they would rebuild the church. Steps were taken to raise money for financial assistance. Money was received from the Stewart Lumber Company, the logging camps, and from Polish immigrants who lived in Stevens Point, Custer, Polonia, Amherst, Junction City, Menasha, Pike Lake, Wausau, the southern part of Chicago, and parishioners of St. Casimir Parish in the Town of Hull.[230] Collected donations brought the days of rebuilding closer.

On October 3, 1895, the church was rebuilt and dedicated by Bishop Sebastian Gehard Messmer.[231] Rebuilding required more than $6,134.68, but the church that was built was much larger, and the exterior walls were covered by bricks. The church had a length of 100 feet and a width of 45 feet. In 1895, the next parish priest Rev. Joseph Kominek arrived. The following year, he was replaced by Rev. Adam Lopatto. However, on February 4, 1897, Rev. Garus returned. He was replaced in 1898 by Rev. James Kulla. The next pastors were Rev. Leo Jankowski in 1899, Rev. John Adamowski in 1900, and Rev. Nicdolemus Kolasinski in 1901. Two years later in 1903, Rev. Stanislaus Elbert became the parish priest, and in 1904, he was succeeded by Rev. James Kulla.

Church of St. Michael, Wausau 2012
Source: Author's Collection

The year 1905 was a breakthrough year for the Parish of St. Michael as a result of the reorganization of the diocesan structure. The parish was transferred from the Diocese of Green Bay to the Diocese of La Crosse.[232] At the same time, a new parish priest Rev. Ladislaus Slisz was appointed. Later in 1912, pastor Rev. Theophil Wojak built a school

---

230   Malcolm Rosholt, *A Photo Album of Marathon County 1850-1925,* Wisconsin 1978, p. 35

231   Sebastian Gerhard Messmer (1847-1930) – the Bishop of the Diocese of Green Bay in the year 1892-1903: Archbishop of Milwaukee 1903-1930.

232   Parish Book, *Church of St. Michael, Wisconsin 1887-1977,* Wisconsin 1977, p. 7

building and organized the four grades. He invited the Felician Sisters to administer it. The sisters accepted the invitation and took over the responsibility of the school in which 150 children attended. In 1947, the Parish of St. Michael in Wausau received a new pastor Rev. Bernard Hoppa. After four years of pastoral work, he was replaced by Rev. Maximilan Kluczykowski. In 1956, the bishop of the diocese appointed a new pastor Rev. John Krasowski who completed the modernization and reconstruction of the church. The rebuilt church was dedicated on November 26, 1972. The modernization of the church and the school cost half a million dollars. Two years later in 1974, the bishop appointed a new pastor Rev. Joseph Rafacz.

TABLE 13: Associate Pastors who worked at St. Michael Parish, Wausau

Rev. Taddeus Szczerbinski	1940
Rev. Roman Papiernik	1941
Rev. Jerome Kamla	1942
Rev. Hester Wrzaszczak	1944
Rev. Hilary Simmons	1946
Rev. Edward Masalewicz	1948
Rev. Augustine Sulik	1951
Rev. Stanley Swikowski	1951
Rev. Joseph Marx	1952
Rev. Aloysius Wozniak	1953
Rev. Myron Meinen	1954
Rev. Harles Donahue	1955
Rev. John Hodges	1956
Rev. Mark Walljasper	1959
Rev. Stephen Boehr	1962
Rev. Lyle Schulte	1962
Rev. Donald Klauke	1963
Rev. Lawrence Zawadzki	1964
Rev. Thomas Donaldson	1968
Rev. John Olson	1970

TABLE 13: Associate Pastors who worked at St. Michael Parish, Wausau

Rev. Michael Lynch	1974
Rev. Thomas Abraham	1974
Rev. Lawrence Dunklee	1978
Rev. David Kunz	1981
Rev. Robert Schaller	1987
Rev. Edward Shuttleworth	1992
Rev. David Olson	1999

During the years 1940-1999, seventeen associate pastors worked in the Parish of St. Michael. The associate pastors were assigned for a duration of one year.

4. St. Michael, Junction City

In the early 1870s, the Polish immigrants also came to Junction City. They settled in and began a new life mostly working hard in the fields. The origins of the pastoral ministry in Junction City were similar in most cases to those of other Polish parishes. Initially, the priest and the faithful met in homes where often in very simple ways, they celebrated Masses, prayed together, and provided the Holy Sacraments. One of the few missionaries arriving in Junction City with the pastoral ministry was Rev. Schaller from Marshfield.[233] Soon the community of Junction City set a goal of building their own church and rectory. They tried to acquire and retain a permanent pastor. In 1882 with the arrival of Rev. August Krogulski, hope for the building of the church became more real. The townspeople were able to make huge sacrifices to meet their goal. Rev. Krogulski was strongly supported as he lived with the Polish immigrants.[234] The first step toward building the church occurred with a donation by John Beatz who offered two acres of land for the church and parsonage. The committee intended to erect a church and

---

[233] H. H. Heaming, *History of the Catholic Church in Wisconsin,* Milwaukee 1895, 1896, p. 821
[234] Parish Book, *St. Michael Church Junction City,* Wisconsin 1958, p. 2

rectory for the next pastor. Work had already started by the next year. The name for the church was elected to be St. Michael the Archangel. The church was built and completed in 1888.[235] In 1885, one acre of land was purchased for a newly formed cemetery. The purchase was again made by John Beatz.

Church of St. Michael,
Junction City around 1895
Source: H. H. Heaming History of the Catholic Church in Wisconsin

Rev. A. Krogulski after four and one half years was transferred to another parish and was succeeded by Rev. August Babinski. Two years later, Rev. Theophil Lugowski arrived. He became not only the pastor of the Parish of St. Michael the Archangel but also the administrator of the parish in Mill Creek.[236] At the time, he received assistance from other priests: Rev. F. Jachiniak, Rev. A. Bursera, and Rev. L. Gabowski.[237] Another change occurred when Rev. Joseph Miller came to the parish. He rebuilt the church which was too small for the rapidly growing community of believers. Also at this time, two sacristies were built, and the heating appliances were installed in the interior of the church. Rev. James Gara was the parish priest in 1900. Two years later due to cramped space, the rectory was expanded. In 1904, Rev. J. Gara was transferred to Pine Creek. Over the next two years, the Parish of St. Michael in Junction City had four more pastors. They were Rev. George Kiepier, Rev. Romuald Mayott, Rev. James Korczyk, and Rev. Walter Stepaniak.

In the year 1905, another change took place at the administrative level. All parishes in the western portion of Portage County passed from the jurisdiction of the bishop of the Diocese of Green Bay and were

---

235 W. Kruszka, *A History of the Poles. Part 4*, p. 26
236 H. H. Heaming, *History of the Catholic Church in Wisconsin*, p. 822
237 Parish Book, *St. Michael Church Junction City*, p. 3

placed under the jurisdiction of the bishop of the Diocese of La Crosse. Rev. Anthony Malkowski was appointed the new pastor in Junction City in 1906, and he decisively took the initiative to build a school. Its construction began in 1907 and was completed a year later. The new school began operation with eighty students. In 1908, Rev. Wenceslaus Krzywonos was appointed pastor. In the same year, the parish bought two bells. The consecration of them was performed by the parish priest from St. Peter's Church in Stevens Point Rev. Lucas Pescinski.[238] After two years of ministry in the parish, Rev. Krzywonos died. He was succeeded by Rev. W. B. Polaczyk who performed his ministry in Junction City for the next seven years.

Rev. Andrew Farysiak became the next pastor in Junction City. During his tenure, he built a new bell tower in the church, and the heating system was exchanged for a newer and more functional one. In 1922, Rev. Farysiak was transferred to another facility, and Rev. Novitski was appointed to replace him. Two years later, he was transferred and in his place the bishop assigned Rev. Peter Kurzejka. This pastor served the parishioners in Junction City for ten years. After his death, the new pastor was Rev. Stanislaus Lapinski. During his pastoral ministry, all the parish buildings were renovated and refurbished. Rev. Florian Marmurowicz the subsequent pastor served for eleven years. He put a great deal of energy into the restoration of the church. He installed new stained glass windows and replaced the roof and the chimney on the church.

In 1949, Rev. Marmurowicz was replaced by Rev. Joseph Schulist. Unfortunately two years later, Rev. Shulist was moved to Polonia, and his place was taken by Rev. John Nowak. In June 1955, he retired, and the position of the administrator of the parish was given for two months to Rev. James Crosgrove. On August 31, 1955, Bishop John P. Treacy appointed Rev. Ernest J. Kaim as pastor. A year later, the resident pastor presented plans for a new hall and church. The hall was completed in spring of 1956 at a cost of approximately $25,000. Most of the work was done by volunteer parishioners.[239] In late 1956 and early 1957, the pastor began an active campaign to build a larger church. In

---

238 Parish Book, *St. Michael Church Junction City*, p. 4
239 Ibid., p. 10

the plan, the new interior of the church was designed to accommodate 360 people.

On June 29, 1958, Rev. George Hammes dedicated the cornerstone for the new church. The consecration of the church took place on September 28, 1958, by Bishop John P. Treacy. The next day, the bishop of the diocese consecrated the main altar and celebrated the Mass of Thanksgiving for the intention of the parishioners of Junction City. The Holy Mass was celebrated in the company of more than forty priests who came from nearby parishes. Parish life then returned to normal. In 1964, Rev. Kaim was transferred, and in his place was appointed Rev. Raymond Bornbach. Parishioners decided to create many fundraising opportunities to pay off the debt incurred by building the church. Therefore, they organized dances, dinners, wedding receptions, and they sold paczki (doughnuts). In April 1968, Rev. Dominic Eichman took over the position of pastor. In that same year, the parish school was closed due to the high cost of maintenance and the lack of nuns who were willing to teach in the school.[240] In June 1974, Rev. Raymond Schultz became pastor. True to his pastoral duties, he served parishioners for over seventeen years, and after that he retired. In June 1991, Rev. John Wisneski the newly appointed parish priest arrived. He also was assigned to the Parishes of St. Wenceslaus in Milladore and St. Kilian in Blenker. During his work in the parish, Rev. Wisneski supervised the construction of restrooms in the church in 1992. In the hall was built a kitchen, classrooms and restrooms during the years 1999 and 2000.

Church of St. Michael, Junction City 2012
Source: Author's Collection

---

[240] Parish Book, St. *Michael Catholic Church, Junction City, Wisconsin 125th Year Anniversary 1883-2008,* Wisconsin 2008, p. 10

5. St. Peter, Stevens Point

Before 1860, the first Poles settled in the town of Stevens Point. The first Polish priest was Rev. Jan Polak who came to Stevens Point from Pomerania on July 20, 1860. He left his homeland because of persecution by the Prussian government.[241] He was soon appointed as pastor of the Parish of St. Stephen Martyr which included Catholics of German, Irish, and French nationalities. Six Polish families were also recorded in this parish because these families sought a spiritual ministry. In 1861, the Bishop of Milwaukee John Martin Henni[242] came to visit Stevens Point for the first time. While there, he administered the sacrament of Confirmation. On March 15, 1862, Rev. Jan Polak left Stevens Point. By then forty families had already started to attend Sunday worship and celebrations in St. Joseph Church.[243] In June 1876, Rev. Antony Bogacki was sent by Bishop Henni with instructions to organize a Polish parish in the city.

Church of St. Peter, Stevens Point 1897
Source: Portage County Historical Society & University of Wisconsin

The first step of the new pastor was to convene a meeting of Polish families in the school at St. Stephen's. About fifty families came to this meeting. They made a decision to begin construction of a church, and they took a collection for that purpose. They collected $800 and thus were able to purchase the four square lots at First and Second Streets. On one of the square lots was a house which was adopted for liturgical celebrations while parishioners waited for the completion of their new church.

---

241 *Księga pamiątkowa złotego jubileuszu 50-tej rocznicy założenia parafii św. Piotra,* Stevens Point 1926, p. 9

242 John Martin Henni was born on June 15, 1805 in Misanenga in Switzerland. He was ordained on February 2, 1829 in Bardstown, Kentucky. In 1843 he was appointed the first bishop of the Diocese of Milwaukee. On March 19, 1844 he accepted the bishop position in Cincinnati. In 1875 the diocese was raised to the level of an Archdiocese and Metropolis and Bishop Henni became Archbishop of the Metropolis. After 37 years of ministering he died on September 7, 1881 in Milwaukee.

243 W. Kruszka, *A History of the Poles. Part 4,* p. 18

In August 1876, construction was completed, and the house was converted into a rectory. It was used until 1882 when the new rectory was finished. The church was a wooden building with two towers. The cost of construction amounted to $3,000. The successor of Rev. Anthony Bogacki was Rev. January Czarnowski who worked in this parish for only five months. After him came Rev. Wojciech Bukowski who was in the parish from September to May 1878. From May to October in that same year, the parish remained without a pastor. Finally, in October 1878, the newly appointed parish priest Rev. Jozefat Walun arrived. On September 1, 1881, after three years of work, he went into retirement because of very poor health. At that time, the parish administrator was Rev. J. Zawistowski who held the office until November of that year. The following year was a repeat of the previous year for the parish. Again, it remained without a pastor until November 1882 when a new parish priest Rev. E J. Slowikowski was appointed. This zealous priest began to build a new parsonage with the cost of this construction being $2,500.

Another pastor in the Parish of St. Peter in Stevens Point was Rev. Anthony Lex[244] who arrived on May 23, 1884, and remained as a pastor until November 1888. During his residence, the wooden church was covered with bricks. In 1887, Rev. Lex for the price of $1,000 bought a public school from the city and transformed it into a parish school.[245] The management and care of the school was handled by the Sisters of Notre Dame. From 1888 until 1891, the pastor of the Parish of St. Peter was Rev. Walter Grabowski. In 1890, he built a home for the nuns for the price of $2,400 and also enlarged the existing church for a cost of $1,200.[246] In 1891, the parish received a new pastor in the person of Rev. Zygmunt Wozny. During his tenure, he reconstructed the church towers and purchased a bell and new altar. Three years later in May 1894, Rev. Kwiryn Zielinski arrived at the Parish of St. Peter. He changed the roof of the church, remodeled and modernized the rectory, expanded and modernized the choir loft, and divided the cemetery into quarters. The same year, the Sisters of Notre Dame left the parish so temporary

---

244 The different last name is given by H. H. Heaming, *History of the Catholic Church in Wisconsin*, p. 849. And it listed the last name as Father A. Lex but in the book *Księga pamiątkowa złotego jubileuszu*, p. 11 the last name is listed as Father A. Leks. I have chosen to use Lex.

245 *Księga pamiątkowa złotego jubileuszu*, p. 11

246 W. Kruszka, *A History of the Poles. Part 4*, p. 19

custody of the school and children was handled by lay teachers. Soon, the Sisters of St. Francis from the Monastery of St. Joseph in Milwaukee arrived and took over the responsibility of the school from lay personnel. On October 18, 1896, after vespers for an unknown reason, the parsonage and the church burned down.[247] Soon after, Rev. Zielinski left the parish, and the care of this parish was taken for one month by Rev. Mikolaj Kolasinski who commuted there from Hull. The celebration of the Holy Eucharist was said during that time in the school.

On December 23, 1896, the parish received a new pastor Rev. Lucas Pescinski. Archbishop Messmer sent him to Stevens Point with the task of comprehensively reconstructing and reorganizing the parish. On July 11, 1897, less than one year after the fire, the church cornerstone was blessed. Later in December of the same year, Archbishop Messmer blessed the new church and two bells.

Church of St. Peter, Stevens Point 2012
Source: Author's Collection

The total cost of the new church with new altars, pews, and pipe organ was $24,000. The number of families in the parish was 434. Five nuns taught in the school where a total of 350 Polish children were pupils. The school building was completely finished in 1905. From September 1906 to September of the next year, Rev. L. Pescinski was in Europe, so he was replaced by Rev. Ladislaus Stefaniak. After his return, the parish received for the first time an associate pastor Rev. Andrew Forysiak. He worked at that position until June 1909. Rev. Pescinski was moved from the Parish of St. Peter in December 1909. He was succeeded by Rev. Stanislaus A. Elbert.

The first parish picnic took place in the summer of 1912. On December 19, 1915, Bishop Rohde came to visit the parish. Construction of the house for the nuns began in 1924. Two years later, they began the

---

247   *Księga pamiątkowa złotego jubileuszu*, p. 13

preparation for the celebration of the golden jubilee of the parish. In the spring of 1927, Rev. Elbert went to Europe for six months. During his absence, the associate pastor served as the administrator of the parish. After returning from Europe, Rev. Elbert was appointed the chaplain of the religious house of St. Joseph in Stevens Point.

The new pastor Rev. Julius Chylinski was appointed on June 22, 1929. In September of 1930, the parish benefited from the Bukolt Family who were generous enough to donate the funds needed for a new organ. Meanwhile, Rev. Chylinski bought property at a cost of $11,600 for construction of the new school. Construction soon began. On March 13, 1932, Bishop Rohde came personally to dedicate the school. Until 1952, Rev. Chylinski led the Parish of St. Peter successfully with the assistance of twenty-one associate pastors.

In autumn 1943, work began on revamping the church. In the renovation, the east and west side entrances were added. Confessionals were recessed into the church walls. In spring of 1944, the pulpit was moved to the sanctuary while the interior of the church was renovated, and new light oak pews were installed. In the next two years, more remodeling was completed. The church tower clock was electrified, and in 1947 the steeple was remodeled. The exterior masonry was sandblasted, and the interior was thoroughly washed and cleaned. In 1963, the communion rail was lowered, and the worship area received a complete cleaning. The parish always worked to maintain their temple and school. As a result in 1969, more work was done including the addition of new steps at the front entrance to the church and the cleaning and renovation of the organ. The church hall had kitchen equipment installed in 1970. During 1973, the roof was replaced, new wiring and light fixtures were installed, and carpet was added to the church.

The '90s found the parish making additional improvements such as renovating the organ from mechanical to electronic, changing the steam heating system to hot water, and replacing the church roof. The reconciliation room was designed and installed. Redecoration included the statues, ceiling paintings, and the Stations of the Cross. Bishop Raymond Leo Burke of the Diocese of La Crosse rededicated the worship area in September 1995. Later, the church clock tower faces were replaced, and an electronic clock system installed.

The Diocese of Madison was founded on December 22, 1945, although at that time, Portage County still belonged to the Diocese of La Crosse. Pope Pius XII elevated Rev. Chylinski to the level of Monsignor. During the diamond jubilee in 1951, the parish consisted of 1,900 families. That same year two vicars Rev. Dominic Eichman and Rev. Joseph Walijecki helped Msgr. Chylinski in his pastoral ministry. Three years later, Rev. Eichman was moved, and in his place came Rev. Bernard Nowak. Rev. Walijecki was transferred in 1956, and his position was taken by Rev. Edward Masalewicz. At the end of 1957, Msgr. Chylinski blessed the new cornerstone for the chapel at the cemetery. After his death, the function of administrator of the parish was held by Rev. Nowak. On June 3, 1959, Bishop Treacy appointed Rev. Stephen P. Mieczkowski as the resident pastor. After eight years, his position was taken over by Rev. Stanley A. Andrzejewski. Two years later in June of 1969, a new pastor Rev. Chester A. Zielinski was appointed.

TABLE 14: Pastoral Registry at St. Peter Parish, Stevens Point

PASTORS	
Rev. Anthony Bogacki	1876–1887
Rev. January Czarnowski	1877
Rev. Adalbert Bukowski	1877
Rev. Josepha Walun	1878–1881
Rev. J. J. Zawistowski	1881
Vacant	December 1881 to January 1882
Rev. E. J. Slowikowski	1882–1884
Rev. Anthony Lex	1884–1888
Rev. Walter Grabowski	1888–1891
Rev. Zygmunt Wozny	1891–1894
Rev. Kwiryn Zielinski	1894–1896
Rev. Nicholas Kolasinski	1896
Rev. Lucas J. Pesinski	1896–1909
Rev. Stanislaus A. Elbert	1909–1929
Rev. Julius Chylinski	1929–1959

TABLE 14: Pastoral Registry at St. Peter Parish, Stevens Point

Rev. Bernard Nowak	1954–1960
Rev. Stephan S. Mieczkowski	1959–1967
Rev. Stanley A. Andrzejewski	1967–1969
Rev. Chester Zielinski	1969–1980
Rev. Chester Moczarny	1980–1982
Rev. Chester Osowski	1982–1987
Rev. Francis Manci	July 1987 to November 1987
Rev. Robert Cook	December 1987 to April 1988 Interim
Rev. Gerald Fisher	1988–1998
Rev. Robert Schaeller	1988
ASSOCIATES	
Rev. Andrew Forysia	1907–1909
Rev. Paul Sokol	1909–1910
Rev. Wladimir Pruc	1913–1914
Rev. Ignatius Grad	1914–1915
Rev. Peter Banka	1915–1916
Rev. B. J. Walejko	1916–1918
Rev. Peter Nowicki	1918–1919
Rev. John Landowski	1919–1920
Rev. Victor Hoppa	1920–1922
Rev. Stanley Ziolkowski	1922–1923
Rev. Korwin Szymanowski	1923
Rev. Franciscan Fathers	1923–1924
Rev. Joseph Szupryt	1924–1926
Rev. Florian Marmurowicz	1926–1929
Rev. Alois Trzebiatowski	1929–1930
Rev. B. Platta	1930–1931
Rev. Michael Wasniewski	1931
Rev. J. Labno	1931–1932

TABLE 14: Pastoral Registry at St. Peter Parish, Stevens Point

Rev. C. Tomczyk	1931–1934
Rev. E. Horyza	1932–1934
Rev. J. Tomczyk	1934–1938
Rev. Hubert Wojak	1934–1945
Rev. Joseph J. Schulist	1935–1937
Rev. A. Betley	1937–1939
Rev. Leo Przybylski	1938–1941
Rev. J. Garstka	1939–1940
Rev. John J. Nowak	1940–1941
Rev. C. Krauklis	1941
Rev. Francis Wengier	1941–1945
Rev. Chester Zielinski	1941–1947
Rev. Edward Sobczyk	1945–1950
Rev. Dominic Eichman	1947–1954
Rev. Hilary Simmons	1950–1951
Rev. Joseph Taczala	1951
Rev. Joseph Walijewski	1951–1956
Rev. Bernard Nowak	1954–1960
Rev. Edward Masalewicz	1956–1957
Rev. Richad Tomsyck	1957–1960
Rev. Roy Mish	1960–1962
Rev. Patrick Devine	1961–1962
Rev. John Wisnecki	1963–1972
Rev. John Hodges	1967 1972
Rev. Dan Kozlowski	1972–1975
Rev. Ambrose Blenker	1976–1976
Rev. Donald Przybylski	1978–1985
Rev. Leo Schneider	1985–1988
Rev. Bogdan Werra	1987–1992

6. Sacred Heart of Jesus, Polonia

The first Polish immigrants who came to Portage County in Wisconsin were members of the family of Michael von Koziczkowski.[248] Michael and Frances Koziczkowski came to Stevens Point in September 1857 bringing with them only $50.[249] After their arrival, many Polish immigrants decided to settle in the vicinity of Stevens Point. Families who came to this area were the families of Jozef Jazdzewski, Kazimierz Lukasiewicz, Tomasz Kuklinski, Valenty Reszczynski, Jozef Kleman, and Jan Szelbracikowski.[250] They came because they had heard about Rev. Jan Polak [251] who was a very popular priest arriving in Stevens Point in the 1860s. Most Polish immigrants were farmers. Their goal was to work diligently and persistently to build a better future for themselves and their families. They settled in the town of Sharon on farms where they created a Polish enclave.[252] This area was known as "Polish Corner" which means a Polish nook or small intersection. To those families, Rev. Jan Polak commuted to perform his priestly ministry. He also met the needs of the Germans who also settled nearby. During his pastoral ministry for the Polish settlers, Bishop John Martin

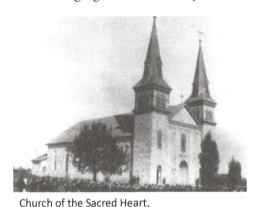

Church of the Sacred Heart, Polonia between 1875–1903
Source: http://www.pchswi.org/archives/church/sacred_heart/sacredheart

---

248 The difference in the application name and last name: in W. Kruszka, *A History of the Poles. Part 4*, p. 7. The last name is Michal Kozyczkowski while in the parish book *Sacred Heart Congregation Polonia, Wisconsin 1864-1964*,Wisconsin 1964, p. 18, the name and the last name is Michael Koziczkowski.

249 H. H. Heaming, *History of the Catholic Church in Wisconsin*, p. 714

250 *Księga pamiątkowa złotego jubileuszu*, p. 9. In the book W. Kruszka, *History of Poles, Part 4*, p. 7 we find completely different information about the first Polish settlers in Stevens Point, Wisconsin. The author gives completely different names of the first settlers in this area. Accordingly to the author they were Jacob Werechowski, Michel Kozyczkowski, Adam Klesmit, Jozef Szulfer, Jozef Daczyk, and Jan Zynda. However, according to M. J. Goc, *Native Realm*, Stevens Point, 1992, p. 31 they were Michael Koziczkowski, Jan and Anna Zynda, Jan and Jozefina Platta, Adam Klesmit and his children.

251 The difference in the surname in M. J. Goc, *Native Realm*, p. 46, is Polack, and in W. Kruszka, *A History of Poles, Part 4*, p. 8, is Polak.

252 W. Kruszka, *History of Poles, Part 4*, p. 8

Henni from Milwaukee came for a visit[253] and gave the sacrament of Confirmation. In order to practice their faith, Polish immigrants together with immigrants from Germany built a small church under the title of St. Martin.

For the next eight years, Rev. Polak tried to support the spiritual needs of the Polish people attending St. Martin Church.[254] This Polish center developed rapidly and in 1864 had already reached a population of forty-four families. It was then decided by the Polish parishioners to create and organize their own parish. This occurred because the Poles saw the German factor of fifteen families as being selfish and arrogant. Also, the Germans would not allow the Poles to look at the finances of the parish. Additionally, the Germans made fun of and mocked Polish prayers and the Polish National Anthem.[255]

A petition was sent to Bishop Martin Henni of the Diocese of Milwaukee with a request to approve the proposal for the establishment of a new Polish parish. In 1862 in order to organize a new parish with Polish settlers, Bishop Martin Henni sent Rev. Bonaventura Buczyński OSM. Rev. Polak unhappy with the turn of events left the parish in 1863 and returned to Milwaukee where he died in 1865. In a short time, a church building committee was established and work soon started. Less than one year later at the end of 1863, the church was completed. The newly built church received the title of St. Joseph and was situated near the Church of St. Martin.[256]

A conflict between the owners of the bars and saloons who built their businesses on property surrounding St. Joseph Church arose. Drunkenness and swearing in the vicinity of the church upset the young pastor as well as the parishioners. They were concerned about the lures tavern and saloon owners used to entice churchgoers into their establishments. It reached a point where there were few male churchgoers attending Mass because they spent their free time in the liquor establishments. People who sat in the taverns and drank said that God created the church, and

---

[253] H. H. Heaming, *History of the Catholic Church in Wisconsin*, p. 714

[254] Zdzisław J. Peszkowski, *Ojciec Seminarium Polskiego w USA: ks. Józef Dąbrowski*, Warszawa 1942, p. 42, Father Jan Polak came from a noble family, was born in 1818. He arrived in this area around 1850 first he became the pastor of Sharon and since 1860 worked in Stevens Point.

[255] *Księga pamiątkowa złotego jubileuszu*, p. 9

[256] H. H. Heaming, *History of the Catholic Church in Wisconsin*, p. 714

the devil created the saloons.[257] Rev. Buczyński many times requested that owners close their bars which surrounded the church during the time of services, but his requests remained unanswered. Rev. Buczyński left the parish in 1866 and moved to Milwaukee. He was replaced by the following pastors: Rev. Francis Wenglikowski (who worked there for three years), Rev. S. Szczepankiewicz, Rev. Joseph Juszkiewicz, and Rev. J. J. Zawistowski.[258] In the years 1868 and 1870 because of disputes and conflicts with immigrants of German origin, a decision was made by the bishop that the Parish of St. Joseph would have an interdict imposed upon them.

In December 1870, the bishop of the diocese sent as pastor Rev. Jozef Dąbrowski[259] who remained until September 30, 1882. The unrest and anticlericalism continued in this split community. Although Rev. Dąbrowski worked to resolve the problems in the community, it was to no avail. He concluded that drastic measures were required. After a Sunday Mass, he proposed to the parishioners that St. Joseph Church be physically moved to a more suitable location on a hilltop two miles east of the old site. It was a unanimous decision, and volunteers stepped forward to accomplish the move. Rev. Dąbrowski asked Mr. McGreer a man of Scottish origin and a Protestant to sell the land under the church. When the landlord found out the whole truth about the issue, he offered twenty acres of land to Rev. Dąbrowski. Later, he became a practicing Catholic.[260] Farmers throughout the county came with wagons, team horses, axes, and other necessary equipment to complete the move which took one week.

The new site was renovated, and a new rectory was built. On September 12, 1872, renovations to the church were completed, and it was blessed by Bishop Joseph Milcher of the Diocese of Green Bay.[261]

---

257 W. Kruszka, *A History of the Poles. Part 4*, p. 11.

258 The sources say that successors of Father Buczynski were the following priests, but they did not give the exact time of their stay nor the time spent working in the Parish of St. Joseph in Sharon.

259 Here is a difference in the last name in H. H. Heaming, *History of the Catholic Church in Wisconsin*, p. 714. The author gives the last name Father Jozef Dombrowski, but W. Kruszka, *A History of the Poles. Part 4*, p. 11, gave the last name Father Jozef Dąbrowski. I am choosing to use in this work the Polish spelling Dąbrowski.

260 Alexander Syski, *Ks. Jozef Dąbrowski*, Orchard Lake, Michigan 1942, p. 72.

261 Joseph Milcher was born on March 19, 1806, in Vienna. He was ordained on March 27, 1830, in the Diocese of St. Louis. On March 3, 1868, Pope Pius IX nominated him to be the first Bishop of the Diocese of Green Bay which was created on July 12, 1868. He died in Green Bay on December 20, 1873.

The church was placed under the patronage of the Annunciation of the Blessed Virgin Mary. The area where this church was placed was given the name Polonia in memory of Rev. Jan Polak the priest who worked among the Polish immigrants, organized, and built their parish.

The opponents of Rev. Dąbrowski brought legal action for loss of business because of his decision to move the church. The process in the court resulted in a loss for the bar owners. However, because the business owners didn't want to give up on the old church property, they built their own new church and invited Rev. Jan Frydrychowicz to minister in this church. He was a priest who had been suspended in Mulberry, Texas, in 1871. As a result, the church received the name "Red" church due to its red roof. It was a schism that lasted briefly because Rev. Frydrychowicz died shortly after his arrival in Polish Corner.[262]

In the summer of 1874, Rev. Dąbrowski received permission from the bishop to bring Polish nuns from the Congregation of Felician Sisters of Krakow to the Polish parish. On August 15, 1874, the request was introduced to the sisters and was accepted positively. The religious authorities decided to send five nuns to America as missionaries.[263] When the sisters came to the parish, a religious house was not yet finished. Rev. Dąbrowski rebuilt the rectory and adopted it as temporary living quarters for them. Six months later, the convent house was built and ready for the nuns.

The next decision was to begin construction of the school. In the meantime in the rectory, two rooms were prepared for use as classrooms for the children. On December 3, 1874, the sisters began teaching in this makeshift school. The joy did not last long because on March 16, 1875, during a storm, lightning struck the church property resulting in the rectory and convent house being completely burned. The convent quickly was rebuilt, and on May 4, 1875, Rev. J. Dąbrowski dedicated it under the patronage of St. Francis. In the evening of May 18, 1875, history suddenly repeated itself. The convent burned down again. In October 1876, the nuns once more received the opportunity to live in a new convent house, and on November 21, 1876, it was opened up as a

---

262   Z. Peszkowski, *Ojciec Seminarium Polskiego w USA: ks. Józef Dąbrowski*, p. 48
263   H. H. Heaming, *History of the Catholic Church in Wisconsin*, p. 715

novitiate for the sisters.[264] In 1882, the Congregation of Felician Sisters community was moved to Detroit to a former convent house that had been intended as a home for poor boys.

Bishop Francis Xavior Krautbauer,[265] of the Diocese of Green Bay blessed the cornerstone for the new Church of the Sacred Heart of Jesus on September 29, 1875. Fire again destroyed the church building in 1879, but it was rebuilt in the same year. A year later, the church and rectory burned down again. The insurance paid the parish as compensation $5,000. Rev. J. Dąbrowski immediately invested this into the construction of the new church which was dedicated in 1881. Due to lack of funds, this church was built without a foundation. This omission soon led to complete devastation. The temple could not be saved though much effort was used to try to do so.[266] Rev. Ladislaus Grabowski[267] who on October 1, 1882, replaced Rev. J. Dąbrowski in the position of pastor remained at the parish until April 16, 1888. In the three years following 1889, patronage of the parish was taken over by Franciscan Fathers. They were Fathers Stanislaus Jeka, Erasmus Sobocinski, and Jerome Schneider. A new pastor Rev. Thomas Grebowski was appointed in 1891. On July 26, 1902, during Rev. Grebowski's patronage, the cornerstone was blessed for the new temple. The church was completed, and it was dedicated on October 20, 1903. It was a new Gothic style church. Its length was 167 feet, and the width was 70 feet. The total construction cost was $45,000.

During the pastoral ministry of Rev. Grebowski, many things were accomplished. School construction was completed; the new roof was put on the church; the new pipe organ was purchased for the church at a cost of $2,500. The high altar was restored, and the Stations of the Cross were purchased.[268] In 1902, the parish consisted of approximately 375 families, and it had about 2,400 worshipers. A new priest Rev. Theophil

---

264 Parish Book, *Sacred Heart Congregation Polonia*, p. 29-30

265 Francis Xavior Krautbauer was born on June 12, 1828, in Bruck, Bavaria, Germany. He was ordained on June 16, 1850, in Buffalo, New York. Pope Pius IX nominated him as a 2nd Bishop of the Diocese of Green Bay, and he was ordained to the episcopacy on June 29, 1875. He died on December 17, 1885, in Green Bay.

266 W. Kruszka, *A History of Poles, Part 4*, p. 14

267 H. H. Heaming, *History of the Catholic Church in Wisconsin*, p. 715

268 W. Kruszka, *A History of the Poles. Part 4*, p. 13

Malkowski arrived at the parish in 1904. During his pastoral work in 1914, the orphanage for the boys burned. However, it was rebuilt in just one year.

The New Year, 1916, brought another change in the position of pastor. The new parish priest was Rev. Lucas J. Pescinski. He worked in the parish for twelve years. His pastoral ministry was very active. During his stay, a new brick rectory was built, and Polonia became the first place in Portage County to receive electricity. From April 28, 1928, to September 27, 1946, the pastor in Polonia was Rev. Leon Jankowski. On St. Patrick's Day, March 17, 1934, Polonia again experienced adversity. Lightning struck the church, and it burned down. Because the church was insured, the parish received $65,000 as compensation. This sum was used for the building of a new church, and it was completed before Christmas 1934. On September 27, 1946, Rev. Jankowski died, and Bishop John Treacy of the Diocese of La Crosse appointed Rev. John Gruna as the next pastor.

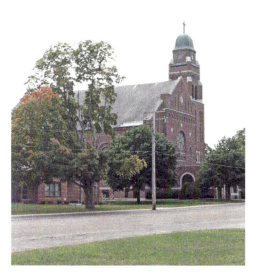

Church of the Sacred Heart, Polonia 2012
Source: Author's Collection

During his term of office, renovations were made in the school, church, and rectory. Rev. J. Gruna retired on November 15, 1951, after serving the parish for five years.

By November 15th of the same year, a parish priest was assigned, Rev. Joseph J. Schulist. During his stay in the parish, heating systems in the church and school were installed. In 1952, the rectory was renovated and modernized. The interior of the church was renovated by the artist Louis Shrovnal.[269] Rev. J. Schulist celebrated his silver jubilee of the priesthood in 1960. He initiated the construction of the new school building in the parish. This goal was reached on December 15, 1961,

---

269   Parish Book, *Sacred Heart Congregation Polonia*, p. 34

when the construction was completed. The official opening took place on January 3, 1962, and the number of students was 196.[270] The bishop of the Diocese of La Crosse dedicated the school building on April 19, 1962. The total cost of the construction was $94,327.53.

TABLE 15: Pastoral Registry in Sacred Heart of Jesus Parish, Polonia

Rev. Joseph Schulist	1951–1974
Rev. Thaddeus Szczerbicki	1974–1978
Rev. Herbert Zoromski	1978–1988
Rev. Al Wozniak	1988–1995
Rev. Joseph Konopacky	1995–1998
Rev. Marcin Mankowski	1998

7. St. Casimir, Town of Hull

Five miles north of Stevens Point and nine miles west of Polonia in the Town of Hull proudly stands the Parish of St. Casimir. In 1871, Rev. J. Dąbrowski came to this small town parish community.[271] The history of the parish began with the building of a small chapel. It was built by the residents with the encouragement of Rev. J. Dąbrowski. This priest came to Hull once a month as the pastoral minister to celebrate the sacraments and to preach the Word of God.[272] With time, the Town of Hull transitioned from a mission station into a separate self-contained parish. In autumn 1875, the first permanent pastor Rev. Josephat Walun was

Church of St. Casimir, Town of Hull 1906
Source: http://www.pchswi.org/archives/church/st_casimir/hist_stcasimir.html

---

270 Ibid., p. 35
271 Parish Book, *St. Casimir Parish, Town of Hull, 100 Anniversary 1871-1971*, Wisconsin 1971, p. 7
272 W. Kruszka, *A History of the Poles. Part 4*, p. 16

appointed by the bishop.[273] A new church was built in 1877. After three years in the Parish of St. Casimir in October 1878, Rev. J. Walun was transferred to Stevens Point. He was succeeded by Rev. January Czarnowski. He arrived in Hull in October 1878 and stayed until May 1886 when he was moved to another parish. During his stay in the parish, many changes occurred which included the purchase of three altars for the sum of $1,000. During this time, there was a significant increase in the number of parishioners.

After Rev. Walun left the parish, the church remained without a pastor for the next seven months.[274] The newly appointed permanent pastor was Rev. Lucas Pescinski. His pastoral work in the parish began on November 28, 1886. For a total cost of $3,500, he built a multi-storied school building and convent house for the nuns who led the school activities. He also purchased a bell. The school was opened on October 11, 1888. Three sisters from the Congregation St. Francis of Assisi were invited to run the school. The number of students was 180, and the salary of the teachers was $20 a month.[275] Already in 1893, the number of students grew to 213 pupils. In the same year, a small bell for the church was purchased for the sum of $104.03. In 1894, the whole parish community voted to change the name of the Town of Hull to St. Casimir in Portage County.[276] Rev. Pescinski remained in the parish until April 15, 1895. He was replaced by Rev. Wladyslaw Grabowski who worked there until February 1896. Rev. Grabowski promoted the building of a new church and the creation of a new separate parish in Torun.

Rev. Nikodemus Kolasinski arrived in March 1896. Two years later in November 1898, he was succeeded by Rev. Teofil Malkowski. During his time at St. Casimir's, a portion of the parish was separated as a mission church in Torun. After four short months of work, Rev. Malkowski left the parish and was replaced by Rev. J. Kula. After three years in June 1902, the bishop appointed a new pastor Rev. L. Kasperski. In October 1904, he was succeeded in this position by Rev. B. Polaczyk.

---

273 The differences in pronunciation and use of last names: W. Kruszka, *History of the Poles, Part 4*, p. 16, gives the last name J. Wałuń but Parish Book, *St. Casimir Parish*, p. 7 says J. Walun.

274 W. Kruszka, *A History of Poles, Part 4*, p. 17

275 Parish Book, *St. Casimir Parish*, p. 7

276 Ibid., p. 9

This priest built a new rectory for a total cost of $5,018.[277] By 1905, the parish had grown to 160 families.[278] Another change occurred in September 1909 when Rev. Leo Jankowski was appointed to St. Casimir Parish. During his seven years of work, the old St. Casimir Church burned, and he rebuilt a brick church on the same plot. The church was dedicated and put into operation in November 1913. The construction of the new church was for the sum of $5,000. In August 1916, the bishop made personnel changes at the parish with the assignment of a new pastor Rev. Paul Sokol. After six years of work in the parish in August 1921, Rev. Sokol left and was succeeded by Rev. W. Pruc. After five months, another change was made. The position of pastor was granted to Rev. J. B. Gruna. The parochial school which had remained closed for several years was then reopened.

Church of St. Casimir, Town of Hull 2012
Source: Author's Collection

The next pastor assigned to St. Casimir Church in May 1938 was Rev. F. Disher. He left the parish in 1942 and joined the Army as a chaplain. In his place in July 1942, Rev. S. A. Elbert came and remained until June 1948. At this time with only thirteen students enrolled, the school was again closed. On June 29, 1948, Rev. F. Brzostowicz arrived. During his stay, the buildings were renovated. He built an extension onto the church and put a new roof on it as well. On August 6, 1969, the newly appointed pastor was Rev. Arthur Redmond. He held his pastoral ministry until 1982. From 1982 to 1994, Rev. Edwin Stanek worked as the parish pastor. Another change to this office occurred in 1994 when Rev. Donald Walczak took up residence.

---

277   Ibid., p. 10
278   M. J. Goc, *Native Realm*, p. 38

TABLE 16: Pastoral Registry St. Casimir Parish, Town of Hull

Rev. Jozef Dąbrowski	1871–1875
Rev. Josaphat Wałun	1875–1878
Rev. J. Czarnowski	1879–1886
Rev. Lucas Pescinski	1886–1895
Rev. Ladislaus Grabowski	1895–1896
Rev. Nicodemus Kolasinski	1896–1898
Rev. T. Malkowski	1898–1899
Rev. J. Kula	1899–1902
Rev. L. Kasperd	1902–1904
Rev. W. B. Polaczyk	1904–1909
Rev. L. Jankowski	1909–1916
Rev. Paul Sokol	1916–1921
Rev. W. Pruc	1921
Rev. J. B. Gruna	1922–1938
Rev. F. Disher	1938–1942
Rev. S. A. Elbert	1942–1948
Rev. F. Brzostowicz	1948–1969
Rev. Arthur Redmond	1969–1982
Rev. Edwin Stanek	1982–1994
Rev. Donald Walczak	1994–

8. St. Mary of Czestochowa, Stanley

The Parish of Our Lady of Czestochowa is located one half mile east of Stanley, five miles west of Thorp, and four miles north of Highway 29.[279] The first immigrants of Polish descent settled in this area around 1901. They initially searched through Pennsylvania and Chicago looking

---

[279] The parish of Stanley counted 60 families. The small town does not have detailed information about starting and running a parish school. During the past 25 years until 1967 besides the church of Lady of Czestochowa, classes were conducted on catechistical teachings on Sunday mornings. The children were taught by the priests and then these duties were taken over by nuns. Children were taught catechism to prepare them for reception of the sacraments.

for opportunities before coming to the Stanley area.[280] Here they found very good soil although it had to be prepared for cultivation. So regularly, they prepared this area by cutting and clearing the forests. The land over time became very productive and yielded abundant crops. But life was not easy, and the Polish immigrants were initially in a very difficult economic situation. However, they did not give up, and their perseverance, sense of duty, and love for family allowed them to survive the most difficult moments. The Polish settlers were characterized by a strong faith in God and a devotion to tradition. Their belonging to the Catholic Church always played an important part in their lives. Since their conversion ages ago, they had always been faithful to the true church which was confirmed by Polish history.[281]

From the beginning, the Polish settlers were tied to the nearest Catholic Church which was located in Stanley. On foot or horseback regardless of the weather or the distance, the Poles went there to worship on Sundays and Holy Days. During this time, the pastor of St. Mary's in Stanley was Rev. Byrne.[282] English was used in the parish which made for a lot of difficulties for the Poles who didn't know the English language very well. Because of this, the Polish settlers living there went to a more distant parish in Thorp to the Church of St. Hedwig. The Polish language was used during the Liturgy of the Word. Rev. Pudlo the pastor in Thorp welcomed them kindly and helped them to adapt to life in a new area. This seemed a good solution because many of the Poles from the Junction in Stanley were unable to attend church services on Sundays due to bad weather and/or generally poor conditions for travel.

After 1906, there was a marked and significant increase in the population of settlers of Polish descent. New families arrived, and the city continued to grow. Soon the Polish residents of Stanley formed a committee to build a new church and therefore to establish a new Polish parish. The first meeting for the construction of the church was held by the committee on December 8, 1906. At the meeting, a plan was presented to build a new church. In the meantime, several residents of Stanley offered property for the purpose of the church. They were Paul

---

[280] www.usgennet.org/usa/wi/county/clark/webbs/records (February 9, 2009)
[281] Parish Book, *Diamond Jubilee 1908-1983,* Wisconsin 1983, p. 8
[282] There is a lack of first names in sources.

Zapisek who gave two acres, Ignatius Wisniewski donated six acres, and Anthony Misiewicz who made a contribution of two acres. Because the properties which were donated to the parish were situated in different locations, a problem existed as to where a new church should be built. Each of the donors wanted the church to stand near their home.[283] John Janik another resident of Stanley offered five acres of his land to the parish, but his offer was rejected. The settlers could not agree on a location of the church. The next meeting was held on June 9, 1907. During this meeting, people wanted to end the debate which was full of discrepancies and differing opinions and to finally begin the work on the church.

During a subsequent meeting, John Janik (one of the residents already cited) made another offer. This time, he would give a single plot of ten acres. The participants welcomed with joy this new proposal.[284] The decision was made for this plot to be used as the ground for the future temple. During the meeting, another resident John Cot donated four acres for the future cemetery which was also accepted with joy. Construction of the church was accompanied by extensive public support and enthusiasm. Many parishioners offered their assistance. One of them, Stephen Pluskwa promised to donate the stone needed for the construction of the foundation of the new church. A new committee was chosen for the oversight of the construction project. The chairman of this committee was Paul Zapisek, and the treasurer was Joseph Kapuscinski who was later replaced by John Janik as financial secretary and S. Pluskwa as the accountant.[285] Rev. Francis Pudlo the pastor of Thorp was invited to join the board committee and was asked to supervise the construction of the church.

During one of the meetings, Rev. Pudlo seeing the great passion and enthusiasm of the parishioners promised to ask Bishop James Schwebach for permission to organize the parish and build a new church. This request was sent to the bishop. In the fall of 1907, the church building committee received a response from the bishop. Permission was granted, and the blessing was given by the bishop for this project. People after hearing the decision of the diocesan bishop were very excited. The plan prepared be-

---

283 Parish Book, *Diamond Jubilee 1908-1983,* Wisconsin 1983, p. 9
284 www.usgennet.org/usa/wi/county/clark/webbs/records (February 9, 2009)
285 Parish Book, *Diamond Jubilee 1908-1983,* Wisconsin 1983, p. 9

forehand became operational. The first step made in this direction was to collect the needed money. Some residents sacrificed greatly in order to donate a significant amount of money. One of them, John Staszko donated the sum of $125. In addition, many local families offered physical help.

Unfortunately, the collection of money went very slowly, and over time, the church building costs increased significantly. Therefore, during the next meeting, Rev. Pudlo advised the gathered people that the committee did not have any other choice but to go to the bank to borrow the shortage of $600 which was needed to cover the shortfall. The loan was requested, and the borrowed money helped finish the church. On November 13, 1907, everything was finalized. The new church building could accommodate about one hundred people. Shortly after the completion of the church, a request to the bishop of the diocese was sent in which he was invited to come to dedicate the temple. The bishop could not attend the dedication, but he sent his blessing to the newly created parish. He also appointed Rev. Pudlo as a delegate to preside at the first Mass in the new church on his behalf. The first Mass was celebrated by Rev. Pudlo on the Solemnity of the Immaculate Conception on December 8, 1907.

In February 1908, the parish was officially adopted administratively by Bishop James Schwebach while Rev. Pudlo was made the first pastor of the missionary church.[286] On August 15, 1908, during the celebration of the Assumption of the Blessed Virgin Mary, the church was solemnly blessed and dedicated to Our Lady of Czestochowa. The parish now began a period of normal operation. The first sacrament of marriage was granted in the new church on May 13, 1908, between Stella Wozniak and John Pacholdki and between Anna Slowiak and Michael Symbala. One of the first sorrowful worship services in the church was the funeral of Constanty Zapisek who tragically drowned at the age of 22. He was buried on July 8, 1908, at the cemetery of St. Mary's next to the church.

From the date the church was erected in 1907 until 1913, it went through various changes. It is difficult to determine the exact date on which the parish was a mission under the pastoral care of the pastor from Thorp and when it became an independent mission with official membership to the Parish of St. Mary in Stanley. The first appointed pastor for

---

[286] Ibid., p. 10

the mission was Rev. E. Pudlo who was also a pastor in Thorp. During the next six years, the following priests worked in the parish: Rev. Pudlo, Rev. Joseph Mueller, Rev. E. C. Ciszewski, and Rev. J. Orlowski.[287]

This uncertainty lasted until 1913 when the bishop established the parish as an independent administrative unit and appointed newly ordained priest Rev. Francis Barszczak as its first permanent pastor. Collaboration between the new pastor and parishioners worked very well. With common strength, they decided to build a new parsonage which was completed in one year. The cost of the construction was $6,000. The time of the pastoral ministry of Rev. F. Barszczak in the parish was rather short. In September 1914, he was moved and replaced by Rev. F. J. Brzostowicz. This priest organized the first choir in the parish. He also became known for organizing the first Community of the Rosary in the parish which was a very important organization. It was led by Anna Ciolkosz and Kathrina Leja. In 1921, Rev. Barszczak returned as pastor. He was replaced by Rev. Karcz who served until 1926. After that, the parish priests who worked there were Rev. S. T. Szymczak, Rev. A. Kulig, Rev. Edmund Krystyniak, Rev. Louis Sobieski, and Rev. Roman Papiernik.

Church of St. Mary of Czestochowa, Stanley 2012
Source: www.usgennet.org/usa/wi/county/clark/webbs/records

After thirty-seven years of worship in a wooden church, in 1944 parishioners from the Church of Our Lady of Czestochowa decided the time had come to build a new, enlarged church. For the next two years, not too much happened regarding this matter. However, meetings were held for planning purposes. During a meeting on September 15, 1946, a decision was made, and the committee was elected for the construction of the new church. This committee created and prepared the plans and made a list of steps needed to begin work on the building. When

---
287 Parish Book, *Diamond Jubilee 1908-1983,* Wisconsin 1983, p. 10

the plans were presented to the bishop of the Diocese of La Crosse, he gave permission to begin construction. Although the preparations continued, it was not easy to start the project because the years following World War II were a difficult time for everyone.

In May 1949, land was purchased for the church, and in early autumn the work began. On December 8, the Solemnity of the Immaculate Conception of the Blessed Virgin Mary, the foundation stone was blessed and laid by Rev. Francis Brad who was a consultant for the diocese and also the pastor of the Parish of St. Patrick's in Eau Claire. In March 1950, the church was completed, and the construction cost was $74,946.26. On July 9, 1950, the church was consecrated by Bishop John P. Treacy of the Diocese of La Crosse. During the Mass, Rev. Stanislaw Andrzejewski preached the homily in the Polish language. After the ceremony in the church, the congregation prepared a dinner for 500 people. The newly built temple could hold 240 people. Inside the church, a special area was dedicated for the choir. In addition, a special room was built for children so that they would not interfere with the other participants during the service.

The church was built in the new Gothic style and had a basement under the entire foundation. This part was soon adopted as a parish meeting place. This church was known as Our Lady of Czestochowa the patron of Poland to whom the whole nation was under her protection and to whom prayers were said.[288] In the church was hanging a picture of Our Lady brought from Poland by Pawel Zapisek in 1907. It was solemnly dedicated and was placed on the main altar. The image was also known as the Black Madonna painting.

On July 9, 1952, there was another change in the position of pastor. The new priest was Rev. Ernest Kaim. During his pastoral ministry, the rectory was restored; the church was renovated; the benches were replaced; a new altar and a new tabernacle were built; and the debt of the parish was reduced. Soon there were more changes. The successor to Rev. Ernest Kaim, Rev. Sobczyk arrived on August 31, 1955. Two years later on September 3, 1957, the new pastor of the parish Rev. Edward A. Masalewicz arrived. Since all the repairs in the church were complet-

---

288   Parish Book, *Diamond Jubilee 1908-1983*, Wisconsin 1983, p. 15

ed, the new pastor focused on the typical pastoral work. He expanded the existing Group of the Rosary and the Holy Name Men's Group. A little later through his initiative, a new heating system was purchased and installed in the church.

On June 1, 1958, the parish celebrated its golden anniversary of establishment. In the first fifty years of existence, parish statistics showed 702 baptisms, 138 marriages, and 141 funerals.[289] Rev. Andrew Karoblis served the parish from 1961 to 1963. During these years, the parsonage was renovated; the church debt was repaid; changes were made in the lower church. He was succeeded by Rev. Rudolph Urbic who arrived at the parish in 1963 and worked until 1969. Rev. R. Urbic was moved and was succeeded by Rev. Stanley Andrzejewski who served from 1969 to 1980. However, in the years 1974 to 1975 while Rev. Andrzejewski struggled with illness, Rev. Stanley Chilicki served in the position of pastor. Rev. Andrzejewski served as pastor again from 1975 to 1980. In 1980, Rev. John B. Pinion came to the parish followed by Rev. John Puerner. During these years, the number of members in the parish decreased. This was partially due to the loss of small farms and the smaller number of children born in the families. Moreover, the younger generation to gain a good education and better paying jobs began to flee to larger cities. The church was closed on June 9, 1996, the Solemnity of Corpus Christi.

9. Our Lady of Scapular, Fancher[290] (also known as the Church of Our Lady of Mount Carmel)

The beginning of this parish dates to 1884. In the town of Fancher in Portage County south of Stevens Point, there were about thirty-five to forty Polish families. Once acclimated to the area, Poles settled here as farmers. They bought five acres of land for the church. This land was acquired from the family of August Dulak for a sum of $50. It was di-

---

289 Parish Book, *Diamond Jubilee 1908-1983*, Wisconsin 1983, p. 15

290 Another name for the church is presented in D. Kolinski, *The Origin and Early Development of the Polish Settlements in Central Wisconsin*, "In Polish American Studies," Vol. 51: 1994, No. 1, p. 89 and reads: The Parish of Our Lady of Mt. Carmel. Another different name we can find in: www.rootsweb.ancestry.com/wispags/ch-stmary.html (February 5, 2009), where it is Our Lady of Mt. Carmel.

vided into several parts. Two acres were allocated for the cemetery, and the remaining acres were divided into plots for the construction of a church, school, and rectory.[291]

Rev. Antoni Lex was responsible for the construction.[292] At that time, he stayed and lived in Stevens Point. In 1884, the church was complete. It was a small church with a length of 30 feet, width of 20 feet, and a height of 14 feet. Later that same year, the church was enlarged, as well as two rooms were built as quarters for the priest who came to minister to the parish. At that time, there were several priests who undertook the pastoral care in Fancher. Rev. Maczynski arrived in the autumn of 1866 and worked at Fancher until 1888. During his stay, a simple parsonage was built which had three small rooms. Rev. Lebnicki administered in the parish from 1889 to 1891 followed by Rev. Sikorski in 1892. Then in 1893, Rev. Lugowski worked at Fancher for a period of one year. The church in Fancher was rather small and soon parishioners outgrew it.

Church of St. Mary of Mount Carmel, Fancher 1905
Source: http://www.pchswi.org/archives/townships/heritagetrail.html

Shortly after he arrived in 1893, Rev. Mikolaj Kolasinski began the construction of a new, larger church. This church was 100 feet long, 40 feet wide, and 27 feet high. The building was finished and consecrated by Bishop Messmer on July 16, 1894.[293] Two years later on March 9, 1896, Rev. M. Kolasinski was transferred to Hull, and his successor was Rev. R. Wawrzykowski who remained in the parish until September 15, 1898. At that time, the number of parish families was 160. The newly appointed pastor in Fancher then became Rev. L. Staroscik.

In 1901, a very energetic pastor, Rev. Stanislaw Kubiszewski came to

---

291 W. Kruszka, *A History of the Poles. Part 4*, p. 20

292 Ambiguous spelling of the name of Father Leks working in Fancher: W. Kruszka, *A History of the Poles Part 4*, p. 20, the name is Lex, while D. Kolinski, *The Origin and Early Development of the Polish Settlements in Central Wisconsin*, p. 89, is Leks.

293 W. Kruszka, *A History of Poles, Part 4*, p. 21

the parish. In 1902 with the permission of the bishop, he opened a parochial school. The organist was a school teacher as was Rev. Kubiszewski who taught a few hours a day.

On March 19, 1904, for unknown reasons the wooden church burned down. Soon a meeting was called in the parish in order to decide on the construction of a temple. The construction work started very quickly. With the involvement of the parishioners and pastor, the church was finished and consecrated by Bishop Fox in the spring of 1905. It was a brick structure and cost $25,000. On July 18, 1908, Archbishop Francis Albin Symon[294] the first Polish bishop in the United States blessed the bells for this parish.[295]

In 1912, a separate school building was finished next to the church. Three nuns from the Congregation of St. Joseph in Stevens Point were asked to come and administer in the school and educate the children and youth. During that time, a house was built as a dormitory in which some children who lived far away from school could stay from Monday through Friday. On Saturday and Sunday, they returned to their families. Parents of children who attended the school paid a subsidy, but the parish was responsible for providing the meals.[296] On an evening in 1934, parishioners experienced another tragedy when the school building exploded and was consumed by fire. It being winter, forty students living in the boarding school were forced to leave the building immediately. The

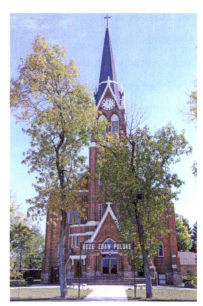

Church of St. Mary of Mount Carmel, Fancher 2012
Source: Author's Collection

---

294 Franciszek Albin Symon (March 13, 1841-May 28, 1918) became a Bishop of Płock, was a professor and rector of the Theological Academy in St. Petersburg, and a professor in the seminary in Żytomierz. He defended the church against Russification. He could not cover the function of the Bishop of Płock due to opposition by the Czar's authorities. He was deported to Odessa in the years 1897-1901. After his release, he went to Rome. He visited the Polish parishes in the United States. He was the author of many publications of historical and biblical topics.

295 W. Kruszka, *A History of the Poles. Part 4*, p. 22

296 www.rootsweb.ancestory.com/wispags/ch-stmary.html (February 5, 2009)

school was rebuilt soon, and the education in it continued until 1970 when low enrollment eventually caused its closing.

TABLE 17: Pastoral Registry of Our Lady of Mount Carmel Parish, Fancher

Rev. Stanislaus J. Kubiszewski	1900–1908
Rev. Leon Jankowski	1908–1909
Rev. Anthony S. Elbert	1909 briefly
Rev. Lukas Pescinski	1909–1916
Rev. Julius Chylinski	1916–1929
Rev. Stanislaus Kubiszewski	1929–1934
Rev. Peter Borowski	1934–1939
Rev. Anthony Kauza	1939 briefly
Rev. Stanislaus Lapinski	1939–1945
Rev. Maxmillian Kluczykowski	1948–1951
Rev. Stephen Mieczkowski	1951–1959
Rev. Thaddeus Szczerbicki	1959–1974
Rev. Dominic Eichman	1974–1977
Rev. Roy Mish	1977–1981
Rev. Stanley Krupa	1981–1986
Rev. Robert Pedretti	1986–1988
Deacon Gene Shaver	1988–1999
Deacon Thomas Jirous	1999–2000
Rev. Raymond Pedretti	2000

10. St. John the Baptist, Belmont[297]

Around the year 1890 in the town of Belmont located in the southeastern corner of Portage County, several Polish families settled. They came from the nearby town of Berlin. Most of them before settling in the state of Wisconsin had already resided in the Chicago area.[298] Soon

---

297   There are two names for the village. One comes from the name of a very wealthy family Heffron, and the second name of the same village where the church was built was Belmont.

298   D. Kolinski, *The Origin and Early Development of Polish Settlements in Central Wisconsin*, p. 38-39.

there was a small community of Polish immigrants who wanted to build a church. The history of the church began with the donation of the land for the church as well as land for the future cemetery. This land was donated by the John and Martin Heffron Family for a sum of $1.00. This family also donated wood for the construction of the church. One of the residents, Andrew Izydor, a carpenter, made a wooden altar and also made a few pieces of furniture needed in the church.[299] The number of Polish families settling in Belmont was not very high with only twenty-five to thirty-five families. Records prepared by Rev. Kurzejka who commuted from Plover to St. John the Baptist in Belmont (the church was a parish mission of St. Patrick in Lanark) show that Mass was celebrated twice a month but only on weekdays.[300]

Church of St. John the Baptist, Heffron (Belmont) around 1950
Source: http://www.pchswi.org/archives/townships/heritagetrail.html

In the spring of 1896, the Heffron Family donated an additional five acres of land for the church. At the same time, more Polish families were arriving in Belmont. A new church was soon built, and on March 25, 1896, the first Mass was celebrated[301]. In 1898, Rev. Michael Klosowski from Fancher arrived at the Parish of St. John the Baptist. After that, the acting pastor was Rev. John Pociesha who received permission from the bishop of Green Bay to celebrate Mass and permission to dedicate a new church. In 1900, although he still commuted, Rev. Franciszek Wlaslowski was the first pastor of St. John the Baptist. He arrived in Belmont from Lanark.[302] He held custody of the

---

299   W. A. Guyant, *A History and Memories: Portage County, Belmont Township*, p. 133

300   W. A. Guyant, *A History and Memories: Portage County, Belmont Township*, p. 133. The report was written on January 23, 1899, and was sent to the Diocese of Green Bay to the Diocese Archives.

301   There is a mismatch between the first church building W. Kruszka, in *A History of the Poles. Part 4*, p. 24, is giving information that on March 25, 1896, the church was built and during that time the first Mass was celebrated. While W. A. Guyant, *A History and Memories: Portage County, Belmont Township*, p. 132 gives 1895 as the year of construction of the first church.

302   In the book, W. Kruszka, *A History of Poles, Part 4*, p. 24, the information is given that Father Franciszek Wlaslawski changed his name to Francis Laslow.

parish until 1904.[303] In 1901, a newly ordained priest Rev. Michal Kolosowski also came to Lanark to help Rev. Wlaslowski. The successor of Rev. Wlaslowski in the parish was Rev. Pociecha who in 1903 built a magnificent rectory. By this time in order to celebrate Mass, a priest came to the church in Belmont every other Sunday. His arrival was dependent on good weather conditions.

The first permanent resident pastor who lived at the Parish of St. John the Baptist was Rev. Franciszek Pruss. In December 1905, Rev. R. Margot who was quite elderly lived at the parish.[304] Rev. Pruss received a challenge from the bishop to build a new church designed to be very solid. After talks with parishioners, Reverend Pruss decided to start the construction. In 1906, the cornerstone was laid. In the same year, there was another change in the position of pastor with the assignment of Rev. Warzynski. To pay for the church construction, a bank loan of $4,500 was obtained. It was assumed that each family would make an annual offering of $10 for this purpose. During a parish meeting in 1908, the decision was made that the old altar from the former church would be donated to the church in Custer.

Church of St. John the Baptist, Heffron (Belmont) 2012
Source: Author's Collection

In June 1908, the new church was dedicated. A special collection was taken for the diocesan bishop which amounted to $51.82. In 1909, a new parish priest Rev. Victor Zareczny was assigned to St. John. The church was painted in 1917, and in the old church, a new floor was laid and the roof tiled. Pavement was placed around the parsonage as well as the old and new churches. An interesting occurrence was the regular collection of money during the Mass for the victims of World War I in Poland.[305]

---

303 W. Kruszka, *A History of Poles, Part 4*, p. 24

304 W. A. Guyant, *A History and Memories: Portage County Belmont Township*, p. 134 mentioned a different spelling of the last name of the pastor, and it is Father R. Maggot.

305 W. A. Guynat, *A History and Memories: Portage County Belmont Township*, p. 135

In 1922, another room was added to the rectory, and the church basement was finished. The following year, the parish debt was retired. The church was closed in 1960.

11. St. Adalbert, Rosholt

The Church of St. Adalbert in Rosholt was separated from the Parish of the Sacred Heart of Jesus in Polonia, Portage County. This was due to a large group of immigrants who arrived from the Polish territory. They needed land to settle, and the parish in Polonia was too small and too far from other centers. The arriving Poles settled in the city of Alban which was a separate part of the city of Sharon. On January 14, 1895, to meet the needs of the newly arrived immigrants, Rev. Tomasz Grembowski the pastor of Sacred Heart of Jesus in Polonia called for a meeting of all residents. It was decided that a new school would be built in Alban to enhance the development and education of the immigrant children. In addition, a chapel was to be erected.[306] That was the beginning of the Parish of St. Adalbert, and the school under the title of St. Joseph was founded beside the chapel. In order to achieve the proposed plan, one acre of land was purchased for the price of $15.[307]

Church of St. Adalbert, Rosholt 1923
Source: Parish Book, Celebrating 100 years, St. Adalbert Catholic Church Rosholt, *Wisconsin 1998*

On June 18, 1895, a wooden school was completed for a total cost of $328. That same year, the school started its activities with fifteen students. The school also fulfilled the function of a temporary chapel. At a subsequent meeting when the number of families increased to sixty, a decision was made to build a new church. The Bishop of Green Bay, Sebastian Messmer, gave permission to begin construction of the church and the

---

306 Parish Book, *Celebrating 100 Years St. Adalbert Catholic Church, Rosholt*, 1988, p. 8
307 D. Kolinski, *The Origin and Early Development of Polish Settlements in Central Wisconsin*, "Polish American Studies," Vol. 51: 1994, nr 1, p. 36-37

formation of the parish. On March 4, 1898, Rev. Grembowski was appointed to be responsible for the construction of the church. The building project started in the spring of 1898.[308] Land for the future church was partly purchased and partly donated. The construction work was completed in December of that same year. The total cost to build the church was $10,000. In 1899, the first pastor Rev. Michael Miklaszewski came. A small parsonage for the pastor was also built.

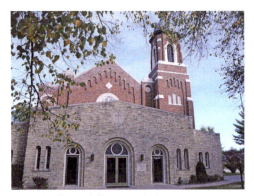

Church of St. Adalbert, Rosholt 2012
Source: Author's Collection

Over the next two years by 1900, the parish grew to 150 families. The next priest who took charge of the parish was Rev. Jan Adamowski on January 21, 1900. He was succeeded by Rev. L. Jankowski.[309] In March 1908, another change occurred with the assignment of Rev. John Pociecha as the new pastor. During his stay in the parish, a new brick school was built which had four classrooms. The cost of the school came to $5,000. During the new school year 1909-1910, nuns from the Congregation of St. Joseph served as administrator and teachers at St. Joseph School. On October 13, 1909, Bishop Paul Rohde consecrated the school building.

In 1916, a new parish priest Rev. Francis Nowak built a rectory for a total sum of $21,000 which still stands today. In June 1924, Rev. Michael Klosowski was transferred to the parish. During his administration and pastoral care, the church burned after being struck by lightning. A week after this event, parishioners met and decided to rebuild the church. In a short time, the construction began, and on May 3, 1935, a new church was dedicated. This church was much larger than the former church. Everyone attending Mass in the church had his own seat as this church had 725 seats. The construction cost $57,000. Rev. Michael Klosowski remained until his death in 1957.

---

308   Ibid., p. 37
309   W. Kruszka, *A History of the Poles. Part 4*, p. 22

In June 1957, Rev. John Nowak assumed the position of pastor. Cardinal Karol Wojtyla who later became Pope John Paul II visited this parish in August 1973. Rev. John Nowak served this parish until 1981 when he was succeeded by Rev. Don Walczak.[310] While he served the parish, an addition to the school complex was built. Also constructed were an entrance, bathrooms, elevator, and a special ramp as access for the disabled. In 1995, Rev. Joseph Konapacky was transferred to St. Adalbert Parish. He served in two churches: St. Adalbert and Sacred Heart in Polonia. As of 1998, a new pastor Rev. Marian Mankowski managed the parish of 300 hundred families.

12. Immaculate Conception of the Blessed Virgin Mary, Torun

At the end of the 19th century to this charming corner in Wisconsin came Polish settlers. They were searching for a job and a way to better themselves and their children. In the very beginning, there lived approximately one hundred people in this area. The local parish was founded in 1895. To establish this parish, a donation was made by Julian and Martha Fierek. They donated six acres of land for the future church to the bishop of the diocese.[311] They also donated the first $100 to start the construction of the new church. Bernard and Kathy Zylka donated an additional two acres at the beginning of construction work to create

Church of St. Mary, Torun 1898
Source: http://www.pchswi.org/archives/church/stmarytorun.htm

---

310 Parish Book, *Celebrating 100 Years, St. Adalbert Catholic Church Rosholt*, 1998, p. 17
311 www.pchswi.org/archives/church/stmary_torun (August 19 2008). Article gives information about 4 acres.

the parish church. These two acres of land were later earmarked for use as a local parish cemetery. Moreover, other donations were collected in the amount of $700 to be used for the purpose of building a church. The supervisor of the construction in Torun was Rev. Nicodomus Kolasinski the pastor of St. Casimir Parish. Construction of the church did not happen easily because only forty-five parish families in the area were able to provide financial assistance and/or physical assistance. The construction of the church was completed in late 1897 and named Immaculate Conception of the Blessed Virgin Mary. With time, the church became more commonly known as the Church of St. Mary.[312] The church was dedicated on December 5, 1897, by Bishop Messmer of the Diocese of Green Bay. Initially, the Church of the Blessed Virgin Mary was a missionary church to which the priest from St. Casimir Parish commuted for his pastoral ministry.[313] In 1898, St. Casimir Parish welcomed a new pastor Rev. Theophil Malkowski. After two years when the construction of the church was finished in December 1899, Torun welcomed its first pastor Rev. Romuald Magott. At the church, a small school was also opened for children. From the very beginning, two lay teachers taught the students.

The church in Torun had two levels. One level was the main church where the celebration of the liturgy took place while the second level was used for classrooms and by the pastor. Another pastor in Torun was Rev. Joseph Smith who came to the parish in 1900 and remained until 1902. In 1902 Rev. T. Maluszewski arrived, but he remained in the parish only a few months. In the same year, Rev. Magott returned and took over the administrative and priestly duty in the parish until 1904.[314] Rev. Magott was followed by Rev. James Kula, and his successor was Rev. Felix Nowak[315] who served as pastor until 1905. After 1905, the parish again became a mission church, and the commuting priest was Rev. W. B. Polarczyk from St. Casimir Parish. Although soon after, Rev.

---

312   This church has four different names which appeared in the history of this parish: The Church of St. Mary, Church of the Immaculate Conception, Church of Blessed Virgin Mary of Perpetual Help, or The Church of Virgin Mary.
313   D. Kolinski, *The Origin and Early Development of Polish Settlements in Central Wisconsin*, p. 37
314   www.pchswi.org/archives/church/stmary_torun (February 10, 2009)
315   W. Kruszka, *A History of Poles, Part 4*, p. 23

F. M. Fierek arrived in Torun as the parish priest and remained there until January 1906. Rev. Stephen Phazal remained in his position as pastor only until November 1907. After that for eleven months, the pastoral duty was held in Torun by Rev. W. Kolaczyk. In December 1908, Rev. S. Kasperski arrived and remained until 1911.

During Rev. Leon Jankowski's administration, the parsonage was built with construction completed in 1916. Unfortunately, at the same time after eighteen years of operation, the school was closed due to lack of teachers. The pastor remained the sole teacher of catechism for the children. Another priest in the parish was Rev. V. Pruc who administered in the years 1916-1918. His successor was Rev. Stanisz (working in Torun until 1919) followed by Rev. Ignatius Grad (who remained in the parish until 1929). After these successive pastors came Rev. A. Forysia who died shortly after arriving and was replaced by Rev. S. Elbert. After that, Rev. B. Plaza worked in Torun until June 1931. For the next eight years, the priestly duty was taken by Rev. S. A. Janczewski. Rev. Anthony Kraus was at this post until 1940. In the years 1940 to 1943, Rev. Peter Novicki worked in Torun. Rev. Joseph Schulist was the parish priest in the following years. In 1946, the parishes in Portage County including Torun were annexed to the Diocese of La Crosse.

Church of St. Mary, Torun 2012
Source: Author's Collection

The new Bishop of the Diocese of La Crosse, John P. Treacy, in July 1947 appointed Rev. Chester Zielinski who served in the parish until 1954. He was replaced on November 24, 1954, by Rev. Ed Klimaszewski. A year later, a successor Rev. Dominic Eichman was appointed. During his ministry in the parish of Torun, a new pipe organ was purchased for the church and the church renovated. The successor of Rev. Eichman was Rev. Alois Szerafinski. He died at the age of forty-four in August 1965. The next pastor was Rev. Richard Tomsyck who administered in the parish until 1978. At that time, the parish in Torun became a mission with the pastoral ministry being handled by Rev. Arthur Redmond the pastor of St. Casimir Church who commuted to Torun.

13. St. Stanislaus, Lublin

Immigration from Europe also reached a small village in Wisconsin which the settlers called Lublin. The first of those who came and settled in this area were the families of J. Wasielewicz, J. Albimiak, J. Cieciora, M. Skrzypczak, M. Barca, and M. Orzechowski.[316] In 1902, a small group of Polish settlers had a meeting at which time the decision was made to build a church and to establish a new parish. The pastoral ministries were done at that time in Lublin by Rev. Francis Pudlo and Rev. Francis Orlik. The most important reason justifying this decision was the fact that the nearest Catholic parish and church was located in Thorp, a distance of twelve miles. The roads were of poor quality, and the method of travel to church was on foot or by horse carriage. Efforts to obtain a building permit started in 1902, but only in 1908 did the residents of Lublin receive permission from Bishop Augustin Schinner of the Diocese of Superior.[317] In the early days, the church was dedicated to All Saints. Later, on April 4, 1920, the title was amended, and the patron of the church became St. Stanislaus, Bishop and Martyr.

The first pastor in Lublin was Rev. T. F. Malecki.[318] He was succeeded by Rev. B. J. Barca. During their stay in the parish, these two pastors built and finished a parsonage. Rev. Stanislaus Topolski worked in the parish during the years 1911 to 1916. During his administration, the cemetery was established, and the facilities in the church were completed (including the purchase of vestments).

---

316 *History of St. Stanislaus Bishop and Martyr Church, Lublin,* in: The archives of the Diocese of Superior (Catalog of the Parish of St. Stanislaus, in Lublin), Superior 1910, p. 1, but in *WI History Records Survey (Series 1953) 1936-1942 Inventory of the Church Records by County,* Box 252, Folder 20, County: Taylor states that the church was organized December 27, 1907, and dedicated in the same year.

317 *History of St. Stanislaus Bishop and Martyr Church, Lublin,* in: The archives of the Diocese of Superior (Catalog of the Parish of St. Stanislaus, in Lublin), Superior 1910, p. 1, but in *WI History Records Survey (Series 1953) 1936-1942 Inventory of the Church Records by County* Box 252, Folder 20, County: Taylor p. 1

318 *History of St. Stanislaus Bishop and Martyr Church, Lublin,* in: The archives of the Diocese of Superior (Catalog of the Parish of St. Stanislaus, in Lublin), Superior 1910, p. 1 states that the first permanent pastor was Father Edward Casterz in the years 1907-1908.

The next pastor was Rev. L. S. Nowacki who worked there in the years 1916 and 1917. His successor was Rev. P. Raczaszek who worked in the years 1917 to1922. During his period of service in the parish, the church was painted, and the inside of the church was also decorated. The priest's annual salary was also established as well as a fee was introduced for renting a space in the church (pew rent). Rev. John Balcer was transferred to the parish and worked in the years 1922 to1931. Soon after he assumed his position, the rectory burned. At the beginning of 1923 during a parish meeting, everyone agreed that the rectory should be rebuilt.

Over the next fifteen years from 1931-1946, pastor Rev. Joseph Rapala tended to the needs of the parish. After him from 1946 to 1950, the parish priest was Rev. Thaddeus Augustyn. During his service, a decision was made to change the roof on the church and the rectory. The next pastor of the Parish of St. Stanislaus was Rev. Eugene Konopka who worked in Lublin from 1950 to 1961.[319] During his pastoral ministry, construction of the new church lasted from 1958 to 1961. The new church was completed in 1961 for a total cost of $132,000. This church had 300 seats. The first Mass was celebrated on December 25, 1961.

Church of St. Stanislaus, Lublin 2012
Source: Author's Collection

In the years 1961 to 1968, Rev. Edward T. Cyz served as next pastor. In the years 1968 to 1970, his successor was Rev. West. From 1970, the responsibility of administration was led by Rev. Casimir Paul.[320] He worked in the parish until 1984 when he retired. Rev. Nowak replaced him and remained until September 1986.[321] A temporary pastor was appointed. Rev. George Tsanakas arrived in December of that year and remained until January 1987. After that, Rev. Brian Przyborowski was appointed and worked until June 1999 when his position was taken by Rev. Phil Juza.

---

319 www.rootsweb.com/-witaylor/histories/lublinhistory (February 20, 2004), p. 9-10
320 www.rootsweb.com/LublinHistory (September 18, 2008), p. 10
321 www.rc.net/superior/mjpps/stanshistory.html (July 2, 2012)

14. St. Ladislaus, Bevent

The town of Bevent is located by Pike Lake in Marathon County. A parish and church were founded there with the title of St. Ladislaus. Under the spiritual guidance of Rev. Grabowski, this community began operation on March 15, 1886.[322] The parish of Bevent was primarily founded by Polish immigrants. They faced many difficulties including language problems and financial hardships. For most immigrants, the origins of life in a foreign land were very difficult. However, their enthusiasm, determination, perseverance, hopes for a better future, and a deep faith allowed them to survive the most difficult moments. This survival was evident with the Polish immigrants in Marathon County near Bevent. After their arrival, they were determined and willing to take any job including the felling of trees regardless of how much discomfort they experienced. These poor people had no money for woolen socks for their shoes. They had to work in the winter in the woods clearing forests with no socks.[323]

Church of St. Ladislaus, Bevent
Source: Record Herald Newspaper

Within the young Polish community in the area, there was a need for a place of worship. These people built a small building with the title of St. Ladislaus in which they organized prayer meetings. Soon, however, it was evident that it was too small of a building. The parish swelled as a result of immigrants arriving from Poland. Rev. Romuald Magot who was appointed the pastor of this new parish in November 1895 came to address the needs of the population. As a leader, he mobilized the parishioners. In the same year, construction of a new, larger church

---

322 W. Kruszka, *A History of the Poles. Part 4*, p. 102. In L. Marchetti, *History of Marathon County Wisconsin*, p. 256 states the first Catholic Church built in Bevent was in 1883.

323 M. Rosholt, *The Wisconsin Logging Book 1839-1939*, Wisconsin 1980, p. 103

began. The church was completed in 1897.[324] The dimensions of the church were 122 feet long and 50 feet wide. The total cost of the church structure was $15,000.[325]

In 1898, Rev. Stefan Kasperski arrived to shepherd the parish until 1901. The next pastors appointed to the pastoral ministry in Bevent were Rev. Walslowski followed by Rev. Jan Pociecha in 1904. The parish numbered about 800 worshipers. Rev. Francis Pudlo was the next successor who stayed in this community until 1926.[326] In 1913 during his stay, the parochial school was built.

Church of St. Ladislaus, Bevent 2012
Source: Author's Collection

For the first nineteen years, lay personnel taught in the school due to a lack of housing for nuns. School attendance was eighty students. Children were also taught religion in school. Religion was also offered to children attending public schools. In 1932, nuns from the Congregation of Felician came to the parish and assumed the teaching positions at the school. Rev. Francis Pudlo died in 1927 and was buried in the parish cemetery.

His replacement was Rev. Stefan Kasperski, and he was later succeeded by Rev. Ignatius Mordarski. In 1932, Rev. F. J. Brzostowicz lived in the parish as a resident. In May 1935, a leaky chimney caused a fire to break out in the school. However, the fire was put out in time to save the building. Another pastor in the Parish of St. Ladislaus in Bevent was Rev. Peter Rombalski who started in 1936. In 1938-1939, the parish school added two classrooms: one for ninth and the other for tenth grade,[327] in the

---

324 Ibid., p. 103
325 Parish Book, *St. Ladislaus Parish, Bevent, Wisconsin*, 1985, p. 15 to compare L. Marchetti, *History of Marathon County, Wisconsin,* p. 567
326 L. Marchetti, *History of Marathon County Wisconsin,* p. 567. This author is the only one to mention Fr. Ignatious Latorski as pastor of St. Ladislaus at this time. The book was published in 1913.
327 Parish Book, *St. Ladislaus Parish, Bevent,* Wisconsin 1985, p. 20

church the tabernacle was changed, a new main altar was purchased, and a new heating system was installed. In 1944, Rev. John Krasowski arrived as pastor at St. Ladislaus. His successor in 1956 was Rev. Florian Marmurowicz who worked there for twelve years until 1968. After his death, the newly appointed priest was Rev. Bernard Nowak. He cared for the souls of this parish for the next twenty-two years until 1990.

15. St. Florian, Hatley

The village of Hatley is situated along the Plover River in Marathon County. This town owes its name to Matthew La Arien who called this area as well as the city of Quebec his city of origin. The first residents who came here were of Polish origin. They spoke either very little English or none at all.[328] They were Catholics who were characterized by a strong attachment to their family. From Poland, they brought their ancestral traditions. Therefore, all family ceremonies: weddings, funerals, and baptisms were held in the "Polish Fashion". In 1885, six Polish families began to meet regularly for the Eucharist in the home of Jan and Franciszka Petarski.

Church of St. Florian, Hatley
Source: Parish Book, St. Florian's Parish Hatley, WI 1885-1985

However, over time due to the constantly growing number of participants, this place was no longer sufficient. New settlers came to Hatley in greater numbers. Spiritual care over this area was provided by the priest from St. Michael Parish in Wausau and was also offered by the Franciscan Fathers from the monastery in Marathon City. The priest commuted by train to Hatley for the celebration of the Holy Eucharist and sacraments.[329] Among these priests were Rev. T. S. Wojak, Rev. L.

---

[328] Parish Book, *St. Florian's Parish Hatley, WI 1885-1985*, Wisconsin 1985, p. 14
[329] W. Kruszka, *A History of Poles, Part 4*, p. 102

W. Slisz, Rev. S. A. Elbert, and Rev. James Kula.[330] The first service was celebrated in the former school building. Due to the expanding ranks of the faithful, a decision was made to build a church. R. E. Parcher owner of a wood company offered fifteen acres of land for this purpose.[331]

Construction started very quickly on the new church named after St. Florian, the patron of Krakow, Poland, and patron of firefighters. The church was completed and dedicated in 1898. At that time, the Parish of St. Florian belonged administratively to the Diocese of Green Bay. St. Florian's as a result of border changes was added to the Diocese of La Crosse on May 3, 1905. The first permanent pastor Rev. Modiarski was appointed in 1906 to St. Florian's. He also commuted to several other parishes with his pastoral ministry including St. Agnes (Callon), St. Francis of Assisi (Norrie), and St. Joseph (Galloway). Rev. Modiarski was responsible for the Polish community taking over that responsibility from Rev. Garus. There is no information about the building of the rectory.[332]

The first pipe organ for the church was purchased from the Parish of St. James in Wausau. The pipe organ was transported by horse drawn carriage to Hatley by Frank Kobus and his neighbors. For several months in late 1906 and 1907, the bishop of the Diocese of La Crosse appointed Rev. Jozef Miller as the second pastor of St. Florian. Rev. J. Miller worked in the parish only for a brief period of time because he could not speak Polish very well. He was succeeded for a short time by Rev. J. Orlowski and then Rev. John Karcz. As the fourth newly appointed pastor, Rev. John Karcz saw the need to build a new church. He, therefore, organized a committee for the project of building a church and parsonage. Ten acres of land for the church and other facilities were donated by Jones Land Company. Sixty Polish families decided to build a larger church and hired architect Frank Spalenka from Stevens Point. The debt from building the original church was repaid during the

---

330   L. Marchetti, *History of Marathon County Wisconsin*, p. 568. This book states that the priests who commuted to the Hatley with their pastoral care before the erection of the parish of St. Florian were Fr. Garus, Fr. Leo Jankowski, Fr. Jan Adamowski, and Fr. Kula.

331   L. Marchetti, *History of Marathon County, Wisconsin*, p. 568. Here is information stating that fifteen acres of land were donated for the construction of the new church, but in *Hatley History of a Central Wisconsin Village*, Edina, MN 2009, p. 43, this information is given as a six acre land donation, but in Parish Book, *St. Florian's Parish, Hatley, WI, 1885-1985*, p. 14, the amount is ten acres of land for the new church in Hatley.

332   Parish Book, *St. Florian's Parish Hatley, WI 1885-1985*, Wisconsin 1985, p. 14

period of the ministerial care of Rev. John Karcz. At the same time, parishioners with considerable influence in the parish started a fund with $1,200. It was used to initiate the building of a new church with the dimensions of 135 feet long and 50 feet wide. The church plans called for brick construction on a foundation. The parish had now grown to 135 families.[333] The parsonage was built in 1914 also under the leadership of Rev. J. Karcz. In the same year, Bishop James Schwebach of the Diocese of La Crosse consecrated the new church and rectory. Soon after the consecration of the church and rectory, Rev. J. Karcz was transferred to Texas because of his health.

Church of St. Florian, Hatley 2012
Source: Author's Collection

He was replaced by Rev. Joachim Orlowski who was from the Congregation of Sacred Heart. In Hatley, he worked from 1911 to 1912. After the consecration of the new church, the old wooden church which had served local families for sixteen years was sold to Chester Warpechowski. He used it for years as a large barn on his farm. Another pastor appointed by the bishop for the Parish of St. Florian in Hatley was Rev. Stanley A. Krakowiecki. He continued his pastoral ministry for twenty-seven years uniting many people. His work was not only limited to the parish in Hatley but also to the nearby villages of Eland and Galloway where there were no priests and a large pastoral expectation. He was able to do this because of his great personal commitment.

In 1941 during the morning Mass, lightning struck and completely burned the parsonage.[334] On November 16, 1949, Rev. Raymond H. Rucki was appointed as parish administrator. A few years later in 1955, Sister Mary Thomasilda from the Congregation of the Mother of Good

---

333 L. Marchetti, *History of Marathon County Wisconsin*, p. 568-569
334 Parish Book, *St. Florian's Parish Hatley, WI 1885-1985*, Wisconsin 1985, p. 16

Counsel from the Providence of Felician Sisters in Chicago became the first director of the parish school. In the same year on July 29, Bishop John P. Treacy came to bless the middle school complex and the convent.[335] In 1968, the Felician Sisters left their post in Hatley. This position was taken over by the sisters from the Congregation of St. Joseph who continued the educational work in the school.

Rev. R. H. Rucki was replaced by Rev. Edwin Klimaszewski and on November 5, 1966, a new pastor Rev. Chester Moczarny was appointed. On June 18, 1968, the bishop of Diocese of La Crosse appointed Rev. Sigismund Lengowski as pastor. He served the parish until May 12, 1980. The position of pastor changed on July 1, 1980, when Rev. Chester Osowski was appointed pastor. He was replaced by Rev. Thomas J. Abraham on July 1, 1982.

16. St. John the Baptist, Peplin

A few miles to the east of the small city of Mosinee and a few miles northeast of Knowlton, a Polish town was founded that adopted the name of Pelplin. This town was established in the county of Marathon. The history of this town dates back to 1910 when the Worzalla brothers (Tony, John, and Steven) purchased 26,000 acres of land. This project was inspired because of a large tract of land and the huge availability of forest resources that were used for paper production. The name of the town was later changed to Peplin.[336]

At the very beginning, a saw mill, store, and blacksmith shop were built as was the first boarding house for workers. The next step in creating the town was advertising in Polish language newspapers and in brochures printed for the cities. Pictures of beautiful lands and farms were posted in order to persuade others to come to Peplin and settle. The intended goal was reached. The first who came to Pelplin were Albert Wonsil, Alex Dyda, and Vince Ruzga.

A few years later when the town had grown and added more residents,

---

335 Ibid., p. 17
336 www.Marathoncountyhistory.org/PlacesDetails.php (February 3, 2011)

the community of settlers made the decision to build a church with the possibility of establishing a parish in the future. This decision to build was made January 31, 1915. The church was to be named St. John the Baptist. The organizer for the construction work on the church was Rev. John Rolbiecki pastor of St. Paul Parish in Mosinee.[337] A committee was formed to oversee the building of the church. The committee established a monetary commitment for each family in the parish of $15 for construction purposes. In the meantime, the Worzalla family made a donation to the church of $1,500 and donated ten acres of land for construction of the church and the parish cemetery.[338] The work lasted more than a year but was crowned by the construction of the temple. The Peplin community stood together for the thanksgiving devotion which was organized in the new church on April 9, 1916.

Church of St. John the Baptist, Peplin
Source: Record Herald Newspaper

In order to care for the parish and the faithful, the pastor of St. Paul Parish continued to come to Peplin once a month until 1917. Another year brought changes in the nearby parish of Knowlton where a new pastor Rev. S. F. Szymnczak was appointed. He was responsible for the pastoral care of Peplin. This assignment continued until 1920.[339] In the same year, further changes for the church and pastoral care occurred with the assignment of Rev. J. T. Brzezinski from Mosinee. Rev. Brzezinski stayed for seven years. In 1927, there was another change when pastoral care was given to Rev. Bernard Dykowski pastor of the parish of Galloway. Less than a year later in 1928, Peplin lost independence from Knowlton. Due to lack of time, the pastor could not come often to Peplin. Therefore, the mission church declined because of neglect.

---

337   Parish Book, *Saint John the Baptist*, Wisconsin 1991, p. 2
338   Ibid., p. 3-4
339   Ibid., p. 3

The pastor seeing what happened with the Parish of St. John the Baptist suggested it would be good to build a rectory and with that create an independent parish. This did not occur however because on Christmas Day in 1937 the church burned. The following year in 1938, a new pastor Rev. Edward Roskos was appointed by the bishop. He received an order to rebuild the church in Peplin as soon as possible. This time, the church was built of brick at a total cost of $14,000. The pastoral care for St. John the Baptist was given to the pastors of Knowlton until 1962.

Church of St. John the Baptist, Peplin 2012
Source: Author's Collection

Bishop John Treacy then appointed Rev. Aloysius Wozniak as the first pastor of the newly, independent Parish of St. John the Baptist.[340] Rev. Wozniak decided to live next to the church in a home donated to the parish. With time, this house became the pastor's rectory. After four years, Peplin again became a mission parish and pastoral care was passed to Rev. Thomas Weyer. During the 50th jubilee celebration of the church's construction, St. John the Baptist again received an independent pastor Rev. N. Kriebach who served in the parish until 1972. The next pastors assigned were Rev. Vincent Schwartz (1972-1975) and Rev. George Becker until 1980. After Rev. Becker's transfer, the pastoral care was provided by older priests or those in retirement. These priests were Rev. Thomas Abraham (1980-1982), Rev. Eugene Trainer (1982-1984), Rev. Ray Kaluzny (1984-1989), and finally Rev. Wladyslaw Kowalski who is currently a resident at St. John the Baptist Parish.

During the early years of Peplin, it continued to grow very quickly. Numerous new homes were built and part of the area became industri-

---

340   Parish Book, *Saint John the Baptist,* Wisconsin 1991, p. 4

alized. The larger portion of this area, however, remained in a natural state. Many residents of Peplin worked at the paper mill in Mosinee. Every day they had to go 6-7 miles to get to work. A large number of families worked at clearing land and preparing it for agricultural use. Because of the very difficult living conditions in this area, many Polish families ultimately left.

17. St. Methodius, Pilot Knob

In 1884 in Adams County in the town of Pilot Knob, a small group of Polish settlers built a wooden church that could accommodate one hundred people. From the very beginning, it was a mission church which lasted nine years (1887-1896). Rev. Anthony Abb[341] commuted from Briggsville on the first Sunday of the month to conduct services. He was succeeded by Rev. Stefan Kasperski who came from the Polish Kingdom (Królestwo Polskie).[342] There was no parsonage. Sacred vessels to celebrate the liturgy were not available. For the celebration of the Holy Eucharist, the mission even lacked vestments.

Seeing the enormous needs of the faithful and at the same time knowing the poverty of the faithful, Rev. Kasperski began collecting vestments and vessels necessary for the liturgy and use in the church. He also organized fund-raising in the neighborhood and sometimes went long distances to other Polish parishes in search of necessary funds. He visited

Church of St. Methodius, Pilot Knob 1895

Source: H.H. Heaming, History of the Catholic Church in Wisconsin

---

341 M. J. Goc, *From the Past to the Present: The History of Adams County*, 1999, p. 182
342 W. Kruszka, *A History of the Poles. Part 4*, p. 105

Milwaukee, Wisconsin; Chicago, Illinois; Buffalo, New York; and Detroit, Michigan; where he preached sermons. After collecting funds, he built and equipped the rectory and the church. He left the parish in Pilot Knob in August 1897 and was succeeded in September of that year by Rev. Piotr Kurzeja. Seeing no possibility of the church maintaining his position because the parish was too small to provide for the needs of the priest, Rev. P. Kurzeja moved to Plover where he commuted to Pilot Knob.

Church of St. Methodius, Pilot Knob 2012
Source: Author's Collection

During this time, the church again became a mission church, and a priest commuted just once a month. The parish had about thirty families. In addition to immigrants from Poland, a few families from the Czech Republic also resided in the area. In 1969, the church was closed due to the small number of parishioners. Next to the church is a cemetery. Every year a celebration of the Holy Eucharist takes place, and a collection is taken for the maintenance, restoration, and repairs of the church and cemetery.

CHAPTER III

DIOCESAN AND RELIGIOUS CLERGY AND NUNS

The origin of the Diocese of La Crosse is associated with the movement of immigrants from Europe in the early 19th century. This movement was caused by a search for a better life for hundreds of thousands of Europeans who in their home countries could not make an adequate living. Emigration to America was an opportunity for parents and their children. With the number of immigrants, a few priests came. Their task was the spiritual care of fellow countrymen in this new homeland. The priests who came here were educated and ordained in Europe. In the initial period, priestly activity was limited only to occasional visits to their countrymen and the celebration of the sacraments in their private homes. At a later period when the diocesan structure along with the pastoral ministry was formed and consolidated, the focus was then placed on parish churches and centers. In addition, the priests working in the newly created diocese were appointed to offices of the church and performed a variety of functions.

The first appointed bishop for the Diocese of La Crosse in La Crosse, Wisconsin, was Michael Heiss in 1868.[343] He arrived from Pfahldorf village which lies north of Ingolstadt in Bavaria (Germany). He was ordained to the priesthood in 1840 in the Diocese of Louisville, Kentucky. Rev. Michael Heiss was nominated to the office of bishop of the Diocese of La Crosse on March 3, 1868, and served this

---
343 H. H. Heaming, *History of the Catholic Church in Wisconsin*, p. 756.

diocese until March 14, 1880. He was succeeded by Bishop Kilian Casper Flasch[344] from Retzstadt which is located north of Wurzburg in Bavaria (Germany). He was appointed bishop on June 14, 1881, and he served in this diocese until his death on August 3, 1891. His successor was Bishop James Schwebach[345] from the small town of Platen in northern Luxembourg. Bishop Schwebach shepherded in the Diocese of La Crosse having been appointed bishop on December 14, 1891, and exercised the authority until June 6, 1921. After him, the leadership in the Diocese of La Crosse was given to Bishop Alexander Joseph Mc Gavick.[346] He was born in Fox Lake, Illinois, and was appointed to the office on November 21, 1921. This position was held by him until his death on August 25, 1948. From August 25, 1948, until October 11, 1964, the head of the Diocese of La Crosse was Bishop John Patrick Treacy.

On December 30, 1964, Bishop Frederick William Freking[347] became the head of the Diocese of La Crosse. He remained in this office until May 10, 1983. On October 14, 1983, Bishop John Joseph Paul was appointed.[348] He served in this position until December 10, 1994, when he was replaced by Bishop Raymond Leo Burke. Bishop Burke served until December 2, 2003, when he received the nomination to

---

344   L. Rummel, Rev., *History of the Catholic Church in Wisconsin*, O. Prem., Madison, Wisconsin 1976, p. 254. Kilian Casper Flasch was born July 16, 1831, in Germany. He graduated from the Seminary of St. Francis in Milwaukee. He was ordained into the priesthood on December 16, 1859, in La Crosse by Bishop John Martin Henni from Milwaukee. He was appointed bishop on June 14, 1881, and he was consecrated on July 24, 1881, by the laying of the hands of Archbishop Michael Heiss from Milwaukee.

345   L. Rummel, Rev., *History of the Catholic Church in Wisconsin*, Madison, Wisconsin 1976, p. 260. James Schwebach was born on August 15, 1847, in Luxembourg. He graduated from the Seminary of St. Francis in Milwaukee and ordained to the priesthood on June 16, 1870, in St. Paul, Minnesota, by Bishop Thomas Langton Grace from St. Paul. He was appointed bishop for the Diocese of La Crosse on December 14, 1891, and was consecrated on February 25, 1892, in La Crosse.

346   L. Rummel, Rev., *History of the Catholic Church in Wisconsin*, Madison, Wisconsin 1976, p. 257. Alexander Joseph Mc Gavick was born August 21, 1863, in Fox Lake, Illinois. He graduated from the seminary in Bourbonnais, Illinois, and was ordained to the priesthood on June 11, 1887, by Bishop Patrick Augustine Feehan of Chicago. He was appointed to be a bishop of the Diocese of Marcopolis on November 2, 1898. On November 21, 1921, he became the bishop of the Diocese of La Crosse.

347   L. Rummel, Rev., *History of the Catholic Church in Wisconsin*, Madison, Wisconsin 1986, p. 255. Frederick William Freking was born on August 11, 1913, in Huron Lake, Minnesota. He graduated from the Seminary of the Immaculate Heart in Winona, Minnesota. He was ordained to the priesthood on July 31, 1938, in Rome, Italy, by Archbishop Luca Emenegildo Pasetto. He was appointed to the office of bishop of Salina, Kansas, on October 10, 1957. He was consecrated November 20, 1957. On December 30, 1964, he became bishop of the Diocese of La Crosse.

348   G. E. Fisher, *257 Things You Should Know About the Diocese of La Crosse 1868- 1993*, Stevens Point 1993, p. 74-75.

the position of Archbishop of St. Louis, Missouri. As of December 29, 2004, the bishop of Diocese of La Crosse was Jerome Edward Listecki.[349]

The Origin and Place of Education and Formation

In the years 1772 to 1918, Poland was divided between the three neighboring powers of Russia, Prussia, and Austria. Because of the occupation by these invaders, immigrants came to America in three waves that were closely related to the political situation of the country. The first wave began after the fall of the Confederation of Barska in 1772. After the first partition of Poland, the second wave of immigration began in 1793 and the third in 1795.

After successive partitions, the next influx of immigrants from Poland occurred after the uprising in 1830. Generally, immigrants were soldiers and people of higher classes. In the year 1855, the first Catholic Church (St. Mary Virgin) was built for Poles in Texas.[350] During this time, hundreds of Polish families because of economic and political issues made the decision to emigrate to the United States of America. These families joined together to go "to their country of dreams" carrying all of their belongings, their habits, national traditions, and deep faith. A great number of Polish clergymen followed the immigrant Polish families to America.

At the beginning of the twentieth century, a practice was established in Poland to inform resident pastors of a family's plan for a departure to America. When this decision was made by the family, they received a very special blessing offered by the priest for this journey. Also, this information helped to establish contacts between the home country and the new homeland. Often, however, the priest encouraged families to remain in the fatherland and to abandon their decision to leave. For this purpose, priests used different arguments. Local priests tried to inhibit this process in order to stop the depopulation of their parish. Priests spoke of the many difficulties of getting work as well as the difficulties of receiving equitable remuneration. This attempted persuasion did not bring the desired effect. It was difficult inhibiting the process of emigra-

---

349   www.DioceseoflaCrosse.com (September 25, 2008)

350   Ch. G. Herberman, E. A. Pace, C. B. Pallen, T. J. Shahan, J. J. Wynne, *The Catholic Encyclopedia*, New York 1911, p. 205.

tion. With immigrants arriving in America, there soon was a need to ensure their spiritual care. Immigrants, after arriving in the new country, showed the same spiritual and religious needs they had demonstrated in their home country. These needs and expectations meant that the number of clergy must be increased. However, the path of priests taking responsibility for immigrants in America was not simple or easy.

Spiritual responsibility for immigrants decided upon by clergy in the United States progressed in two different directions. The first direction was to assume that the aid for immigrants should only involve the dimension of their religious lives and nothing else. The second focused on cultivating and upholding ethnic diversity in the existing national groups.[351] Before deciding how spiritual assistance to immigrants should occur, priests accessed differences in the needs of individual ethnic groups. Pastoral care for immigrants primarily took into account the needs of Catholics. Poles needed to find themselves and get acclimated in a new environment. With reference to the existing spiritual needs of individual ethnic groups, barriers were the language and traditions of individual nations. It was a huge challenge. Most of the churches were not prepared to grant such aid.

Because of this, steps were taken to incorporate a means to sustain and foster the existing cultural and ethnic diversity of its members. For the immigrants who came from Poland, it meant maintaining the mother language, cultivating traditions of religious fathers, and habits of the parents while in a new situation in a new country. The Poles in their new homeland, like no one before or after them, were a great force in organizing the construction of churches and schools.[352]

The spiritual care of the Polish immigrants was handled by Polish priests who arrived with them. Their fates were similar to other immigrant families. They inhabited the places where visible spiritual and religious care was needed. This meant they were in small communities where Poles lived and worked. At the turn of the 19th and beginning of the 20th centuries, the group of Polish Catholic priests was very small. This very small number of clergy who immigrated tried to support the existing needs of the Poles. In order to address the enormous needs of the Poles, they estab-

---

[351]   F. Renkiewicz, *The Polish Presence in Canada and America*, Toronto 1982, p. 389
[352]   F. H. Miller, *The Polanders in Wisconsin*, Milwaukee 1896, p. 239

lished a visiting ministry which meant the priests traveled from village to village, from town to town, and to the farms. They offered the sacraments, and at the same time, they celebrated the Holy Eucharist for gatherings in family homes.

Very soon however, it appeared that this was not sufficient. During the same time, there appeared a need to increase the number of Polish priests in order to form Polish parishes. To remedy this need, decisive steps were taken. An idea emerged to start organizing seminaries here for clergy who then could serve the Poles already living in America. Therefore, the younger generation who already lived in this country was able to go into the priesthood. Rev. Joseph Dąbrowski[353] was a precursor to the formation of a seminary for Polish immigrants in the United States. He was a long term pastor in the Parish of the Sacred Heart in Polonia, Wisconsin. The number of Polish priests increased to twenty-five in 1870 and to seventy-nine in 1877.[354]

In 1889, the number of Polish churches in America amounted to 132. There were 126 Polish priests as well as 122 Polish schools. The large number of Polish immigrants who arrived in America forced the American bishops of the Catholic Church to send several formal requests to the bishops in Poland asking for a large number of clergymen who would be willing to come and provide for the spiritual needs of the Poles. With the same request, they turned to Cardinal Mieczyslaw Ledóchowski the Prefect of the Congregation for the Propagation of the Faith in Rome to send more Polish priests to America. Cardinal Ledóchowski in response to this request suggested the American bishops offer education to local clergy and future descendants for the needs of their dioceses.

Rev. Joseph Dąbrowski was an early leader in locating space to educate future priests from the Polish immigrant families. In 1883, he resigned from the pastor position in the parish of Polonia, Wisconsin, and moved along with the nuns of the Congregation of Felician Sisters to Detroit, Michigan. He became their chaplain. The Felician Sisters were brought by Rev. Dąbrowski to work in the schools. They were the first nuns who arrived from the old country to teach the younger generation of Poles. The

---

[353] W. Kruszka, *A History of the Poles. Part 1,* Washington 1993, p. 144

[354] Ch. G. Herberman, E. A. Pace, C. B. Pallen, T. J. Shahan, J. J. Wynne, *The Catholic Encyclopedia,* New York 1911, p. 205

city of Detroit became very favorable for the actions and projects of Rev. Dąbrowski. In this area, construction started on a new seminary under the name of Saints Cyril and Methodius. To achieve his intended purpose, Rev. Dąbrowski began collecting money among the Poles. He accomplished his goal, and the seminary foundation was built on 2.5 acres. On July 24, 1885, the cornerstone was laid by Bishop Ryan from the Diocese of Buffalo, New York.[355] The building of the seminary was completed, dedicated, and made available on December 15, 1887. The dedication of the building was made by Bishop Casper Henry Borgess of the Diocese of Detroit.[356] When the seminary started, it had two education levels. The first was classic and was a two year course. The second was philosophy and theology and lasted for three years. When the seminary opened, it had only six student seminarians. This number, however, grew rapidly over time. At the end of 1888, the number of seminarians increased to twenty-six men.

TABLE 18: Number of Seminarians in Detroit

YEAR OF ACTIVITIES	NUMBER OF SEMINARIANS
1888–1889	35
1889–1890	65
1890–1891	66
1891–1892	77
1892–1893	80
1893–1894	105
1894–1895	125
1895–1896	123
1896–1897	133
1897–1898	131
1898–1899	153
1899–1900	156*

* W. Kruszka, *A History of the Poles. Part 1*, Washington 1993, p. 142

---

355 W. Kruszka, *A History of the Poles. Part 1*, Washington 1993, p. 141
356 No Author, *Millennium of Christianity in Poland*, Stevens Point 1966, p. 15

As seen in the table, the number of seminarians joining the seminary in Detroit increased with each year of its activity. It was a very positive decision. This seminary helped American dioceses through the ordination of men to the priesthood. Priests were ready to work with Poles in their dioceses. Priest professors played a huge role in the seminary. Rev. J. Dąbrowski went to Europe (Italy and Poland) in 1885 in order to seek future cadres to study at the seminary in Detroit. He did not achieve much in talks with Rome. He did, however, receive assurance that with more opportunities a few volunteers (professors) might step forward. In fact, it happened. Rev. Witold Buchaczkowski[357] was an example of a professor who came to this seminary from Rome. Fellow priests from Krakow, Poland, who joined Rev. Buchaczkowski at the seminary in Detroit were Rev. Baran and Rev. Bronikowski. The only Polish seminary in the United States was in Detroit, Michigan.

Later, throughout the state of Wisconsin, many different kinds of seminaries for clergy were established. This was because of the arrival of many religious orders and congregations of religious seminarians. These congregations established seminaries for their own needs. Dioceses were also sending candidates to the seminaries in order to prepare them for work within the diocese. In the Diocese of Green Bay in the town of Pulaski[358] near the city of Green Bay, the second seminary in America was established. It was also for Poles because it had a Polish character. The Franciscan Monastery was formed in the city on April 27, 1887, by Brother Augustine, Rev. Erazm Sobocinski, Rev. Jeka, and Rev. H. Schneider. It was at this time that the second group of Franciscan monks came to America.[359] The first group of monks had arrived in Chicago twelve years earlier. Franciscans in America were very active and formed five parishes, six schools, and the seminary in Pulaski.[360]

The Wisconsin seminaries that were Polish or of Polish origin were:
- St. Francis Seminary in Milwaukee, Wisconsin, established in 1845

---

357 W. Kruszka, *A History of the Poles. Part 1*, Washington 1993, p. 142

358 L. Rummel, Rev., *History of the Catholic Church*, Madison, Wisconsin 1986, p. 89

359 W. Kruszka, *A History of the Poles. Part 1*, Washington 1993, p. 144

360 P. Taras, "The Contribution of Polonia into the Development of the Roman-Catholic Church in the United States," *Biblioteka Polonijna*, Vol. 4:1979, p. 96

- St. Wawrzyńca in Mount Calvary, Wisconsin, established in 1864
- Word of God in East Troy, Wisconsin, established in 1921
- School of Theology, Sacred Heart of Jesus in Hales Corners, Wisconsin, established in 1929
- The Formation Home for Missionary of St. Francis Xavier in Franklin, Wisconsin, established in 1947
- Holy Name Seminary in Madison, Wisconsin, established in 1962

Holy Cross Seminary was founded in the city of La Crosse for the needs of the Diocese of La Crosse. During the spring of 1947 at a meeting of the clergy, Bishop John Treacy of the Diocese of La Crosse announced to all gathered priests that a decision had been made to establish a seminary for the diocese. The first appointed rector of the seminary was Rev. Edmund Bettinger. Later, Rev. Joseph George Andrzejewski was nominated to procure the funds and to prepare the plans for the building. It was suggested that a collection for money for the construction occur between the 2nd and 10th of November. The collection of money was carried out under the spiritual patronage of the Poor Souls in Purgatory. The new seminary was to be built on approximately sixty-seven acres of land.

When the initial preparation was completed, beginning of the construction work was celebrated. Many respectable guests were invited including some staff from the local newspaper and the inhabitants of the city of La Crosse. The inauguration of the start of construction on the future seminary was held October 17, 1948. In attendance were 10,000 faithful, several dozen priests, and twenty-five archbishops and bishops. For this celebration, the delegate from Rome from the Holy See Rev. Amleto Giovanni Cicognani[361] blessed the land.

Construction began on August 21, 1949. It continued without interruption until the end of construction in 1951. During this time, the seminary's chapel was built as were part of the bedrooms for the seminarians, the auditoriums, and the refectory. During the same time, the high school building located near the new seminary was completed.

---

[361] The Staff of the La Crosse Register, *Holy Cross Seminary 1951*, La Crosse, Wisconsin 1951, p. 40-41

The new seminary building was blessed and completely available for students of theology in September of 1951. In the newly, opened building were several Polish priests who spoke Polish and English fluently. One of them was Rev. Joseph Rafacz who began working at the seminary in 1956. He ended his work in 1968 when the seminary was closed because of the small enrollment of seminarians.[362]

Female Congregations of Religious Communities in Wisconsin

A large contribution to the development of the Catholic Church in America can be attributed to female congregations and religious communities. Just as clergy came with immigrants, nuns also came to America. Their task was to disseminate the works of mercy and to educate children, youth, as well as adults. The needs of the country were enormous. To work in America, nuns came from communities and congregations in Europe. However, their number was still insufficient. The missions that were established tried to fulfill the needs as best as possible. The nuns solicited work with the female youth. By doing so, they wanted to create new vocations to the sisterhood. In the state of Wisconsin, many female congregations arrived from Europe and established convents.[363]

Photo 68: Home of Felician Sisters in Polonia
Source: Author's Collection

TABLE 19: Names of Female Congregations and Date of Establishment in Wisconsin

Dominican Sisters	1847
Franciscan Sisters	1849
Franciscan Sister of Perpetual Adoration	1849

---

362 Interview was taken on the December 23, 2008, with Fr. J. Rafacz in St. Agnes Parish, Weston, Wisconsin.
363 L. Rummel, Rev., *History of the Catholic Church in Wisconsin*, p. 153-196

TABLE 19: Names of Female Congregations and Date of Establishment in Wisconsin

Notre Dame Sisters	1850
Society of St. Agnes	1858
St. Dominic Sisters	1862
Franciscan Sisters of Christian Mercy	1869
Society of Good Shepherd (Contemplative)	1877
Franciscan Sisters of Holy Cross	1881
Notre Dame Sisters of Escape and Divine Mercy	1882
Sisters of Divine Mercy	1895
Sisters of St. Joseph – Stevens Point	1901
Sisters of St. Joseph – Superior	1907
Sisters of Mother of Sorrow	1909
Dominican Sisters (Contemplative)	1909
Servants of Mary	1912
Carmelite Sisters of Sacred Heart of Jesus	1912
Sisters of the Holy Cross	1923
Sisters of St. Elizabeth	1931
Szensztackie of Mary	1948
Sisters of St. Bedy Poboznego	1948
Sisters of St. Benedict	1953
Sisters of St. Ida	1957
Sisters of Cloistered Carmelites	1963

In the second half of the 19th century in America, the majority of eight female congregations arrived. These were the Felician Sisters who arrived in 1874, Sisters of Nazareth in 1885, Sisters of St. Bernard, Sisters of the Resurrection, Sisters of St. Dominic, Sisters of the Holy Spirit, Sisters of the Sacred Heart, and the Franciscan Sisters. Already established in America for Poles were the female congregations of the Franciscan Sisters (who were a branch of the Order of St. Kunegunda), Franciscan Sisters of St. Joseph (who were called Josephites), Our Mother of Perpetual Help Sisters (who were from the Franciscan Sisters), the Franciscan Sisters of the Apostolate, the Daughters of Mary of the Immaculate Conception, the Sisters of the Holy Spirit, and the Franciscans from Sylvania. During the second half of the 19th century to the end of the 20th century, 10,300 sisters worked in America. Of this number, 6,900 sisters were in schools, and 300 were in hospitals. Approximately 690 elementary schools were provided instructors from these female congregations. Nuns also worked in eighty high schools, nine academies, and in two colleges. In addition, work was carried out in fifty-one hospitals and more than 146 other institutions such as homes for orphans, the poor, or homeless.[364]

---

[364] P. Taras, "The Contribution of Polonia into the Development of the Roman-Catholic Church in the United States," in: H. Kubiak, G. Babinski, M. Francic, *Biblioteka polonijna*, Vol 4, Wrocław-Warszawa-Kraków-Gdańsk 1979, p. 97

CHAPTER IV

PLACES OF WORSHIP OUTSIDE OF THE PARISH CHURCH

Cemeteries

The majority of Polish cemeteries in the United States were located at parishes. Sometimes, a Polish parish used the cemetery of other Polish parishes. For example, the small town of Stevens Point (in which there were several Polish parishes) benefited from one common grave site which was located outside of the city. When the vast majority of Polish parishes developed their parish, they also started their own burial sites. In most cases, the land for the cemeteries was donated by parishioners or was purchased for a small (often a symbolic) amount of money. After the location of the cemetery was determined, the parish worked on the conditions for its use. The provisions governing the burials and care of the graves were very similar in all parishes. Some of them were:

- Children of the deceased who were not baptized could not use the place of burial of their parents.
- Non-practicing Catholics but those who had received the Holy Sacraments before their death could be buried at the cemetery, however, only in a designated area.
- A person who committed suicide could not be buried in the parish cemetery.
- If someone purchased a plot at the cemetery but did not live according to the rules of the Catholic Church, that person could not be buried.
- If someone wanted to purchase a plot in the cemetery, this per-

- son had one year to pay the fee otherwise the right of ownership was lost.
- The prices of digging graves varied according to the seasons. In winter, the fee was higher due to the difficult weather conditions. The additional charge was actually for snow removal on the roads in the cemetery.
- No one had the right to place a concrete frame on the grave.
- You were not allowed to plant very tall trees or high bushes.
- If anyone did not obey these rules, the manager of the cemetery had the right to remove anything that was forbidden without giving notification to the guilty person.
- If the owner of the plot in the cemetery wanted to bury a different person who was not a member of the family, the family of the deceased had to pay an extra six dollars for the use of this lot.
- Those who were seven years or older at the time of their death were to be buried at a depth of five feet; those younger than seven years were buried at a four feet depth.
- Anything that was not specified in the rules of the cemetery that created problems was reported to the bishop for resolution of that problem.[365]

The cemeteries in the tradition of the Polish parishes played a very important role. Concern for the graves of deceased relatives was a sign of faith and remembrance of those relatives. A very popular custom was to visit the graves of the deceased relatives and pray for their souls. Another custom was to place a wooden cross as a sign of salvation and faith in the resurrection on the fresh grave.

Crosses and Roadside Shrines

Traditions which were brought in the mid-19th century to the United States by Polish immigrants were the customs of placing crosses and the building of shrines beside the roads. Polish immigrants made sacred their surrounding landscape and their places of work and residences with this custom. In Poland, a common practice or tradition was

---

[365] *Księga pamiątkowa złotego jubileuszu*, p. 111

to place a small shrine, altar, or wooden crosses on country roads at the entrances to villages, on the hills, beside cemeteries, and at churches. Near the end of the 18th and the beginning of the 19th century, this tradition spread and became a permanent feature of village landscapes founded by Poles in America. Ethnographer Tadeusz Seweryn in one of his elaborations on the traditions of the Polish immigration suggested the tradition of making crosses and shrines was an expression of romance and longing for the deserted land of their Polish ancestors.[366] Polish parishes, churches, and chapels always had distinctive symbols (crosses and statues) that expressed faith in God and the care and intercession of the saints. Even today in central Wisconsin can be found many roadside shrines and road crosses. They symbolize the great trust and need to offer one's self to the protection of Divine Providence.

The faith expressed in these sculptures and paintings was of the folk art style. They were created by simple Polish farmers. These sculptures and paintings expressed spiritual needs, faith in God, and a yearning for the homeland.[367] The forms and shapes of the sculptures and paintings had a specific origin. They were born of Polish tradition and folk architecture. This folk art was expressed in ecclesiastical art through a classical form. A variety of the historical styles were created primarily by anonymous artists.[368] Some of these road crosses were made of wood and set either individually or in groups. The Polish artists also created small, wooden imitations of a chapel which were hung on trees or attached to buildings. Folk art was very popular on columns made of wood, brick, or on stone bases and utilized various figures of saints. The crosses and shrines and the surrounding areas became sites of prayer. They were designed as places to give thanks to God for received graces or for help and blessings in planned activities. The images of the saints and crosses were very often a way of expressing thankfulness for receiving grace from God or through the saints.

Another motive for building and placing roadside shrines and crosses was a need to guard oneself against the influences and actions of

---

366   D. L. Kolinski, "Shrine and Crosses in Rural Central Wisconsin," *Polish American Studies*, Vol. 5:994, No. 2, p. 33

367   M. J. Goc, *Native Realm*, p. 54

368   T. Seweryn, *Kapliczki i krzyże przydrożne w Polsce*, Warszawa 1958, p. 13

the evil spirits. Some people believed there were wandering souls that needed to be released in order for the deceased to achieve eternal salvation. When the area did not have a church, roadside shrines and crosses became a meeting place for common prayer. The Polish families were required to maintain them in good condition and make necessary renovations and repairs as needed.

To this day in Portage County, Wisconsin, more than fifty roadside shrines and crosses can be found.[369] Over time, the buried parts of many wooden crosses rotted although the upper portion stayed in good condition. To keep these crosses for a longer period of time, the bad section was cut off, removed, and the good section was used over. Shrines and altars were made from stones or bricks. These roadside shrines, altars, and the roadside crosses played an important role in the religious life of the Polish communities. After the shrines, crosses, or altars were built, the owners always requested the local clergyman to offer a blessing of the objects. There were processions to these places although the crosses built close to the church served very often as the foundation for the construction of the altar for the Solemnity of Corpus Christi.

---

369 According to a very long tradition passed orally from generation to generation in the Polish families, beside one of the intersections in Polonia (a town founded by the Poles in the state of Wisconsin) appeared some characters and strange, scary, voices were heard. To guard against this evil spirit, a roadside shrine was built at this place, and it still exists today.

CHAPTER V

RELIGIOUS LIFE PARTICIPATION IN THE DIVINE SERVICES AND SACRAMENTAL LIFE

SACRAMENTAL BAPTISM

In the Polish parishes, the sacrament of Baptism was normally offered on Sunday at midday after the celebration of the Holy Eucharist. A special protocol designed for Polish Americans preceded the celebration of the sacrament of Baptism. When this sacrament was celebrated, it was according to the following rules:

- Parents were obligated to take responsibility for the baptism of their child.
- The sacrament of Baptism was held typically on the eighth day following a child's birth.
- The sacrament of Baptism was celebrated only in the church and only by a priest.
- If the child was in danger of death and the priest was unable to come, every good, practicing Catholic could formally grant the sacrament of Baptism. After the return of this child to full health and to complete the rite of Baptism, parents were obligated to come to church with the child so that the child could be introduced and welcomed into the church family.
- Godparents had to be practicing, confirmed, and adult Catholics. They were bound during the celebration of the sacrament to promise to give a good example of Christian life and help the parents of the child with raising this child in the Catholic faith.

Godparents during this sacrament also had to promise that in the event of the death of the child's parents, they would be ready to take care of and raise this child.

Sacrament of the Sick

The sacrament of the sick was usually offered when someone was in danger of death, or it was offered for those who were very sick. The sacrament was to be offered to a person who was alert and able to receive the sacrament.

Before the arrival of the priest who would celebrate this sacrament, the family was obligated according to strict order to prepare the following things:

- A small coffee table covered with a white cloth.
- On top of this table would be two lit candles, a cross, a glass of water with a small spoon, and cotton balls. The coffee table was to be positioned between the sick person and the priest.
- Family members of the patient were obligated to participate in the sacrament while kneeling in common prayer.
- During the celebration of the sacrament of the sick, the priest gave Holy Communion as viaticum.

In very special cases such as when there was risk of imminent death, the priest could be asked for the sacrament at any time of the day or night. The family was never allowed to have the priest at the same time as the doctor who provided medical aid. After the doctor's visit, the priest was asked to come. The person who was sick usually confessed to the priest. The priest then gave communion and the sacrament of the sick. The presence of the doctor during the celebration of the sacrament of the sick meant a lack of respect for the priest.

Funerals

The right to receive a Catholic funeral in the Polish parishes was given to a person who was a practicing Catholic, who regularly received the holy sacraments, and who was a respectable person of good public opinion. The person belonging to that particular parish could then be buried in the parish cemetery. If the person who died did not fulfill the duties included with the daily practice of their faith, the family was compelled to meet with the pastor in order to receive permission for burial. The place of the burial and the fee for digging the grave had to be determined and paid before the funeral expenses.[370]

Participation of the Faithful in Parish Devotions

The liturgical year in the Polish parishes was divided into two seasons – winter and summer. The celebration of the Holy Eucharist was only in the morning, but the liturgical devotion was always organized in late afternoon. The most important devotion in the parish was to the Sacred Heart of Jesus. This devotion was celebrated on every first Friday of the month. The second most important devotion in the parish was Holy Hour which was celebrated on the first Sunday of each month with the exposition of the Blessed Sacrament in the church. Another very important devotion was to the Blessed Virgin and in a very special way was celebrated in the month of May and also on each Sunday and Wednesday of the year. The celebration of the Rosary was a devotion which occurred in the month of October. Stations of the Cross celebrated each Friday during the Lenten Season for the intention of the conversion and improvement of people's lives was a very popular devotion. Also on Sundays during the season of Lent, "Gorzkie żale" devotion was celebrated. During this, people meditated about the suffering and pain of the Lord Jesus Christ which was undertaken for the salvation of man. Every Sunday evening, vespers were celebrated in church during ordinary time.[371]

Sacrament of Marriage and Celebration of the Wedding

Before two young people were married in the church, the tradition was that the pastor for a period of three weeks prior to the wedding

---

370   *Księga pamiątkowa złotego jubileuszu*, p. 107-110
371   Ibid., p. 106

publicly announced their intentions to the parish. This was done to verify the impeccability of a moral and civil life of the people who wished to be married. During this period of time, if something surfaced such as a public offense or a reprehensible attitude on either side, the right to be married was denied. In the three weeks prior to the wedding, the obligation of the fiancée and fiancé was to go to confession and in detail confess the sins of their entire life. Each believing Catholic who wanted to establish a family had an obligation to be married in accordance with the norms of Canon Law. The fiancée and fiancé had the obligation to ask their own pastor to celebrate the Holy Eucharist for their intention.[372]

In the morning, the wedding celebration would begin in the church. The Polish farmer's family usually avoided having the wedding on Fridays and Saturdays. The wedding celebration would last several days. Although, it was enjoyable; it was very tiring. This resulted in people not being able to fulfill their Sunday obligation or participate in the celebration of the Holy Eucharist. After the marriage in the church was performed, all invited guests went for breakfast at the home of the bride. The wedding band had to play through the entire reception except for at meal time. The bride and groom invited guests to celebrate the next day also. The participants of the wedding reception ate meals that had been freshly prepared to avoid food poisoning. The wedding reception usually lasted until all wedding guests departed, or everyone was very tired, or it was a very late hour.[373]

The wedding reception was celebrated for two to three days for two specific reasons. The first reason was that the farmers were required to fulfill their farming obligations and couldn't leave the farms before they completed them. If any of the invited farmers because of their duties could not be present at the wedding reception in the morning, they could arrive at the afternoon wedding reception and vice versa. It should be noted that the work on the farm was heavy and lasted very long. When the Polish farmers finished their work in the fields, they wanted to wisely use their free time. The second reason was because the journey very often

---

[372] *Księga pamiątkowa złotego jubileuszu*, p. 106
[373] M. J. Goc, *Native Realm*, p. 58

was long and tedious. During this time, travel was by horse with carriage or wagons. In America in contrast to Polish traditional habits, the Polish immigrants married and celebrated their wedding reception during the carnivals which means between the seasons of Christmas and Lent.[374] The wedding reception gave the opportunity for all members of the family to have a common meeting. Because of the long distances and the enormity of the workload of Polish farmers, they could not meet very often. The wedding receptions gave them the opportunity to meet together.

One of the traditional aspects of the wedding reception was to welcome the bride and groom with bread and salt and to dance with the bride known popularly as the dance of the dollar (dollar dance). Near the dance floor, a table was set with an empty plate. When the father of the bride ended the dance with her, anyone who wanted to dance with the bride had to place a coin on the plate. It was expected to be silver (a one dollar coin). The person wishing to dance also had to try to toss the coin on the plate in such a way as to break the plate. If the plate was not broken, the person did not have the right to dance. The more broken plates – the better, as it showed that the wedding was considered to be very successful. The money collected was used by the young couple to pay for their wedding reception.[375] There was a belief that if the wedding reception was great, the couple's life together would also be great.

Traditions and the Religious Customs

Traditions and religious customs came with the immigrants from Poland They were the cornerstones for religious life and family life. The Polish settlers with great respect cultivated rich traditions imported from the motherland. These traditions were closely associated with the possession of land and with farming as a source of income, security, and social respect. The great success of the Poles in America was seen in the high quality of their diet. In the United States, Poles grew and prepared the typical Polish food, breads, cabbage, noodles, and sausage and were very well known for their home grown vegetables.[376]

---
374   www.polishroots.org/history/PAHA/polish_folkways (February 18, 2009)
375   M. J. Goc, *Native Realm,* p. 60
376   Ibid., p. 56

Polish settlers emigrated to America in search of a better lifestyle which included the ability to acquire more acres of land and to have a greater number of horses and cows. As a landlord, a Pole's opinion was valued. He commanded social respect, sat in the front pew of the church and had his own place in the pub and the village.[377]

The Poles brought a rich religious heritage. Many of the traditions were connected with the celebration of Christmas. During the season of Advent, the time before Christmas, was the celebration on December 6th of St. Nicholas. Traditionally on this day, children received sweets. Just before Christmas, the organist or the nun in the parish prepared *opłatki* for the vigil. The blessed *opłatki* were sent to the homes via servers.[378] This momentous event occurred directly before Christmas when the family celebrated the common Christmas dinner (vigil dinner). On the vigil table, they had to have *opłatki* which represented the host and was embossed with the symbol of the Nativity of Jesus Christ. The sharing of *opłatki* was done before starting dinner. The father of the family took his piece first then shared with his wife, then with children and invited guests. At the end, if there was a little piece left, people used to say, "No matter how little I have, I will always split it with you, and no matter how small you have, I will always accept it from you."[379] After the sharing of the *opłatki* among the entire family, the special supper began.

It was tradition to prepare twelve different dishes. They were served one after another. A very important rule during this evening dinner celebration was the tradition that the meals should include four or five sources of the family food. These dishes were from the field such as grains, vegetables from the garden, fruits from the orchard, mushrooms from the forest, and fish from the water.[380] No meat was offered during this vigil dinner. On the table, one plate was prepared for the unexpected guest or visitor. Sometimes a candle was lit and set up in the window. This was for people who traveled or for the poor who could

---

377 J. S. Pula, *Polish-Americans an Ethnic Community*, p. 27
378 www.polishroots.org/history/PAHA/polish_folkways (February 18, 2009)
379 Parish Book, *St. Mary of Czestochowa Catholic Church,* Wisconsin 1983, p. 60-61
380 www.polishroots.org/history/PAHA/polish_folkways (February 18, 2009) and Parish Book, *St. Mary of Czestochowa Catholic Church,* Wisconsin 1983, p. 62.

take advantage of the invitation and eat with the household. This idea came from the belief that on such a wonderful day when God was born, no one should be alone. The cooking of a birthday cake for Jesus Christ was also a tradition of Polish families.

When the supper ended, the family began to sing Christmas carols, and afterwards they got ready go to Midnight Mass at church which could be a great distance from their home. During the celebration of this Midnight Mass, the gathered people sang carols. The solemn celebration of the Holy Eucharist was preceded by a procession during which a young girl was selected to bring a little statue or figure of the baby Jesus and to put it in the manger.[381] A few days before the celebration of the birth of Jesus Christ in Polish parishes, another tradition was for parishioners to receive the sacrament of reconciliation in order to bring peace to the hearts of the faithful at that very specific time. Also during the Christmas season was the celebration of the Solemnity of the Three Kings. On that day, the priest gave to the faithful a special blessing in the church. He then visited their homes to bless their farms and to initial the three kings (K+M+B) on the front door of their homes. In the church, the priest blessed the charcoal, gold, and myrrh.[382] During the season of Christmas, children of the parish prepared a special performance about the birth of Jesus Christ which was commonly called *Jasełka*.

Another very important holy day celebrated by Poles was the feast of the Mother of God called "Gromniczna" which was celebrated on February 2nd. During this very special day, candles called *gromniczna* were blessed. It was a custom to light the small candles in a very small container with water. In addition to this, holy water was sprinkled on a person who was sick or to protect them from disease. The Our Father was said as a prayer. The tradition meant that this person would recover from illness in the near future.[383]

Another strong religious tradition of Polish settlers was associated with the Easter season. In the season of Lent which occurs prior to

---

[381] G. Hollnagell, "Polish Traditions Adds to Arcadia Christmas," in: *La Crosse Tribune*, December 7, 1985, p. 10

[382] www.polishroots.org/history/PAHA/polish_folkways (February 18, 2009)

[383] D. A. Silverman, *Polish-American Folklore*, Illinois Press 2000, p. 95

Easter, the faithful gathered together in the church to celebrate the devotion of the Stations of the Cross.[384] The Lenten season was fulfilled by fasting, personal sacrifice, and almsgiving. On the evening of Good Friday or the morning of Holy Saturday during Holy Week before Easter, there was a custom of hanging a herring on a string. It meant the end of the six weeks of Lent. On Good Friday, people followed the custom of covering mirrors with dark canvas.[385] People also believed that water taken from a stream or lake before sunrise on Good Friday had the power to heal people. Farm animals and those who used the water that day would be saved from diseases of the skin. Another tradition was the evening procession in the streets or villages during which the cross was carried to commemorate the burial of Jesus. The procession was accompanied by servers with special rattles. The sound heard was to remind one of the nailing of Jesus to the cross. Then they sang songs such as "People of My People" and "In the Cross Suffering."[386]

Until noon on Holy Saturday, food was blessed that was to be prepared for the traditional Easter Sunday morning meal. During the Easter morning Mass, a procession was held where people walked around the church three times.[387] The procession was called the Resurrection from the Latin term *resurrectio*. At Easter time, the parish priest gave parishioners a card for confession. They had their numbered cards which were given to the priest in the confessional and then were returned to the office.

A traditional celebration observed by Polish people was "Name Day" (*imieniny*). In Europe and Latin America, the Name Day tradition consists of celebrating the day associated with one's given name. This tradition is associated with the Roman Catholic and Greek Orthodox Calendar of Saints. The newborn child was given a name of a particular saint. This gave the child an opportunity in the future to celebrate the saint's feast day. The Name Day celebration included

---

384 M. J. Goc, *Native Realm,* p. 56

385 www.polishroots.org/history/PAHA/lenten_customs (February 18, 2009)

386 A. H. Gunkel, "The Sacred in the City: Polonian Street Processions as Countercultural Practice," *Polish American Studies*, Vol. 60:2003, No. 2, p. 10

387 Ibid., p. 13

gathering with friends and family at which time gifts and flowers were given to the child. People didn't celebrate their birthday.

Each year at the beginning of the month of May, the children of the parish would make a wreath from fresh flowers and would place it on the head of the statue of the Blessed Virgin Mary. On May 15th, the Holy Day of St. Isidore, patron of the farmer, was celebrated. On that day, oats were brought to be blessed with hopes for a good harvest and favorable weather.

Every year on August 15th, they celebrated the Assumption of the Blessed Virgin Mary which is commonly called the Feast of Our Lady "Zielna." On this day, parishioners brought flowers, oats, corn, fruits, and vegetables from their own gardens to be blessed. After Mass, the priest blessed all that was brought and prayed a blessing for the families.[388]

A beautiful celebration was held on the feast of Corpus Christi. Outside of the church, four altars were built, or the priest selected four houses which were set on the corners of the village or town. The altars were covered with white tablecloths on which a cross and candles were placed. Around this altar, small green trees were set. The children who during this year received their First Communion were dressed in their Sunday best. At the front of the procession, the cross was carried along with candles. After that, decorated pictures, banners, and statues of saints were carried. Next in the procession came the servers, clergy, and people of God.[389] The Blessed Sacrament in the monstrance was moved from place to place.

A variety of processions for special feasts were also very popular in Polish parishes.

The following prayers and hymns were used during the Lenten Season.

---

[388] Parish Book, *St. Mary of Czestochowa*, p. 62

[389] A. H. Gunkel, "The Sacred in the City: Polonian Street Processions as Countercultural Practice," *Polish American Studies*, Vol. 60:2003, No. 2, p. 14

GORZKIE ŻALE

Pobudka

1. Gorzkie żale, przybywajcie, –
Serca nasze przenikajcie.
2. Rozpłyńcie się, me źrenice, –
Toczcie smutnych łez krynice.
3. Słońce, gwiazdy, omdlewają, –
Żałobą się pokrywają.
4. Płaczą rzewnie Aniołowie, –
A któż żałość ich wypowie?
5. Opoki się twarde krają. –
Z grobów umarli powstają.
6. Cóż jest, pytam, co się dzieje? –
Wszystko stworzenie truchleje!
7. Na ból Męki Chrystusowej –
Żal przejmuje bez wymowy.
8. Uderz, Jezu, bez odwłoki –
W twarde serc naszych opoki!
9. Jezu mój, we krwi ran Swoich –
Obmyj duszę z grzechów moich!
10. Upał serca swego chłodzę, –
Gdy w przepaść Męki Twej wchodzę.

CZĘŚĆ PIERWSZA

Intencja

Przy pomocy łaski Bożej przystępujemy do rozważania Męki Pana naszego Jezusa Chrystusa. Ofiarować je będziemy Ojcu niebieskiemu na cześć i chwałę Jego Boskiego majestatu, pokornie Mu dziękując za wielką i niepojętą miłość ku rodzajowi ludzkiemu, iż raczył zesłać Syna Swego, aby za nas wycierpiał okrutne męki i śmierć podjął krzyżową. To rozmyślanie ofiarujemy również ku czci Najświętszej Maryi Panny, Matki Bolesnej, oraz ku uczczeniu Świętych Pańskich, którzy wyróżniali się nabożeństwem ku Męce Chrystusowej.

W pierwszej części będziemy rozważali, co Pan Jezus wycierpiał od modlitwy w Ogrójcu aż do niesłusznego przed sądem oskarżenia. Te zniewagi i zelżywości temuż Panu za nas bolejącemu ofiarujemy za Kościół święty katolicki, za najwyższego Pasterza z całym duchowieństwem, nadto za nieprzyjaciół krzyża Chrystusowego i wszystkich niewiernych, aby im Pan Bóg dał łaskę nawrócenia i opamiętania.

Hymn

1. Żal duszę ściska, serce boleść czuje, –
gdy słodki Jezus na śmierć się gotuje; –
Klęczy w Ogrójcu, gdy krwawy pot leje, –
Me serce mdleje.
2. Pana świętości uczeń zły całuje, –
Żołnierz okrutny powrózmi krępuje, –
Jezus tym więzom dla nas się poddaje –
Na śmierć wydaje.
3. Bije, popycha tłum nieposkromiony –
Nielitościwie z tej i z owej strony, –
Za włosy targa; znosi w cierpliwości –
Król z wysokości.
4. Zsiniałe przedtem krwią zachodzą usta, –
Gdy zbrojną żołnierz rękawicą chlusta; –
Wnet się zmieniło w płaczliwe wzdychanie –
Serca kochanie.
5. Oby się serce we łzy rozpływało, –
Że Cię mój Jezu, sprośnie obrażało! –
Żal mi, ach żal mi ciężkich moich złości –
Dla Twej miłości.

Lament duszy nad cierpiącym Jezusem

1. Jezu, na zabicie okrutne, –
Cichy Baranku od wrogów szukany, –

Jezu mój kochany!
2. Jezu, za trzydzieści srebrników –
Od niewdzięcznego ucznia zaprzedany, –
Jezu mój kochany!
3. Jezu, w ciężkim smutku żałością, –
Jakoś sam wyznał, przed śmiercią nękany, –
Jezu mój kochany!
4. Jezu, na modlitwie w Ogrójcu –
Strumieniem potu krwawego zalany, –
Jezu mój kochany!
5. Jezu, całowaniem zdradliwym –
od niegodnego Judasza wydany, –
Jezu mój kochany!
6. Jezu, powrozami grubymi –
od swawolnego żołdactwa związany, –
Jezu mój kochany!
7. Jezu, od pospólstwa zelżywie –
Przed Annaszowym sądem znieważany, –
Jezu mój kochany!
8. Jezu, przez ulice sromotnie –
Przed sąd Kajfasza za włosy targany, –
Jezu mój kochany!
9. Jezu, od Malchusa srogiego –
Ręką zbrodniczą wypoliczkowany, –
Jezu mój kochany!
10. Jezu od fałszywych dwóch świadków –
Za zwodziciela niesłusznie podany, –
Jezu mój kochany!
Bądź pozdrowiony, bądź pochwalony! –
Dla nas zelżony i pohańbiony! –
Bądź uwielbiony, bądź wysławiony, –
Boże nieskończony!

Rozmowa duszy z Matką Bolesną

1. Ach! Ja Matka tak żałosna! –

Boleść Mnie ściska nieznośna, –
Miecz me serce przenika, –
2. Czemuś, Matko ukochana, –
Ciężko na sercu stroskana? –
Czemu wszystka truchlejesz?
3. Co mię pytasz? Wszystkam w mdłości, –
Mówić nie mogę w żałości, –
Krew mi serce zalewa.
4. Powiedz mi, o Panno moja, –
Czemu blednieje twarz Twoja? –
Czemu gorzkie łzy lejesz?
5. Widzę, że Syn ukochany –
W Ogrójcu cały zalany –
Potu krwawym potokiem.
6. O Matko, źródło miłości, –
Niech czuję gwałt Twej żałości! –
Dozwól mi z sobą płakać!

(Jeżeli śpiewa się tylko jedną część, dodaje się 3 razy:
Któryś za nas cierpiał rany...)

CZĘŚĆ DRUGA

Pobudka:

„*Gorzkie żale przybywajcie...*"

Intencja

W drugiej części rozmyślania Męki Pańskiej będziemy rozważali, co Pan Jezus wycierpiał od niesłusznego przed sądem oskarżenia aż do okrutnego cierniem ukoronowania. Te zaś rany, zniewagi i zelżywości temuż Jezusowi cierpiącemu ofiarujemy, prosząc Go o pomyślność dla Ojczyzny naszej, o pokój i zgodę dla wszystkich narodów, a dla siebie o odpuszczenie grzechów, oddalenie klęsk i nieszczęść doczesnych, a szczególnie zarazy, głodu, ognia i wojny.

Hymn

*1. Przypatrz się, duszo, jak cię Bóg miłuje, –
Jako dla ciebie sobie nie folguje. –
Przecież Go bardziej niż katowska dręczy, –
Złość twoja męczy.
2. Stoi przed sędzią Pan wszego stworzenia, –
Cichy Baranek, z wielkiego wzgardzenia –
Dla białej szaty, którą jest odziany, –
Głupim nazwany.
3. Za moje złości grzbiet srodze biczują –
Pójdźmy grzesznicy, oto nam gotują –
Ze Krwi Jezusa dla serca ochłody –
Zdrój żywej wody.
4. Pycha światowa niechaj co chce wróży, –
Co na swe skronie wije wieniec z róży, –
W szkarłat na pośmiech, cierniem Król zraniony –
Jest ozdobiony!
5. Oby się serce we łzy rozpływało, –
Że Cię, mój Jezu, sprośnie obrażało! –
Żal mi, ach żal mi ciężkich moich złości –
Dla Twej miłości!*

Lament duszy nad cierpiącym Jezusem

*1. Jezu, od pospólstwa niewinnie –
Jako łotr godzien śmierci obwołany, –
Jezu mój kochany!
2. Jezu, od złośliwych morderców –
Po ślicznej twarzy tak sprośnie zeplwany, –
Jezu mój kochany!
3. Jezu, pod przysięgą od Piotra –
Po trzykroć z wielkiej bojaźni zaprzany, –
Jezu mój kochany!
4. Jezu, od okrutnych oprawców –
Na sąd Piłata jak zbójca szarpany, –*

Jezu mój kochany!
5. Jezu, od Heroda i dworzan, –
Królu niebieski, zelżywie wyśmiany, –
Jezu mój kochany!
6. Jezu, w białą szatę szydersko –
Na większy pośmiech i hańbę ubrany, –
Jezu mój kochany!
7. Jezu, u kamiennego słupa –
Niemiłosiernie biczami wysmagany, –
Jezu mój kochany!
8. Jezu, przez szyderstwo okrutne –
Cierniowym wieńcem ukoronowany, –
Jezu mój kochany!
9. Jezu, od żołnierzy niegodnie –
Na pośmiewisko purpurą odziany, –
Jezu mój kochany!
10. Jezu, trzciną po głowie bity, –
Królu boleści, przez lud wyszydzany, –
Jezu mój kochany!
Bądź pozdrowiony, bądź pochwalony! –
Dla nas zelżony, wszystek skrwawiony, –
Bądź uwielbiony, bądź wysławiony, –
Boże nieskończony!

Rozmowa duszy z Matką Bolesną

1. Ach, widzę Syna mojego –
Przy słupie obnażonego, –
Rózgami zsieczonego!
2. Święta Panno, uproś dla mnie, –
Bym ran Syna Twego znamię –
Miał na sercu wyryte!
3. Ach, widzę, jako niezmiernie –
Ostre głowę ranią ciernie! –
Dusza moja ustaje.
4. O Maryjo, Syna swego, –

ostrym cierniem zranionego, –
Podzielże ze mną mękę!
5. Obym ja, Matka strapiona, –
Mogła na swoje ramiona –
Złożyć krzyż Twój, Synu mój!
6. Proszę, o Panno jedyna, –
Niechaj krzyż Twojego Syna –
Zawsze w sercu swym noszę.

Któryś za nas cierpiał rany, Jezu Chryste, zmiłuj się nad nami... (3 razy)

CZĘŚĆ TRZECIA

Pobudka:

"Gorzkie żale przybywajcie..."

Intencja

W tej ostatniej części będziemy rozważali, co Pan Jezus cierpiał od chwili ukoronowania aż do ciężkiego skonania na krzyżu. Te bluźnierstwa, zelżywości i zniewagi, jakie Mu wyrządzono, ofiarujemy za grzeszników zatwardziałych, aby Zbawiciel pobudził ich serca zbłąkane do pokuty i prawdziwej życia poprawy, oraz za dusze w czyśćcu cierpiące, aby im litościwy Jezus Krwią swoją świętą ogień zagasił: prośmy nadto, by i nam wyjednał na godzinę śmierci skruchę za grzechy i szczęśliwe w łasce Bożej wytrwanie.

Hymn

1. Duszo oziębła, czemu nie gorejesz, –
Serce me, czemu całe nie truchlejesz? –
Toczy twój Jezus z ognistej miłości –
Krew w obfitości.
2. Ogień miłości, gdy Go tak rozpala, –
Sromotne drzewo na ramiona zwala; –
Zemdlony Jezus pod krzyżem uklęka, –

Jęczy i stęka.
3. Okrutnym katom posłusznym się staje, –
Ręce i nogi przebić sobie daje, –
Wisi na krzyżu, ból ponosi srogi –
Nasz Zbawca drogi.
4. O słodkie drzewo, spuśćże nam już ciało, –
Aby na tobie dłużej nie wisiało! –
My je uczciwie w grobie położymy, –
Płacz uczynimy.
5. Oby się serce we łzy rozpływało, –
Że Cię, mój Jezu, sprośnie obrażało! –
Żal mi, ach żal mi ciężkich moich złości –
Dla Twej miłości!
6. Niech Ci, mój Jezu, cześć będzie w wieczności –
Za Twe obelgi, męki, zelżywości, –
Któreś ochotnie, Syn Boga jedyny, –
Cierpiał bez winy!

Lament duszy nad cierpiącym Jezusem

1. Jezu, od pospólstwa niezbożnie –
Jako złoczyńca z łotry porównany, –
Jezu mój kochany!
2. Jezu, od Piłata niesłusznie –
Na śmierć krzyżową za ludzi skazany, –
Jezu mój kochany!
3. Jezu, srogim krzyża ciężarem –
Na kalwaryjskiej drodze zmordowany, –
Jezu mój kochany!
4. Jezu, do sromotnego drzewa –
Przytępionymi gwoźdźmi przykowany, –
Jezu mój kochany!
5. Jezu, jawnie pośród dwu łotrów –
Na drzewie hańby ukrzyżowany, –
Jezu mój kochany!
6. Jezu, od stojących wokoło –

I przechodzących szydercо wyśmiany, –
Jezu mój kochany!
7. Jezu, bluźnierstwami od złego –
Współwiszącego łotra wyszydzany. –
Jezu mój kochany!
8. Jezu, gorzką żółcią i octem –
W wielkim pragnieniu napawany, –
Jezu mój kochany!
9. Jezu, w swej miłości niezmiernej –
Jeszcze po śmierci włócznią przeorany, –
Jezu mój kochany!
10. Jezu, od Józefa uczciwie –
I Nikodema w grobie pochowany, –
Jezu mój kochany!
Bądź pozdrowiony! Bądź pochwalony! –
Dla nas zmęczony i krwią zbroczony, –
Bądź uwielbiony, bądź wysławiony, –
Boże nieskończony!

Rozmowa duszy z Matką Bolesną

1. Ach, ja Matka boleściwa –
Pod krzyżem stoję smutliwa, –
Serce żałość przejmuje.
2. O Matko, niechaj prawdziwie, –
Patrząc na krzyż żałośliwie, –
Płaczę z Tobą rzewliwie!
3. Jużci, już moje Kochanie –
Gotuje się na konanie! –
Toć i ja z Nim umieram!
4. Pragnę, Matko, zostać z Tobą, –
Dzielić się Twoją żałobą –
Śmierci Syna Twojego.
5. Zamknął słodką Jezus mowę –
Już ku ziemi skłania głowę, –
Żegna już Matkę swoją!

6. O Maryjo, Ciebie proszę, –
Niech Jezusa rany noszę –
I serdecznie rozważam.

Któryś za nas cierpiał rany, Jezu Chryste, zmiłuj się nad nami... (3 razy)

Stations of the Cross were said regularly during Lent by Polish immigrants as follows:

Stacje Drogi Krzyżowej

I. Pan Jezus skazany na śmierć.
II. Jezus Chrystus bierze krzyż na swoje ramiona.
III. Jezus Chrystus upada pod krzyżem po raz pierwszy.
IV. Jezus Chrystus spotyka swoją Matkę.
V. Szymon Cyrenejczyk pomaga nieść krzyż Chrystusowi.
VI. Weronika ociera twarz Jezusowi Chrystusowi.
VII. Jezus Chrystus upada pod krzyżem po raz drugi.
VIII. Jezus Chrystus pociesza niewiasty jerozolimskie.
IX. Jezus Chrystus upada pod krzyżem po raz trzeci.
X. Jezus Chrystus z szat odarty.
XI. Jezus Chrystus przybity do krzyża.
XII. Jezus Chrystus umiera na krzyżu.
XIII. Jezus Chrystus zdjęty z krzyża.
XIV. Ciało Jezusa Chrystusa złożone do grobu.

CHAPTER VI

INSTITUTIONS, ORGANIZATIONS, AND RELIGIOUS ASSOCIATIONS

SCHOOLS

The first Catholic bishop in the United States of America was John Carroll who hoped that there would be no need to create new schools and separate religious teaching. History has shown the opposite to be true. Those who were born here or those who came as immigrants had to start their life here a little differently. In order to raise their children in the Catholic faith, they had to establish their own schools. The Polish parochial school system was created in America in the 19th century. It was designed to meet the needs and requirements of Polish immigrants. The aim of this system was to build and open Polish schools in addition to the Polish churches and parishes. The Polish immigrants wanted to keep Polish traditions and pass them on to their children. The Polish schools became the best places to promote Polish culture and patriotism.[390] In Polish parish schools, children were not only taught subjects that were offered in the public schools, but also they learned the truth and principles of faith and patriotism from the Polish homeland.[391] These schools also separated the children from some degree of secularization which was present in the public schools. Very often, schools were built and opened before the parish was organized or the church structure built.

Polish Catholic schools were created in a large part through the ef-

---

[390] E. M. Kuznicki CSSF, "The Polish American Parochial Schools," in Frank Mocha, *Poles in America*, Stevens Point 1978, p. 436

[391] W. Kruszka, *A History of the Poles*, p. 111

forts of the Polish clergy and the administration of the Polish parishes. That is why they were called parish schools, unlike public schools which were supported by the government. The political situation in Poland in the 19th century contributed to the emigration to America. Immigrants came not only for economic reasons but also because of the political exile of groups of prominent Catholic educators, clergy, land owners, and the Polish intellectual elite. One of the most important people who helped create the system of Polish education in North America was Rev. Francis Dzierzynski who was a Jesuit. He came to America in 1821 and two years later was appointed as Superior of the Society of the Jesuits in America.[392]

The first Polish school was built in 1867 in Panna Maria, Texas. The oldest Polish parish and the first Polish church dedicated to the Blessed Virgin Mary were also built there. The school in Panna Maria was founded by Rev. Adolf Bakanowski who was a Polish teacher in America. Teachers in this school were the pastor who taught religion, the organist, and an American who taught both English and sewing. The school was erected and dedicated to St. Joseph. The children in this school learned Polish and English[393] on two levels depending on their abilities.

On February 2, 1873, Rev. Felix Zwiardowski the pastor of the Parish of the Blessed Virgin Mary in Texas (Panna Maria) wrote a letter to Rome in which he described the situation of Polish parishes. The letter follows. "I brought the nuns to my parish who took over the responsibility of education in the school. The need for teaching in parochial schools is huge. I don't remain passive, we must begin to teach, because otherwise we will only have children and young people raised and educated in public schools, and this is not good. Not wanting to waste time I went to the Provincial Sister in Castorville, and asked for a favor. Please send a few sisters to my parish, to help me with the teaching in the school. The three nuns who came used my rectory as their residence. I, however, moved myself to the church and I lived above the sacristy. These three nuns were of German Alsatian heritage. They did not know

---

392   J. A. Wytrwal, *Poles in America*, Minneapolis 1969, p. 36
393   www.pannamariatexas.com (March 3, 2009)

the Polish language but they decided to learn this language through an intensive study course."[394] Since 1872, the school has been under the protection of the Province of Divine Sisters of Castorville.[395]

The second Polish school in America was a school under the title of St. Stanislaus the Martyr in Milwaukee, Wisconsin. This school was founded in 1869 by Rev. J. Jaster.[396] The bishop appointed Rev. J. Jaster as pastor in the Polish parish although he was a priest of German origin. Shortly after the founding of the Polish school in the parish, Rev. Jaster brought nuns from the Congregation of Notre Dame to administer the school.

The best Polish school in America was a school in Buffalo, New York. St. Stanislaus was founded in 1874. Every year, the number of Polish schools increased and by 1887 when there were over fifty Polish parochial schools in America with approximately 14,000 students.[397] The problem with creating new parochial schools in the rural areas was their financial challenges. Very often in the rural parishes, the pastor became the teacher of the Polish language and religion.[398]

The need for education forced the construction of more schools than churches. Therefore, it became necessary to increase the use of lay teachers. At the end of the 19th century, the salary for the men and women was somewhat different. As an educator, men earned slightly more. The average monthly salary for teachers was between $40 and $60.

Teachers in the Polish parochial school system often used the same titles of books as the public schools. For example, *Elementarz polski* a handbook for primary schools was written by Władysław Dyniewicz. The first Polish primer book written and published in America was titled *Uczenie pisania, czytania i arytmetyki dla szkół i domów polskich katolickich dziaci w Ameryce*. It was released in 1876 and written by Ignatius Wendzinski who taught in Gołańcz in the Wielkie Księstwo Poznańskie. The newer release of the primer book was published in Chicago in 1899. The book *Obrazkowy Elementarz Polski* (*Visual Polish Primer*) was written by J. Smulski.

---

394   W. Kruszka, *A History of the Poles. Part 1*, p. 119

395   E. M. Kuznicki CSSF, "The Polish American Parochial Schools," in Frank Mocha, *Poles in America*, Stevens Point 1978, p. 436

396   J. A. Watrous, *Memoirs of Milwaukee*, Madison 1909, p. 614

397   E. M. Kuznicki CSSF, "The Polish American Parochial Schools," p. 436

398   W. Kruszka, *A History of Poles. Part 1*, p. 111

The Polish school year began in America in September and ended around June 30th. During the school year, classes were held each day except Saturdays and Sundays. Each day had its own strict schedule. The Mass preceded lessons which started at 8:00 AM. The classes at the school continued until 11:30 AM with a 15 minute break at 10:00 AM. In the afternoon, lessons lasted from 1:00 PM until 4:00 PM with a 15 minute break at 2:30 PM. The Polish school curriculum had eight levels and sometimes more. Each grade had a strict educational program.[399] The school year was divided into two semesters.

The classes in kindergarten began with the teaching of religion which included the biblical story of creation and the first parents. They were also taught prayers. Another lesson was language. It involved learning the Polish and English languages. Students learned to properly read, write, and build simple sentences in two languages. During math class, students practiced how to count from one to one hundred, how to write correct numbers, and how to do addition, subtraction, multiplication, and division. During art classes, the children were required to draw simple geometric figures. Children sang simple songs during music lessons which were held twice a week and preceded the physical education classes which included exercises for the arms and legs.

The students in the first grade had religion class which occupied an important place in the curriculum. During religion class, the biblical history of the flood and history of the patriarchs were presented to students. Also, the pupils learned the basics of English and Polish. They learned to memorize various texts and poems, stories, and moral proverbs. Arithmetic involved the memorization of facts, addition, subtraction, multiplication, and division. Other subjects taught in Polish schools were calligraphy, art, music, and physical education.

In the second grade, a very important part of the curriculum was the religion lessons which focused on the use of a book containing an abbreviated version of the history of salvation from all four gospels. Polish and English were taught in language lessons. At this stage, students were taught phonetics and how to write short essays. Arithmetic was more complicated as it already included the use of numbers to one mil-

---

[399] J. A. Wytrwal, *Poles in America*, p. 448

lion and writing four functions of five numbers. A new subject which appeared in the second grade was geography. Students learned the geography of North America as well as the basis and principles of geography. In music, it was important to memorize the most popular Polish and American songs.

In the third grade program, time came for teaching religion from the *Duży katechizm rok 1*. The Polish language was taught with the third Polish textbook written by Władysław Dyniewicz or J. Smulski. History was introduced as a new subject. The students were taught both Polish history and the early history of United States. In English language classes, the book titled *Third Reader* written by Richard Gilmore was used. For spelling, they used the book *Elementary Grammar* written by Thomas Harvey.

At the fourth grade level, religion was taught using a book titled *Większy katechizm rok 2*. Polish language classes used the fourth book written by Antoni Malecki. During music lessons, students performed and learned more complicated songs. English classes had students learning from the book written by R. Gilmore titled *Fourth Reader*. Students continued the study of grammar and spelling. History lessons taught the events of Polish history as well as historical events in North America.

In the fifth grade, religious education classes used a book titled *Duży katechizm rok 3* Part 3 written by J. Chociszewski to learn biblical history, and it was used at the fifth level for students to learn and read in Polish. The book *Szkoła Śpiewu* written by Professor A. Małłeka and the songbook written for Poles in America by A. J. Kwasigroch and S. Zahajkiewicz were used for music lessons.

Sixth grade had an extended program for religion with the book *Największy katechizm* followed by *Historia biblijna* written by Józef Chociszewski. Students were introduced to algebra and physiology. During music lessons, students learned how to sing in two voices and read musical notes. History instruction included American history from the end of the Civil War until modern times.

At the seventh grade level, religion included the teaching of the foundation of the Roman Catholic Church and history in the early centuries of the Church. The study of the Polish language included syntax and contained the main principles of Polish pronunciation. Accounting practices and algebra were learned in math. History classes included lessons about the United States Constitution.

Eighth grade religion classes continued to teach about the Roman Catholic faith and Church history. During history class, students were taught about the Polish nation from its beginning up to modern times. United States history classes covered the events of the American Revolution to the end of the Civil War.[400] The Polish language classes continued with the study of phonetics, pronunciation, and the construction of sentences.

In America, the Polish program in schools consisted of two courses. The first was the basic course which began with preschool and finished with fourth grade. The second course was called higher, or school of grammar, and started at the beginning of fifth grade until the completion of eighth grade. This program was developed and implemented in Polish schools by teachers and offered to all Polish children. Unfortunately, a large number of students attending school did not finish or stopped at a lower level. The reason was often the same. Parents responsible for the education of their children chose to abandon their children's education. They were driven by economic conditions and the need for extra hands in the farm fields. The program prepared for Polish parochial schools was very ambitious compared to the program offered on the same level in public schools. This program gave greater opportunities to children because they were able to learn the Polish language and to develop a strong knowledge of religion.[401]

At the beginning, the parish school buildings were very poorly equipped both in terms of furnishing and classroom supplies. They had poor heating and lighting systems. Often the classes were overcrowded. Many times, these classes held between 140 and 150 children.[402]

Almost from the very beginning, the Polish parochial schools were led by nuns. Most priests were involved with pastoral duties and with activities in their own parishes or the neighboring ones. Therefore for

---

400 W. Kruszka, *A History of the Poles. Part 1*, p. 117
401 Ibid.
402 E. M. Kuznicki, "The Polish American Parochial Schools" p. 436-437. The author of this article was not very subjective and unfairly provided information about people working in the described parishes. The author omitted the names of the clergy, and lay people working at that time and location as well as some of the events in the life of the parish.

this reason, nuns were asked to administer and teach in the schools. The Polish parishes increased in size and the number of families was constantly increasing. In 1870 in America, there were sixteen Polish parishes. While in 1880, there were already fifty-eight. This number increased to ninety-six by 1890 and to 160 parishes in 1900.[403] The demand for nuns was huge. With such a rapid development of parishes and parochial schools, parishes had to wait for two or three years for the arrival of nuns. There was limited opportunity to invite Polish nuns from the old country to work in the schools. For this reason, the curriculum in the schools was shortened.[404]

Polish schools were traditional schools. They were not financially sound when compared to public schools and schools operated by other ethnic groups in America at the same time. The result of this situation was that an employee may have had to wait up to one year for the payment of wages.

The first Polish congregation of sisters who came to the state of Wisconsin to work with children and young people in the schools were sisters from the Congregation of St. Felix Cantilice. In 1874, the sisters began a very active and fruitful effort in the parish of Polonia. The climate and conditions were not the best, but the sisters quickly adapted themselves to the situation in this area. After many years of work and experience in the school, the Felician Sisters became the most active congregation in the United States in terms of teaching responsibilities and for leading Polish parochial schools. In the most fruitful period of time in their educational work, these sisters had 17,822 students under the care of 261 sisters.

The next congregation to become very active in the field of education promoting the Polish culture and educational methods were the Franciscan Sisters of St. Kunegunda. This happened through the work of Rev. Wincent Barzynski who collaborated with Sister Anna Field in 1893.

Two years later in early 1895, the Sisters of Nazareth became very active in the pursuit of education within Polish parochial schools. This congregation was founded in 1894. One hundred twelve sisters taught a total of 9,178 students in 116 parochial schools.[405]

---

403   W. Kruszka, *A History of Poles. Part 1*, p. 81.
404   E. M. Kuznicki, "The Polish American Parochial Schools," p. 450.
405   W. Kruszka, *A History of Poles. Part 1*, p. 124.

Another congregation which began teaching and educating among American Poles was the Benedictine nuns who took over the administration of five parochial schools with approximately 1,000 students. Within the group of Polish nuns who taught in parochial schools in America, there were also six sisters of the St. Joseph Congregation, seven sisters of the Congregation of the Resurrection, three Dominican Sisters, two sisters of the St. Ursuline Congregation, and eight sisters from the Congregation of the Holy Cross. There were also five brothers of the Congregation of the Holy Trinity from Chicago.

In 1920, there was a breakthrough in teaching. The English language had become very popular and more necessary in everyday life. This language was used in homes and elsewhere. Children in primary school began to use English. This situation led to the reversal of the existing situation. With time, the teaching of Polish began to fade, and the knowledge of the Polish language showed a decline. Polish language classes were no longer listed on report cards nor was proficiency in the Polish language required to pass to the next grade level in school.

In 1931, the Polish Union of America restored the teaching of the Polish language in schools. It had soon become apparent that the cessation of teaching the Polish language in schools did not bode well for the next generation of Poles who settled here. Therefore between 1932 and 1952, the Felician Sisters organized ten general meetings in America to resolve the issue of teaching Polish in the schools. The topics of the conferences were how to teach the Polish language, how to make it more attractive in primary schools, how to teach children, and what to do to bring back the Polish language and make it usable on a daily basis.

After the first conference, the nuns decided to publish Polish books for grammar and Polish writing exercises. In an effort to reintroduce the opportunity to learn the Polish language, they collected materials which became very helpful and were thus used for the next thirty years.

After the end of World War II, Polish soldiers who served in the army came to settle in America with their families. It was assumed that this situation would change the image of Polish culture in America. However, the use of the Polish language did not improve. The newly arriving immigrants became more American than Polish. The use of Polish and the continued teaching of this language became superfluous. The language was taught less and less with time and in some places completely forgotten. The liturgy celebrated in the Polish language was becoming not understandable as well. Although the Second Vatican Council gave the opportunity for church celebrations to be performed using a national language, the language commonly spoken by Poles became English. As a result, Poles essentially stopped using Polish for communication in the United States. [406]

The Elementary School of St. Michael, North Creek

In May 1887, the construction project for an elementary school in North Creek was approved and accepted by the bishop of the Diocese of La Crosse. By October 1887, the school was built and put into service for a total cost of $600. The education in school was handled by two teachers: Rev. Dutkiewicz and a secular woman, Mary Wozny. The school grew rapidly as more children came, and responsibilities were added. Therefore after one year, a decision was reached to hire another teacher. After nine years, the school was transferred into the hands of nuns. Seventy-five students attended school during that time.

Unfortunately, this school in 1909 was destroyed by fire.[407] After this tragedy, many parishioners did not want to rebuild the school on the same site in North Creek. They believed that a better solution would be to build a school in nearby Arcadia which was a larger town. A verbal battle raged between the parishioners. After one year, the decision was made to rebuild the school at the old site. The cost to rebuild it totaled $3,000.[408] In 1940, the elementary school of St. Michael merged with the Arcadia public school system.[409]

---

406 J. A. Wytrwal, *Poles in America*, p. 456.

407 J. L. Hauck, *Catholic Church in Trempealeau County*; F. Curtiss-Wedge, *History of Trempealeau County Wisconsin*, 1917, p. 845.

408 J. L. Hauck, *Catholic Church in Trempealeau County*; F. Curtiss-Wedge, *History of Trempealeau County Wisconsin*, 1917, p. 846.

409 Parish Book, *St. Michael the Archangel 1873-1988*, Wisconsin 1998, p. 22; J. L. Hauck, *Catholic Church in Trempealeau County*, p. 845-846.

The Elementary School of St. Stanislaus, Arcadia

The parish in Arcadia was founded in August 1910 by parishioners who primarily came from North Creek. Four years later in March 1914, plans were prepared for the construction of a school as well as for a home for nuns. In a very short period of time, the school building was constructed with two stories at a total cost of $18,000. The school was dedicated by Bishop James Schwebach on October 25, 1914. The official opening occurred in September 1915. On opening day, the enrollment was one hundred students.[410] Soon two nuns from the Congregation of St. Joseph came to teach. They lived in nearby Stevens Point and took over the responsibility of this newly opened school. The school had two large rooms with each holding four classes. In the 8th grade, nuns taught both the English and Polish languages.[411] Over time, the number of pupils increased to 160 while the group of nuns also doubled. In 1925, the decision was made to renovate and modernize this building. Two additional classrooms were added on. At the same time, the home for nuns was completed at a cost of $10,000. The numbers of sisters had grown to five. One of them served for fifty years as the housekeeper for the pastor.[412] With the new construction, the school building could accommodate more students. Unfortunately in 1933, the number of students dropped to 149.[413]

The Elementary School of St. Ladislaus, Bevent

The primary school was built in 1913 of brick which was unique in those days. At that time, the pastor in Bevent was Rev. Ignatius Mordarski. For the first nineteen years, teaching responsibilities were handled by lay teachers. The number of students enrolled was around eighty. However, on Friday afternoons this number increased by an additional 186 students from the public school who came for religious instruc-

---

[410] J. L. Hauck, *Catholic Church in Trempealeau County*, p. 850
[411] www.holyfam.com/St.%20Stanislaus%20History (March 4, 2009)
[412] Ibid.
[413] J. L. Hauck, *Catholic Church in Trempealeau County*, p. 850

tion.[414] In 1932, the environment of the school changed when the Felician Sisters arrived and took over care of the school. A disaster occurred in 1935 when a fire destroyed a portion of the school building. In spite of this loss, the inhabitants of Bevent who knew the value of education decided to rebuild and to partially modernize the burned portion. The school was repaired and was again used by the end of the year.

In the following year, Rev. Peter Rombalski increased the potential enrollment in the school by adding grades 9 and 10. With time, enrollment declined in Bevent due to the small number of families that belonged to the parish and the fact that many families had decided to leave and work in the city. In view of these facts, the bishop decided to close the school on June 9, 1969. Following this decision, the sisters left the parish, and the convent was closed. The school building was renovated and earmarked for the youth. It was later used to teach religion to children attending public schools.[415] To this day, young people use this building.

The Elementary School of St. Michael, Wausau

In 1890, the construction of the church in Wausau was completed, and the basement of the church was assigned and used as a classroom for religious education. The first messengers and promoters of religious education in Wausau were Francis Rybarczyk and Francis Cyman. In subsequent years as the school grew, the sisters of the Congregation of St. Joseph from Stevens Point were invited to conduct the education of students. They taught from 1907 to 1911. Another change in the process of education occurred in 1914 when Rev. Theopolius Wojak built a four class school and invited the Felician Sisters to come. They eagerly joined in the educational work. In the same year (1914), four nuns came to educate 450 students. These sisters worked in the parish and school for years and do so to this day.

In the following years, the number of students began to increase,

---

414 Parish Book, *History of St. Ladislaus Bevent Wisconsin*, 1971, p. 16
415 Parish Book, *History of St. Ladislaus, Bevent Wisconsin*, p. 23

and as a result there was a need to hire more teachers for new positions. Between 1947 and 1952, four more classrooms were added. In the years 1948 to 1954, the number of teachers increased to eight or nine sisters.[416] In 1956, Rev. Krasowski became the new pastor. During his pastoral term, the school was redecorated; floors and new desks were added. The school has worked very effectively over the years. In 1977, the enrollment was 256 students. A kindergarten was added, and in 1977-1978 the pre-school program began. Ground breaking took place on May 1, 1981, for a new school addition which was completed in November 1981. The new addition included a gymnasium, learning center, prayer room, meeting room, and a classroom.[417] The school year 1986-1987 reported an enrollment of 162 students. St. Michael's also provides CCD instruction for students attending public school.

The Elementary School of St. Bronislava, Plover

The residents of Plover who were pioneers in the construction of their church also became pioneers in understanding the needs of education and teaching children and youth. Early on, they decided what would be most important for their children and for future generations. At a meeting of the Polish people living in Plover, a decision was made to build a school. Residents wanted their children and youth to have an opportunity to learn the fundamentals of their faith and to understand traditions and the Polish language. Quickly, a decision was made to build the school, however, the venture proved to be more complicated than expected. The biggest problem was money or rather the lack thereof. Rev. Michael Klosowski met several times with the parish representative. After discussions with parishioners, this problem was presented to the bishop of the diocese. It was not an easy decision because the country's economy was very weak. Also, there was an urgent need for youth education but insufficient time for construction of a school.

The parish was divided into two camps concerning the building of

---

416   Parish Book, *St. Michael's 1887-1977*, Wisconsin 1977, p. 22
417   Parish Book, *St. Michael's 1887-1987,* Irick Studio

a school. Most parishioners wanted to build, but the opponents were many. At the beginning of 1907, families voted on the construction of the school. In favor of construction of the school were thirty-five families and thirty-two opposed. After the third vote regarding this construction project, thirty-two families were for and twenty-six against.[418] At the final meeting, a decision was reached to construct a school within the next three years.

Later in 1907, the decision was made to build the school. The parishioners collected the sum of $1,200 toward the construction. The school was to be a one-room schoolhouse with one lay person or nun as the teacher. The parishioners stood up to the test after all. Soon they created a formal building committee for the construction of the school building, and the plan was implemented in a very speedy manner. The formal committee significantly decreased the amount to be spent on the project. This was critical. An average laborer's pay for one day was $1.00. More skilled workers averaged an annual salary of $1,000.

The school was completed and opened for use in June 1908. Bishop Paul Rohde dedicated the school.[419] A lay teacher was hired to educate the sixty pupils who were enrolled that first year. The school maintained strict discipline which was introduced by Rev. A. J. Rabarczyk. Examples of penalties for students who misbehaved were that they were ordered to kneel in the front of the altar at church, or they had to kneel against the wall in the classroom. A teacher at the school might also use warnings as a penalty. Throwing books at noisy students or hitting them with a stick on the back was allowed. Parishioners of St. Bronislava expected their children to receive specific training and education in religion. Some parents had objections to the methods used for education and punishment of their children, but the school never lacked for students. Participation of children in out of school activities was dictated by economics as well as the location of the parish in relation to their residence. A great number of the parish families lived on farms that were many miles away from the church and school. In this situation, teachers and students boarded at the school Monday through Friday.

---

418   Parish Book, *The History of Saint Bronislava,* Wisconsin 1996, p. 21
419   Ibid., p. 22

The school remained in the hands of lay teachers until 1918 when sisters from the Congregation of St. Joseph took over. The sisters were better prepared for educational work in the school than were the lay people. In the school, three nuns taught sixty to seventy students.[420] The school classes were conducted in the Polish and English languages. At the beginning of 1920, the school, church, and rectory were electrified, and the parish priest Rev. Peter Borowski had the first telephone in town.

In the years of the Great Depression in this country, the economy deteriorated again. For this reason between 1929 and 1932, the number of students fell from eighty to fifty-four. Tuition for attending school was immediately reduced to only a few cents per year. Despite this, many parishioners could not afford to send their children to school. Due to a fire in the school on Sunday, February 9, 1936,[421] caused by a faulty heating system, the school building burned down. The loss amounted to more than $6,000. From insurance on the school building, the parish received only $2,000. As a result of this situation, the sisters left, and the children were sent to public school. In the meantime, religion was taught in the building vacated by the nuns. In 1966, the parish built a new building as a center for youth where students continued their religious education. The building was fully completed in 1974. It took more than fifty years before the decision was made to build a new school in the Parish of St. Bronislava. The new school building was completed and opened in 1995.

THE ELEMENTARY SCHOOL OF ST. STANISLAUS, STEVENS POINT

The first parish school in Stevens Point was built in 1925 at the Parish of St. Stanislaus. The design of the school had been prepared and developed by the construction committee composed of Joseph Zagrzebski, Dominik Martenka, Robert Kostka, Joseph Bemka, Michael Dziekan, Peter Jurgella, Stanislaw Brzezinski, Francis Hintz, and Michael Omernik.[422] Two hundred eighty students attended the newly opened school in 1925. Thirteen students were awarded graduation cer-

---

420　Parish Book, *The History of Saint Bronislava,* Wisconsin 1996, p. 21
421　Parish Book, *The History of St. Bronislava,* p. 32
422　Parish Book, *St. Stanislaus Catholic Church,* p. 12

tificates in 1926. The Parish Council was keenly aware of the need for nuns from the Congregation of St. Joseph in the education of their children. In the collection of parish documents, a letter from Bishop Paul Rohde to Rev. Francis Nowak written in 1937 was found. It mentioned the finances associated with the remodeling of the convent. The bishop noted in this letter to modernize the sisters' house, the parish should not spend $20,000 but should spend $25,000. The nuns of the Congregation of St. Joseph were responsible for the administration and education systems in the school. The original design of the school building was for two levels in the shape of a square. Both floors had six classrooms. Each class had approximately twenty students and was led by one teacher.

Every First Friday of the month, students received Holy Communion. After the celebration of this Mass, children ate a breakfast of egg sandwiches brought from home. Every other morning, the nuns and their students participated in the celebration of the Mass. Normally, they did not receive Holy Eucharist because the fasting requirement was from midnight which was too long for young children.

For many years, the sisters served with care and offered their support to the local school and parish. At a parish meeting in 1950, information was given that suggested a new school be built due to increased enrollment. During this time, the number of students rose to over 500. The school was equipped with sixteen classrooms. Parishioners recommended a high school and auditorium, but unfortunately the plan never came to fruition.[423] This school building held eight grades of education which also included a kindergarten. There were 250 students. In 1987, the local Catholic schools were reorganized. As a result, St. Stanislaus retained the kindergarten and grades one through five which were taught by lay teachers.

The Elementary School of the Holy Family, Poniatowski

The beginning of the school in Poniatowski dates back to 1902 when the shell of a school building was constructed. The school was opened

---

423   www.pchswi.org/archives/church/st_stans (March 5, 2009)

in 1903 with the deep hope that the children would receive the best Catholic education.[424] From the start of the school year, student enrollment continued to increase. The classes were run by a lay teacher. The increased number of students necessitated a need to build a new school. With time, the parish pastor Rev. Ignatius Mordarski prepared plans for a new school building. On July 1, 1909, Rev. Florian H. Kupka became the new pastor. On July 31, 1910, the newly completed school was dedicated and opened for use. Also at the same time, the nuns from the Congregation of Notre Dame were invited to become educators at the school. They taught in the school six years, after which time, they were replaced by Felician Sisters. These nuns came to the parish in 1916 and remained there leading the school until 1970 at which time the school closed.

The school building had two floors and three classrooms. In the first classroom, children in grades 1 to 3 studied; in another classroom were pupils in grades 4 to 6; and the last classroom housed students in grades 7 and 8. One nun was responsible for preparing meals, and an additional three taught students. In 1952 when the parish pastor was Rev. Edward Roskos, work was started to remodel and refresh the school building. The following year in 1953, the school building was enlarged and completely renovated.[425] The number of students ranged between 112 and 125. In 1970, the school building was redesigned for Catholic religious education for students attending public school since the school had closed.

THE ELEMENTARY SCHOOL OF ST. MICHAEL, JUNCTION CITY

In 1906, Rev. Anthony Malkowski along with a group of parishioners met and established a plan to build a primary school. Land for construction of the school was donated by John Kilian. It was a one acre plot that was located on the west side of the church. The school was founded as a result of the special generosity of the parishioners. Con-

---

424 Parish Book, *Holy Family Church*, p. 7
425 Parish Book, *Holy Family Church*, p. 8

struction began the following year.[426] The school was built of stone and brick. The basement in the school was intended for use by the parish as classrooms and a social area. A portion was set aside as a residence for the sisters. The school was opened in 1908, and two lay teachers were hired to teach the children and youth. The number of students in the first year was eighty. After a year, the operation of the school was handed over to sisters who replaced the lay teachers. These nuns came from the Congregation of St. Joseph which was located in the town of Stevens Point.

Modernization of the school and replacement of the school roof took place in 1924. At that time, the pastor of the parish was Rev. Peter Kurzejka. In 1950, the school introduced a hot lunch program. It was offered in an area of the basement which had been adapted as a kitchen and dining area.[427] At the same time, the front of the building was modernized. In 1956, a separate hall was built in the church, and a new oil heating system was installed which warmed the school building also.[428] St. Michael's Grade School ceased operation in the spring of 1968 due to the lack of availability of nuns to teach and the high cost of replacing them with lay teachers. A CCD program was implemented to provide religious education for the children.

THE ELEMENTARY SCHOOL OF ST. PETER, STEVENS POINT

During the ministry of Rev. Anthony Lex from 1884 to 1888, the first parish school was organized at St. Peter Church.[429] In 1887, a three classroom wooden public school and four squares in the city on Washington Avenue were purchased by the parish for a total of $1,000. The dedication of the school was made by Rev. Vincent Barzynski.[430] The leadership in the school was taken over by the sisters of the Congregation of Notre Dame. They worked in the parish until 1896. When they

---

426 Parish Book, *St. Michael's Church Junction City, Wisconsin*, p. 4
427 Parish Book, *St. Michael's Church Junction City, Wisconsin*, p. 5
428 Ibid., p. 7
429 Parish Book, *St. Peter Parish in Stevens Point, Wisconsin*, Stevens Point, Wisconsin 1976, p. 77
430 Parish Book, *Księga pamiątkowa złotego jubileuszu parafii świętego Piotra w Stevens Point*, Wisconsin Stevens Point 1926, p. 11

left, lay teachers were temporarily employed in the school until the arrival at the parish of the Franciscan Sisters of St. Joseph from Milwaukee. The school building was not heated and because of the piercing cold during the winter, classes were held in the insulated basement of the church.

The sisters of St. Joseph in Stevens Point were organized in 1901 and replaced the Franciscan Sisters. In 1904, a commission was established which included Rev. Lukas J. Pescinski whose aim was to improve the conditions in the school. The commission decided to add on and extend the school to twelve classrooms for a total cost of $15,000. The building was to accommodate 600 students.[431] The plan was approved, and construction work on the school began at a rapid pace. It was to be a three-story building supported on a constructed foundation of stone and brick. An auditorium with a stage was added. The new school was opened and consecrated on May 7, 1905, by Bishop J. J. Fox of the Diocese of Green Bay.[432] The original school was demolished.

In the years 1911 to 1913, two new classrooms were added. The school offered education to the eighth grade level. In 1917, further work was carried out including the construction of sewer connections. Work on the construction of the new school which included a spacious auditorium-gymnasium was started in 1931. The new school building cost $200,000. With the completion of the new school in 1932, the old one was demolished, and in its place they made a playground for the children. On March 13, 1932, Bishop P. Rohde arrived in Stevens Point and consecrated this building which was now the third and final one built by the parish. To pay for the cost of the construction of the parish school, parishioners received envelopes in which they could offer money monthly to cover the costs. In order to earn money and to pay off the debt on the school, the parish began to organize various types of appeals such as charity parties and basketball games. A faltering economy was the reason the parish needed to resort to these strategies.

In 1947, the first Catholic boys' high school was established at St. Peter's School. When the jurisdiction changed from the Green Bay Dio-

---

[431] Parish Book, *Saint Peter Parish in Stevens Point, Wisconsin*, p. 84
[432] Parish Book, *Saint Peter Parish in Stevens Point, Wisconsin*, p. 85

cese to the La Crosse Diocese, the high school was terminated at the end of the school year. Later in 1955, the boys' high school was opened as Pacelli High School, but in 1970, it merged with the girls' high school (Maria) under the title of Pacelli High School.

An acute shortage of teaching sisters became a reality in 1960, and lay teachers were required to fill vacancies. This situation continued, and 75% of the faculty was comprised of lay personnel. St. Peter's eighth grade civic club in 1961 established *The Peterette*, a school newspaper. A large carpeted library in 1968 contained over 2200 books and enhanced the educational system at St. Peter's.

The consolidation of parochial schools took place in 1986 after the completion of a thorough study on the matter. The recommendation resulted in the creation of St. Peter Middle School (grades 6 to 8). This decision benefited students by introducing an exploratory art program and a campus ministry. Home economics and industrial arts were available at Pacelli for middle school students.

In 2000, committees reviewed the process of restructuring schools in order to balance class sizes throughout the area parochial schools. Improvements were made to the libraries and the hot lunch program.

The Elementary School of the Sacred Heart of Jesus, Polonia

In September 1872, the parish church in Ellis was moved and put on a new site two miles away. The church was set on a twenty acre parcel. This area of the new church was named Polonia by Rev. J. Dąbrowski. On this occasion, a rectory was built by the newly formed group made up of parishioners. The parsonage was two levels. Rev. Joseph Dąbrowski decided that the first floor of the rectory would be turned into a school.[433] The school started with a lay teacher Mary McGreer[434]

---

433 E. M. Kuznicki, "The Polish American Parochial Schools" in Frank Mocha, *Poles in America*, Stevens Point 1978, p. 440. The author gives facts inconsistent with the information contained in other sources. It is about the date of the arrival of Father J. Dąbrowski to St. Joseph in Sharon and the establishment of the first Polish school. The author says that Father J. Dąbrowski came to the Parish of St. Joseph in the spring of 1870 and also at the same time opened a school. Parish Book, *Sacred Heart Congregation Polonia*, p. 22 gives information that Father J. Dąbrowski was appointed a pastor of St. Joseph in Sharon in December 1871, and the school started its operation in 1872.

434 www.pchswi.org/archives/communities/polonia.htlml (March 6, 2009)

while the Polish teachers were on their way. On June 1, 1874, five sisters from the Franciscans of the Third Order of St. Felix came to America from Poland to begin a new mission. These sisters were Sister Vincentyna, Sister Waclawa, Sister Rafaela, Sister Monica, and Sister Cajetan.

During a church service, a proposal was made to enroll Polish children in the parish school. Over the next two weeks, parents from Central Wisconsin came to enroll their children in the school.[435] With thirty students, the sisters began teaching in the school in December 1874. Since Wisconsin winters were very harsh, some children were taught in their homes. Other children who were attending school often stayed overnight. In the school, nuns taught reading, writing, grammar, and arithmetic as well as Scripture. With time, the sisters took over the teaching of English in the school. The sister who was in charge of training and administrative matters was Sister Mary Cajetan. On March 16, 1875, the rectory and school building were completely destroyed by fire. More than 200 copies of school books which the sisters had transported from Europe were also destroyed. Although parishioners attempted to rebuilt the ruined building and resurrect the school, it was too late to do so that same year. It was decided to close the school.

On October 3, 1876, the house for the nuns was completed of which a portion would be used as a school. The next day, this building was blessed by Rev. J. Dąbrowski and put into use receiving the name and patronage of St. Clare.[436]

In 1895, the number of students enrolled in the school was more than 300. A deepening recession in 1929 meant the country's economy began to deteriorate. This had a destructive effect on many families. Many parishioners who owned their farms lost them. Also, many young people had to leave the rural area to take part in the war. After World War II, many returned to the rural areas. However, many moved to the cities leaving their homesteads behind. The number of families in the rural parishes fell sharply. Plans for the expansion of the school building were suspended.

In 1951, the school and church buildings had a mechanical heat-

---

435 Parish Book, *Sacred Heart Congregation Polonia*, p. 26
436 Parish Book, *Sacred Heart Congregation Polonia*, p. 29

ing system installed for the cost of $1,500. The following year, the hot lunch program for the children was introduced for 112 students.[437] The old bathrooms were remodeled in 1954 for a total cost of $2,600.37, and forty-four benches were purchased for the school. In 1957, four classes were added to the old school building which then offered the opportunity to increase the enrollment at the school to approximately 126 pupils. The total sum for this investment was $1,408.60, but in spite of this effort, the school was still overcrowded.

It was not until the year 1960 that a new spirit and desire came about to expand the school. The new school construction plan was approved by parishioners. On December 16, 1961, the building was completed. The following year on April 29, 1962, Bishop John P. Treacy of the Diocese of La Crosse dedicated the new school building. The student enrollment at that time was 196 children. The cost of construction with all equipment was $94,327.53. The parishioners were very proud of the completed project. A kindergarten was added, and a few years later, a four-year-old preschool program was also established. The seventh and eighth grades were eliminated in 1993.

The Elementary School of St. Casimir, Town of Hull

The idea for a school was born in 1886 among parishioners. It was the result of substantial efforts by the parish priest Rev. Lucas Pescinski and a group of parishioners. A building committee was formed.[438] The decision of the committee prompted the parish to prepare financial statements in order to reduce unnecessary spending in the parish and to save money to spend on the building of the school. One of many proposals which was taken to each family was a request to give four dollars per year earmarked for the building project. Another proposal was that each person attending the church should buy a bench at a cost of $1.50 per year (pew rent). The next step was a plan as to how to encourage and engage parishioners to volunteer their work for the building of the school.

---

437 Ibid., p. 34
438 Parish Book, *St. Casimir Parish 1871-1971*, p. 7

The building committee purchased eight acres of land for the construction of the school. The idea was presented to Bishop F. Kaiser of the Diocese of Green Bay, and he accepted the idea. A new proposal was that each family who had horses and axes for the cutting of trees in the forest should provide one felled tree each year for the needs of the school. If unable to donate a tree, the family was expected to pay a sum of one dollar to a special foundation of the church. Those who did not have horses on their farm had to help with the harvesting of trees in the forest for one day or pay a sum of 50 cents. In this manner, money was collected, and in October 1888, the school was built. The total amount for the construction was $3,400.

The first teacher hired to work in the school was Lucas Dziekan. He worked for a salary of $20 per month.[439] The school was closed in 1948 because of decreased enrollment. Soon the building was used for other purposes including organized meetings for parishioners. In 1970, the parishioners decided to renovate the school building and allocated it as a center for catechesis.[440]

The Elementary School of SS. Peter and Paul, Independence

The school building was constructed and opened in 1887. This building was built of bricks for the total cost of $3,000. The pastor of the parish at that time was Rev. Raphael Tomaszewski, and the administration of the school was handled by sisters of the Congregation of St. Francis from Milwaukee. At the beginning of the 20th century, they were replaced by six nuns from the same congregation but who came from Stevens Point. The sisters stayed in the parish and school until 1933.

A resident Rev. A. W. Gara built a new school for a cost of $11,000 in 1903. In 1927, two lay teachers were hired for two vacant positions, and they taught along with four nuns who remained in the parish. At

---

439 Parish Book, *St. Casimir Parish 1871-1971*, p. 9. This book indicates pay of $20 per month for a teacher's salary, and in other places it is stated that the pay was between $40 and $50 per month. Salaries depended on where the school was located and the financial capabilities of the parish. Therefore in this work, you can find various information concerning salaries of school teachers.

440 Ibid., p. 8-9

that time, the school had 225 students.[441] In 1928, an addition was added to the school which included more facilities. From the very beginning of the school until 1940, all classes were in the Polish language. In 1962, work began on the present school building. Between 1971 and 1972, the school had only two nuns left and six lay teachers. To keep the school in good shape, families of enrolled students were obligated to pay tuition.[442]

The Elementary School of St. Hedwig, Thorp

On November 23, 1919, Rev. James Korczyk called a parish meeting in order to propose the need for a parish school.[443] The meeting was attended by many parishioners, but they saw no need to build the school. The pastor did not give up and called the next meeting on January 18, 1920. Soon there was a change in the parish when the new administrator Rev. Francis Kulig came. During many subsequent meetings with the parish representatives, he tried very hard to present arguments in favor of constructing a school. Discussions continued, but he could not persuade the representatives. On January 9, 1921, during the next parish meeting, the topic concerning the school returned. Rev. F. Kulig the administrator of St. Hedwig Parish asked where a school should be built. At the meeting attended by 148 parishioners, the result of voting was 46 parishioners voted for the construction of the school in Thorp, 36 voted for construction in Poznan, and 67 in general were against the construction of the school at any site. As a result of this outcome, Rev. F. Kulig decided to wait for a better time to propose a construction plan.[444]

Another opportunity appeared in 1935 when during a parish meeting, he suggested that the school should be situated across from the church. During this meeting, the parishioners from Thorp and Poznan made a very important decision affecting the local community when

---

441 J. L. Hauck, *Catholic Church in Trempealeau County*, p. 847

442 Parish Book, *SS. Peter and Paul Church Independence Wisconsin*, Wisconsin 1975, p. 56; J. L. Hauck, *Catholic Church in Trempealeau*, p. 846-848

443 Parish Book, *St. Hedwig's Church Congregation*, Wisconsin 1966, p. 32

444 Ibid., p. 36

they decided to construct a parochial school. The project was approved and adopted on January 24, 1936. However, the development of further plans related to the school construction was stopped because of the death of Rev. F. Kulig.

The newly appointed priest was Rev. Francis Piekarski who in consultation with Bishop Mc Gavick received permission to continue the construction of the school. On March 18, 1943, the pastor called a parish meeting, presented a school building project, and mentioned that it would be good for the parish to invite nuns who could manage and take care of the school. The Felician Sisters came to Thorp on May 7, 1943. This was the first step in beginning the building project. The land for the school was bought for a price of $6,000. The total investment was calculated to be $33,331.02. The total capital investment was completed when the loan was paid in 1964.

School began in 1949, and the following year the Felician Sisters were replaced by the nuns from the Congregation of St. Joseph who came from Stevens Point. The construction of the school was finally completed in 1950, and it could accommodate 225 students. The school had a chapel, four classrooms, and a few other rooms. Bishop Treacy came to the parish on October 1, 1950, and consecrated the newly dedicated school. The next year, the school introduced a hot lunch program for the children.[445] Year by the year, the number of students increased and soon reached 300 pupils. In 1954, a decision was made to create a school library which over time increased by huge volumes.

The Elementary School of Sacred Heart of Jesus, Cassel

Cassel, considered a very small parish, decided in 1910 to build a parochial school. The building materials were stone as well as bricks. The school building was joined to the convent. Parishioners invited the Felician Sisters to lead the school. Three sisters arrived in 1911 to take over the responsibilities associated with running the school. One of the sisters handled the kitchen duties, and the other two sisters taught in

---

[445] Parish Book, *St. Hedwig's Church Congregation*, Wisconsin 1966, p. 33-45

the school.[446] The sisters had a garden and small farm on which they raised chickens that had been donated by parishioners. The school had a chapel which was very often converted into a classroom. Mass was celebrated every day. The school had two levels with the same distribution of rooms on both levels. The school was also used as a meeting place for the parishioners as well as for cultural events such as dances and banquets. The number of students ranged from eighty to one hundred. The last total number of attending students was 121.[447] In 1968, there were only six classes which occupied three classrooms.

In the 1950s, the number of nuns decreased by one, and the position was replaced by a lay teacher. In 1970, the bishop decided to close the school because of the low number of sisters available to teach in the school. The school building was converted and made available to young people and children for the CCD Program.[448]

The Elementary School of SS. Peter and Paul, Weyerhaeuser

In 1936, a parish school was built in Weyerhaeuser. The largest number of students enrolled was ninety. The school had eight grades and nuns from the Congregation of Oblates taught the students. The first teachers at the school were Sister Mary Hyacinth and Sister Mary Augustine. The school building had two levels. In the upper part were classrooms for grades 1 to 4, and the lower level was for grades 5 to 8. Religious education for children from the public schools was offered on Saturdays in the same building. The school was finally closed on May 10, 1967. The building was then devoted to religious education for children from the public schools for CCD.[449]

---

446 Parish Book, *Sacred Heart of Jesus Cassel*, p. 23
447 Ibid., p. 23
448 Parish Book, *Sacred Heart of Jesus Cassel*, p. 23. The CCD Program is the teaching of religion, faith, doctrines, and rites. If was offered as an out of school activity. Children and youth from the public schools had an opportunity to learn about their faith and its history. At the very beginning, the classes offered were called "Sunday School." After Sunday Mass, children attended religion instruction in church or classrooms. The teachers were priests or lay instructors. With time, these duties in the parish were taken over by volunteer teachers. Later, this program was taught during the rest of the week depending on the parish and its capabilities. Children and youth who were attending the parochial schools were exempt from the CCD Program.
449 *Jubilee 2000, Christ yesterday, today, and forever, Diocese of Superior*, p.15

TABLE 20: List of Parishes and Existence of Schools

PARISH	SCHOOL
Hatley, St. Florian	Yes
Fancher, Blessed Virgin Mary of Scapular	Yes
Belmont, St. John the Baptist	None
Mill Creek, St. Barthlolmew	None
La Crosse, Holy Cross	None
Fairfield, St. John Cantius	None
Rosholt, St. Adalbert	Yes
Centralia, Polish Church	None
Grand Rapids, St. Lawrence	Yes
Sigel, Holy Rosary	Yes
Pilot Knob, St. Methodius	None
Torun, Blessed Virgin	Yes
Lublin, St. Stanislaus	No
Pine Creek, St. Wenceslaus and Sacred Heart	Yes
Chetek, St. Boniface	None
Superior, St. Stanislaus	Yes
Ashland, Holy Family	Yes
Hurley, St. Mary's of the Seven Dolores	Yes
Strickland, Assumption of the Blessed Virgin Mary	None
Lublin, St. Stanislaus	None
Peplin, St. John the Baptist	None
North Creek, St. Michael the Archangel	Yes
Arcadia, St. Stanislaus	Yes
Weyerhaeuser, SS. Peter and Paul	Yes
Poniatowski, Holy Family	Yes
Independence, SS. Peter and Paul	Yes
Poznan (Thorp), St. Hedwig	Yes
Cassel, Sacred Heart of Jesus	Yes
Town of McMillan, St. Adalbert	None
Plover, St. Bronislava	Yes

TABLE 20: List of Parishes and Existence of Schools

Stevens Point, St. Stanislaus Kostka	Yes
Wausau, St. Michael	Yes
Junction City, St. Michael	Yes
Stevens Point, St. Peter	Yes
Polonia, Sacred Heart of Jesus	Yes
Town of Hull, St. Casimir	Yes
Stanley, St. Mary of Czestochowa	None
Bevent, St. Ladislaus	Yes

ORGANIZATIONS AND CHILDREN'S ASSOCIATIONS

Association of Scouts of America (Girls and Boys)

The founder of the scout movement was Robert Baden-Powell a long time soldier and a British general. During his military service, he noted that a very large group of soldiers blindly followed orders while a few soldiers in action showed their own initiative. He created a system of military reconnaissance which spread through the whole army of Great Britain.[450] This system provided the defense of the town of Mafeking in South Africa. He saw a huge commitment and dedication of the boys who were used for auxiliary tasks such as message delivery, care of the sick, etc. At last, he came to the conclusion that many young men fulfilled their duty better than the average soldier.

At the time, the apathy of English youth was also evident. Without ideals, they were bored and were unable to take advantage of free time. This prompted Baden-Powell to write an article in 1906 called "Scouting for Boys" which appeared in the newspaper *Boys Brigades*. This article contained basic information and assumptions of the new movement. To see whether the plan was effective, he decided to organize a camp and create a training trip. The camp ended with complete success. From the

---

450 www.scouting.org/cubscouts/aboutcubscouts/history.aspx (March 7, 2009)

twenty participants in 1906, the number of scouts had risen to 100,000 in 1910 in England.

Scouting also created great interest among girls especially after Baden-Powell's sister wrote a book about scouting for girls. In addition, Baden-Powell met Miss Olave Soames who was very enthusiastic about scouting, and several years later, they married. The Girl Scout movement was founded in 1909. Baden-Powell believed that it should be run by women, and in 1910, this was established by law. The symbol of the Girl Scouts became a golden shamrock on a blue background. These colors symbolized the summer shining over the children of the whole world, and the three petals symbolized the scout promise namely serving God, helping others, and obedience to the law.

In 1902, the United States formed a youth organization called the Association of Indian Birch Bark Forest People founded by Ernest Thompson Seton. This was the beginning of and the foundation of the Boy Scouts of America. Ernest Thompson Seton was a pioneer in the world of ecology, a natural scientist, and expert on flora and fauna. He created a program for youth in America that was inspired by the forest Indians. The program included the concept of scouting. The scouting program included several important components for young people. The education of young people in their leisure time through games and learning about the natural world was encouraged. It promoted self-discipline and service of neighbor with both built on the foundation of God's law. This movement was taken over and accepted by the Catholic Church in America. Most Catholic parishes introduced scouting programs for pastoral work.[451] These programs helped in the upbringing of children and young people by teaching them respect for God and others and by providing for the moral education of growing youth. Thus, it became very popular and became a part of parish life. Many priests became chaplains of the scouts, and scouts took an active part in the parish life. Polish parishes in the Diocese of La Crosse had numerous scout groups. These scout groups strengthened parish ties as well as had a positive effect on the morality of children and youth.

---

451   Parish Book, *St. Michael Church, Wausau Wisconsin 1887-1977*, p. 25

Catholic Youth Organization

This youth organization began its operation in the United States in the early 1930s and was known and recognized as the CYO "Catholic Youth Organization." It was created to encourage young people from high schools to be active in their own physical, spiritual, and intellectual development. During the meetings, young people focused on such topics as religion, art, and drama as well as in promoting physical fitness among youth of both sexes. Competitive sports between schools and parishes were used to stimulate the healthy spirit of young people.

In the late 1930s and the early 1940s, a new branch for the female youth was created from this organization, and it was recognized as the Young Ladies Solidarity.[452] The members of the newly formed group met once a month. The purpose of this group was to help raise money for church expenses as well as organize social events at the church.[453] This female group also hung the memory flag which was displayed in the church. On the flag were symbols of stars that represented the various providers for the youth of the parish.

ORGANIZATIONS, FRATERNITIES, AND SOCIETIES FOR ADULTS

Brotherhood of St. Peter

The foundation of every Polish parish had been societies and brotherhoods of the church. The brotherhood in the church became the heart and pulse of the parish. The members became brothers in a common faith, morality, thought, and action. Such was the Fraternity of the Brotherhood of St. Peter founded in the Parish of St. Peter in 1880. The founder was Rev. Walun. This brotherhood was developed and contin-

---

452 Parish Book, *Sacred Heart of Jesus Cassel*, p. 26
453 Parish Book, *St. Michael Wausau*, p. 23-24; Parish Book, *Sacred Heart of Jesus Cassel*, p. 26-27

ued until the early 20th century. Ordinary people including widows belonged to this fraternity. They very often collected money for the needs of the church and parish.[454]

Servers

In the early 20th century, Polish parishes in America began the custom of using adult help in the service of the altar. In some parishes, the scope of the service was increased by the possibility of distributing Holy Communion during the Mass. In addition, lay people were taking an active part in the life of the church and parish including processions. In order to be a server, one needed a mastery of Latin used during the celebration of the Mass and also knowledge of articles used during the celebration.

This practice continued until the Second Vatican Council. After the council, boys who were attending parochial schools were given permission to become active in the liturgical service of the altar. The requirements were to have received First Holy Communion and then to receive through preparation the knowledge of the liturgical actions. The server training meetings were led by the clergy.[455] In the 1980s, girls after receiving First Holy Communion received permission to become servers during the Mass. In the Polish parishes, the participants were very diverse.

The Third Order

The Third Order was formed by lay men and women. They took a very active part in the religious life of the parish, and also these people worked for the selected order. Their origin dates back to the 13th century. The reason for the creation of this order was because of the tardiness of the clergy and the often shocking and outrageous life of the clergy in Europe. It was the member's idea to somehow reform as well as help the

---

454 *Księga pamiątkowa złotego jubileuszu*, p. 18.

455 The server groups occurred in many Polish parishes. Information can be found at Parish Book, *St. Mary of Czestochowa*, p. 32, 73; Parish Book, *SS. Peter and Paul Independence 1875-1975*, p. 68; Parish Book, *St. Michael Church Wausau 1977*, p. 17; Parish Book, *History of St. Bronislava*, Wisconsin 1996, p. 33.

church rebuild its morality.[456] Pope Alexander III was the first pope to open the door to this idea of reform. He approved of the order's ideas as well as their way of proclaiming the Word of God. Some of the members of the Third Order, however, showed a lack of theology.

In 1207, Pope Innocent III ordered the members to summarize their activities and to develop common teaching points which could be passed on to their successors. Many people who belonged to the Third Order chose the path of priesthood and became priests. The rest of them were very close to the church, and they used the development program to help them preach the Word of God.

The Third Order was divided into two groups; one was the clergy who lived in societies; the second were lay people living in the secular world. The religious members took oaths while lay people made solemn promises. Once a Catholic became a member of the Third Order, he or she had to remain in that particular group and could not change from one group to another.

Ladies Scapular Society

Information on the existence of this community was found in the Parish of St. Michael in Wausau, Wisconsin. This group was organized in 1903 with forty-five members. The spiritual leader was Rev. Stanislaus Elbert. The aim of this association was to support the church in a spiritual way as well as to strengthen oneself through proper behavior and morality. This organization was for women only. This association ended in 1921.[457]

St. Isidore Society

On September 8, 1900, the older men of the Parish of the Sacred Heart of Jesus in Polonia formed a community under the patronage of St. Isidore. The purpose of this community was to offer the benefits of an insurance policy that might be needed due to an accident or death

---

[456] www.CatholicOnline (November 10, 2007), p. 1
[457] Parish Book, *St. Michael Church*, Wausau 1977, p. 28

of a member of the parish. This community tried to financially support a family in grief and mourning. The meetings were held once a year in September.[458]

Blessed Virgin Society

In the Parish of St. Michael in Wausau in 1938 this society was founded. The chairman of this society was Rev. Wojak. The aim of this society was to promote the moral principles in the parish and to educate, teach, work for, and provide charity to the members of the parish.[459]

The Parish Council of Catholic Women

In autumn 1955 this society was founded. The guardian for this society was Rev. Kluczykowski. This organization was a combination of small organizations within the parish. The society promoted the spiritual and material needs of the parish and was established based on the law of the diocese. The bishop of the Diocese of La Crosse founded the Diocesan Council of Catholic Women.[460]

Altar Society

This society was organized in the Parish of St. Peter in Stevens Point in 1937. This community established a set of rules to focus on the beauty of the church and especially the care of the altar in the church. The group was not very large but was very active. In addition, for the sanctuary of the church, the members of the group took care of the vestments, albs, and towels, and also decorated the church with flowers.[461]

---

458 Parish Book, *Sacred Heart Congregation Polonia*, p. 76
459 Parish Book, *St. Michael Church,* Wausau 1977, p. 28
460 Ibid., p. 28. The other mention of the same organization is in found in Parish Book, *SS. Peter and Paul Church Independence 1875-1975*, p. 73; Parish Book, *St. Stanislaus Catholic Church*, p. 15; Parish Book, *Parish of St. Michael of the Archangel, North Creek,* Wisconsin 1988, p. 21
461 Parish Book, *St. Peter Parish Stevens Point, Wisconsin*, Stevens Point 1976, p. 83

Third Order of St. Dominic

This was one of the oldest monasteries. The brothers who preached the Word of God represented part of the Order of Penance which was under the authority of the Dominican Order. The monks wore black and white habits. The brothers who preached the Word of God did this with love and great devotion. Their work and words were filled with the spirit of St. Francis. Their preaching of the Word of God began with encouragement and an explanation of the Word of Repentance all the while encouraging listeners to follow the path of purification. Another very important mission of theirs was to defend the Church against attacks. Later, this order worked on the publication of a prayer book. The Third Order still exists today. It is divided into two groups. The first group lives in a religious community and wears habits. The second group is made up of married people who are not religious but secular and live through the secular ideas of this order. They wear some of the symbols of the Dominican habit.

The Third Order of St. Francis

The Third Order of St. Francis was founded in the Parish of the Sacred Heart in Polonia, Wisconsin, in 1905 by Rev. Jerome Schneider, Provincial. Before the establishment, the group in the parish held a retreat in order to prepare people for this event. The aim of this group was to work for the church, to provide financial support, and to pray for seminarians in Orchard Lake, Michigan. In the beginning, this group was supported by Felician Sisters.[462] Through their meetings, assistance was implemented, and spiritual support was organized by them. The meetings always began with the Litany to St. Francis. The group consisted of more than forty members.

Holy Name Society

The main goal of this society was to make atonement for sins by using the love for the name of Holy God and Jesus Christ. Addition-

---
462   Parish Book, *Sacred Heart Congregation Polonia*, p. 71

ally, the society sought to seize and suppress any forms of swearing or perjury and to fight the effects of blasphemy. The society was established in 1274 by the Council of Lyon and has existed since that date.[463] This Council believed that all members who belonged to this society should have a special devotion to the Holy Name of Jesus. On April 13, 1564, this society was accepted and welcomed into the Church by Pope Pius IV. On May 21, 1882, the Archdiocese of New York merged all the representatives of the Holy Name of Jesus into one society. It required its members to receive Holy Communion at least once every three months. After time, the tradition was changed to require members to receive Holy Communion every second Sunday of the month. This society represented a deep love for God and steadfast respect for the name of the Lord Jesus.[464] The activities of this society were to organize the parish picnics, to organize sports competitions and events, to help organize the parish meetings, raise money for missions, and to raise money to recover lost assets of the parish.[465] In the late 1960s, this society ended its activities due to lack of interest in belonging to it.[466]

The Marian Sodality

The founder of this sodality was John Leunis who started it in 1563 with students at the Roman Jesuit College. The slogan under which the Marian Sodality was founded was, "By the love of the Blessed Mother and her faithful service, members strive to acquire outstanding progress in science and Christian virtues."[467] About seventy students founded the Congregation of the Blessed Virgin Mary of the Annunciation. In this organization, they agreed to weekly confession, to fifteen minutes of evening meditation, to examine their conscience, and to recite the rosary daily. This sodality became a force in the defense of the Catholic Church.

Pope Gregory XIII by the Bull *Omnipotentis Dei* officially approved

---

463 www.newadvent.org (December 15, 2007)
464 Parish Book, *Sacred Heart Congregation Polonia*, p. 73-74
465 Parish Book, *Sacred Heart of Jesus Cassel*, p. 25
466 Parish Book, *St. Michael Church*, p. 27; Parish Book, *St. Mary Czestochowa*, p. 42.; Parish Book, *SS. Peter and Paul Independence*, p. 72.
467 Z. Rymarówna, *Przewodnik Sodalicji Mariańskich w Polsce*, Kraków 1997, p. 17.

the Marian Sodality 1584. The Pope called for the establishment of the Roman Prima Primariae Institution (the general house) which could and should be part of an already existing sodality and also called for the future development of worldwide membership. At the turn of the 16th and beginning of the 17th centuries, numerous Marian Sodalities were established that gathered youth and adults from around the world. The Marian Sodality actively engaged in defense of the Church. It also spread the faith and provided assistance to the poor.

Pope Clement XIV dissolved the Jesuit Society in 1773. In connection with this event, the work of many sodalities was stopped. Those that remained were managed by ex-Jesuits, monks from different congregations and dioceses, or by priests. In 1814, the Congregation of Jesuits was reinstated by Pope Pius VII. In 1825, Pope Leo XII at the request of the Jesuit Society agreed to the affiliation of the Roman Prima Primariae Society of Mary that was founded outside of monasteries. Since then, the Marian Sodality has had two sources of origin: one coming from the Jesuits, the other one from the diocesan church with the responsibility of the bishop of the diocese.

The development of the Marian Sodality once again occurred after the announcement in 1854 of the Dogma of the Immaculate Conception of the Blessed Virgin Mary. Between 1855 and 1920, there were 500 sodality groups associated with the Prima Primariae. In 1904, Pope Pius X spoke to the Italian Sodality, "The Marian Sodality expects all good and is to strengthen the Church in the future."[468]

During the Nazi occupation, the Marian Sodality slowed its development while fighting for Christian Europe. When the war ended three years later in 1948, Pope Pius XII published the apostolic constitution about the Marian Sodality *Bis Saeculari*. In this document, the Pope pointed the paths of development for Marian Sodalities. Pope Pius XII approved the creation of the World Federation of the Marian Sodality. The members of these sodalities had to take care of their own moral development and cultivate devotion to Mary and the Eucharist. They had to lead charitable activities, to teach catechism, to defend the faith, and take care of neglected youth. The activities of this Marian Sodality were

---

[468] Ibid., p. 35

expressed in the slogan, *Per Mariam ad maior Dei Gloria* or through Mary to the greater glory of God.

The Marian Sodality until the mid-18th century accepted only men and boys. Later, they also began to accept women. The Marian Sodality had three levels. The first encouraged piety, participation in worship, love for God, and devotion to the Blessed Virgin Mary, the angels, and saints. The second level promoted compassion and spiritualism. The third level referred to the care of the spiritual life.[469]

Catholic Order of Foresters

In July 1879, a few members of the Society of St. Vincent Paolo from Boston, Massachusetts, established the ground work for a new Catholic organization and gave it the name of the Catholic Order of Foresters. Its main purpose was to provide insurance for people. On September 11, 1887, this organization began its activities in the state of Wisconsin.[470] The female part of this organization was formed in 1892 in Chicago. It was created in a similar way, with a low annual premium.

Surprisingly, a large amount of money was collected by this organization, and on December 31, 1908, it amounted to $27,757,000.[471] Catholics between the age of 18 and 45 were eligible for status as permanent members. The annual insurance premium for men and women was just $1.00 per year. On January 1, 1909, an official report said that this organization had 235 branches and 27,757 members including 9,679 women. In addition, the organization supported the needs of the parishes such as new stained glass windows, pews, altars, etc. This organization often worked in the parish and was run by lay people.[472]

---

[469] The information about the Marian Sodality in the Diocese of La Crosse can be found in Parish Book, *St. Michael Church, Wausau*, p. 28; Parish Book, *Sacred Heart of Jesus Cassel*, p. 24; Parish Book, *Sacred Heart Congregation, Polonia*, p. 69-70

[470] H. H. Heaming, *History of the Catholic Church in Wisconsin*, p. 1075

[471] www.catholic.org (December 15, 2007)

[472] Parish Book, *SS. Peter and Paul Independence*, p. 73; Parish Book, *Sacred Heart Congregation, Polonia*, p. 70, 72

Parish Choir

Almost all of the Polish Catholic parishes organized a parish choir which was led by a conductor. The choir was to take an active role in the Sunday liturgy, on Holy Days, and during celebrations of funerals and weddings. In Polish churches, hymns were sung in the Polish language. Masses celebrated with the participation of the choir were often attended by those Poles who wanted to remember their country of origin.[473] Choir members were required to attend weekly rehearsals. The musicians were responsible for the maintenance of their instruments and any repairs. They often engaged in collecting money and other methods in order to purchase music equipment for the parish. For example, the choir of St. Michael in North Creek toured surrounding parishes in order to raise money for the purchase of a pipe organ for the church.[474] The choir also took an active role in secular music events.[475]

Knights of Columbus

The Knights of Columbus was one of the largest Catholic fraternities forming a brotherhood organization. It was founded in 1882 in the United States. The Knights of Columbus were first registered in Green Bay, Wisconsin, on January 1, 1885.[476] The creator of the Knights of Columbus wanted to honor the name of Christopher Columbus as well as to emphasize values like fraternity, patriotism, unity, and support. It was an organization that grew to include more than 1.7 million members who were practicing Catholics. The members of this society could only be men who were faithful to the Catholic Church and were at least eighteen years old.[477]

---

[473] Parish Book, *St. Mary of Czestochowa*, p. 42

[474] Parish Book, *St. Michael the Archangel North Creek*, p. 37

[475] The examples of Polish parishes in which traditional choirs were established can be found in Parish Book, *Parish of St. Michael the Archangel North Creek*, p. 37; Parish Book, *Sacred Heart of Jesus Cassel*, p. 3; Parish Book, *St. Mary of Czestochowa*, p. 42; Parish Book, *Sacred Heart Congregation, Polonia*, p. 78-79

[476] H. H. Heaming, *History of the Catholic Church in Wisconsin*, p. 1072

[477] www.knights.com (December 14, 2007)

This organization was founded by Catholic priest Rev. Michael J. McGivney of New Haven, Connecticut. He gathered a group of men from St. Mary's Parish in New Haven and organized the first meeting on October 2, 1881. This organization was approved by state law in Connecticut on March 29, 1882. The main goal of the creator of the Knights of Columbus was that this organization would work for the common good of the parishes.

As an immigrant priest, Rev. McGivney saw what could become of families who lost the breadwinner and how important it could be to have some insurance for the family. He had the same experience when his father died, and he had to leave the seminary to work to financially support his family. Therefore, if the organization became what he wanted, the insurance would take care of the family in the event of the death of the father. The amount of the insurance paid for the loss of a breadwinner in the family could not be more than $2,000.[478] The organization developed very quickly.

This organization came to Stevens Point on November 25, 1906. At the very beginning, this group had more than 120 members in Stevens Point.[479] Later, the organization of the Knights of Columbus was accepted and began its activities in every parish in the Diocese of La Crosse including the Polish parishes.[480] Men from 18 to 50 years of age belonged to the organization.

Rosary Society

This society was comprised of members prepared to sacrifice time to pray the rosary. Fifteen women belonged to each society, and individuals prayed one mystery of the rosary. These women were expected to pray the rosary at least once a week. They had a duty of at least once a month to receive the sacrament of reconciliation, to receive Holy Communion, and after receiving Holy Communion, they had a duty to say the litany to the Blessed Virgin Mary. While praying the rosary, the fundamental mysteries

---

[478] H. H. Heaming, *History of the Catholic Church in Wisconsin*, p. 1072

[479] *A Standard History of Portage County, Wisconsin*, Chicago 1919, p. 207

[480] The information about the issue can be found in Parish Book, *St. Mary of Czestochowa*, p. 41; Parish Book, *SS. Peter and Paul Independence*, p. 70

of the Christian faith were included. It became for the members of this society an occasion to receive the blessings through the mediation of the Blessed Virgin Mary. In particular, women also prayed for Christian unity and for the extension of the Christian faith among the nations.[481]

One of the oldest Rosary Societies in the Diocese of La Crosse was the society operating at St. Casimir in Stevens Point with origins dating to 1879.[482] Besides saying the rosary, the women from this society gathered and prepared food to be distributed to the needy before Thanksgiving. They also took care of the parish kitchen by purchasing necessary equipment. They prepared the white garments for the Baptism of children which included embroidering on them. These societies very often gathered numerous groups of women.

The Parish of St. Michael in 1930 had ninety women in their society which were divided into six teams. Each team was required to pray daily one decade of the rosary.[483] Praying the rosary played an important role during difficult family events such as the death of a family member. The members of this society gathered at the home of the deceased and joined in saying the rosary. They also sang religious hymns. The family of the deceased also received a small donation with a value of $10.00. During the funeral, the members of this society formed an honor guard in the church.[484]

Catholic Daughters of America

This organization was founded in Utica, New York, on June 18, 1903.[485] The abbreviation for this organization is CDA. It was founded by John E. Carberry and several members of the Knights of Columbus as an association for women who valued the work of charity and patriotism. At the very beginning, Catholic Daughters of America had a different

---

481 *Księga pamiątkowa złotego jubileuszu*, p. 25
482 Parish Book, *St. Casimir Church*, p. 18
483 Parish Book, *St. Michael Church*, p. 28. The mentioning of the same society is also found in Parish Book, *St. Michael Church*, Wausau, p. 28.; *Księga pamiątkowa złotego jubileuszu*, p. 25.; Parish Book, *Sacred Heart of Jesus, Cassel*, p. 24.; Parish Book, *St. Mary of Czestochowa*, p. 40-41; Parish Book, *SS. Peter and Paul Church Independence. 1875-1975*, p. 75; Parish Book, *Sacred Heart Congregation Polonia*, p. 66
484 Parish Book, *Sacred Heart of Jesus Cassel*, p. 24
485 B. L. Marthaler, C. D. Klement, *Catholic Daughters of the Americas*, New York 2003, p. 9

name. The group was called the National Association of the Daughters of Isabella with a motto of unity and charity. In 1908, CDA had ninety registered unions and more than 10,000 members. This association grew rapidly and became so strong and resilient that it was very visible during World War I as charity organizations hurried to assist the victims of the war. The members of this association were very often active nurses who also offered spiritual care, engaged in sewing and repairing warm clothing, and were also very active in the Red Cross. They helped the Knights of Columbus to raise $3 million dollars to benefit the wounded soldiers.

At the 1921 convention, the name was changed from Catholic Daughters of Isabella to the Catholic Daughters of America. Already in 1928, the organization had more than 170,000 members. This organization with time changed their focus and their own profile. CDA became active in missionary work, in strengthening the influences of the Catholic press, and it became committed to social issues and even literacy. When World War II started, CDA again responded by collecting money for family needs during this difficult period. This organization developed in the parishes and became very important in strengthening parish works offered to the needy.[486]

Parent-Teacher Association

This association was founded at Sacred Heart Parish School in Polonia in February 1964 by Rev. J. Schulist. It aimed to develop cooperation between teachers and parents in children's education.[487]

Athletic Association

This association was founded in the Parish of St. Peter in Stevens Point in 1951. This group worked at the parish school to create an exercise program for the young people. Its purpose was to promote the idea that sports contribute to a healthy lifestyle and the spirit of competition.[488]

---

[486] Detailed information about this organization can be found in Parish Book, *St. Michael Church Wausau*, p. 28.; Parish Book, *St. John Cantius 1887 Centennial 1987*, p. 10; Parish Book, *Sacred Heart of Jesus Cassel*, p. 24

[487] Parish Book, *Sacred Heart Congregation, Polonia*, p. 80

[488] Parish Book, *St. Peter Parish in Stevens Point, Wisconsin*, p. 112

Press

In American history, there was a highly visible presence of Poles in the media. The Polish Press played a very important role. From 1863 to 1950 in America, there were more than 600 Polish newspapers and magazines (some in both Polish and English) in publication.[489] The history of the Polish Press in Wisconsin dates back to the very beginning of the settlement of Polish immigrants. Each year, Portage County received new Polish immigrants. They settled themselves and created a very strong ethnic group and only spoke Polish. The Polish settlers who inhabited this area seldom met because they worked so hard and therefore lacked free time. But they wanted to receive information from Poland where there often remained a large part of their family, former neighbors, and friends. In order to help Polish settlers in obtaining information about their homeland as well as to better organize their stay in the Wisconsin, Portage County began publishing newspapers containing information from Poland during the second half of the 19th century.

Initially, they were printed in English. However, this caused many difficulties for Polish immigrants who did not always know English well. They often worked hard on the land or in the woods as it was sometimes the only means of providing their families with a decent existence. Therefore, they did not have enough time for the study of English. The first newspaper in Portage County was *Wisconsin Pinery*. The first copy was issued in 1853 and printed in English. The first Polish newspaper was *Gwiazda Polarna* which was printed beginning in 1872 in Stevens Point. In 1874, this paper was discontinued.

Another weekly Polish newspaper issued in Stevens Point was *Rolnik*.[490] This newspaper was published in the years 1891 to 1960. The editors of this newspaper from 1892 to 1900 were Zigmunt Hunter and T. Krutza. In the years 1900 to 1903, the editor was Viktor Karlowicz. The main editors during 1903 to 1924 were Stephen and Joseph H. Worzalla. In the years 1924 to 1955, the editors were Walter S. Worzalla

---

489 T. Polzin, *The Polish Americans*, Pulaski, Wisconsin 1973, p. 152-153

490 J. Rokicki, *Blednące światło „Gwiazdy": tygodnik Polonii amerykańskiej „Gwiazda Polarna" i jego czytelnicy w świetle badań ankietowych*, in *Zeszyty Prasoznawcze* (147-148) 1996, No. 3-4, p. 124; W. Kruszka, *A History of the Poles*, p. 15

and Paweł Klimowicz. Later in the period 1955 to 1960, the newspaper editor was Adam Bartosz. In this newspaper was information important to the Polish community as well as some educational content. The circulation of the weekly newspaper in Portage County was 5,000 papers.[491]

In Stevens Point in 1892, a printing company was founded that published Polish language newspapers, books, prayer books, and religious pictures. The company was founded by brothers Joseph and Stephen Worzalla. The same printer in 1898 again started to publish *Gwiazda Polarna*,[492] the first Polish language newspaper printed since 1872. The newspaper was brought back to be printed again in Polish.[493] This newspaper continues to be published in Polish under the same title today.

Other Polish language newspapers printed in the state of Wisconsin for a short period of time were *Jaskółka* printed from 1930-1935 and *Słoneczko* a newspaper dedicated to children published from 1938-1940. Both of these newspapers were published in Stevens Point at the Polish company owned by Worzalla.

---

[491] Albert Hart Sanford, "Polish People of Portage County," in *Polish Genealogical Society Newsletter*, Spring 1989, p. 7-28, Stevens Point Wisconsin, p. 14. There is a difference as to the amount of printing of *Rolnik* in the item of J. Rokicki, *Blednące światło „Gwiazdy"*, p. 124-136. The author mentioned that the printing company had its weekly circulation of 3000 newspapers.

[492] J. Rokicki, *Blednące światło „Gwiazdy"*, p. 124-136

[493] M. J. Goc, *Native Realm*, p. 154

CHAPTER VII

NON-ROMAN CATHOLIC RELIGIOUS COMMUNITIES LOCATED IN POLISH COMMUNITIES (DIOCESE OF LA CROSSE)

The Polish National Catholic Church

The Catholic historian John Tracy Ellis described the Polish National Catholic Church (PNCC) as the only major schism of the Catholic Church in America.[494] The church currently has 250 parishes in the United States, Canada, Poland, and Brazil. The schism originated with the Poles in America. In the mid-1890s in Scranton, Pennsylvania, the Independent National Catholic Church was founded. There in the Church of St. Stanislaus in March 1897 was celebrated the first Mass by Rev. Francis Hodur.[495] This schism began because of conflicts between Polish immigrants and the hierarchy of the Catholic Church in America because the Polish parishes were often sent priests who did not know the Polish language. The language used during the Masses was Latin and English which the majority of the Polish community did not understand. Intervention from the bishop of the dioceses did not bring intended results and only deepened misunderstandings and suspicions. Rev. Francis Hodur as a representative of Polish Catholics in America went to Rome to present the problems and attempt to find a solution for them. However, he failed to get support from Rome. He also at the end of that same year was suspended by the Catholic Church.

---

[494] J. S. Pula, *Polish Americans: an ethnic community*, p. 39
[495] J. A. Wytrwal, *The Poles in America*, p. 5

Rev. Hodur then rejected part of the tradition of the Church and some of its dogmas. He had rejected the hierarchy of the Catholic Church. In its place, he installed his own. He changed the language in the liturgy from Latin to Polish and also changed the liturgical calendar. Rev. Francis Hodur during the general synod in 1904 was elected bishop. The church then was characterized as a "Republican Church" in comparison to the "Monarchal" Catholic Church.[496] This was due to the earlier events and the incompetent decision of the American episcopate. In 1896 in Buffalo, New York, the first congress of the Polish Catholic Church was held. It took place under the leadership of Rev. John Picasso. The congress discussed both the risk and also the possibilities for development of the Polish Church in America. This meeting, however, did not produce the desired results. In 1901, another meeting was called at the same place in Buffalo, but as with the previous meeting, issues raised during the congress remained unresolved. A decision was then made to send a delegation to Rome.

In 1903, Rev. W. Kruszka and Rev. R. Mahaney went to Rome to meet the pope and to resubmit to the Holy Father the petitions, rights, and the needs that represented the Polish Church in America. The pope sent Archbishop Albina Symona to investigate the matter. The Polish Catholic Church authorities presented a proposal that the Poles have a representative in America at the episcopate with the rank of bishop. The pope realized that the immigrants in America were not only German and Irish. He recognized that there was also a great number of Polish immigrant Catholics in the Church, and he understood their needs. But instead of appointing a Polish bishop, in 1908 Rev. Paul Rhode became bishop of Chicago. The Polish Catholic Church was not impressed with this decision. Rev. Kruszka and other priests did not express great satisfaction or gratitude with this appointment.

At the same time, Rev. Hodur organized new parishes of the PNCC, and the number of believers in this church began to grow. By September 1904, the PNCC had twenty-four parishes and more than 20,000 members in five states.[497] In the territory of the Diocese of La Crosse

---

496   J. S. Pula, *Polish Americans: an ethnic community*, p. 44
497   J. A. Wytrwal, *The Poles in America*, p. 50

were several parishes of the Polish National Catholic Church. Some of them still exist and operate today. These churches were referred to as the Polish "Independent" Catholic Church.

Wherever the parish church was established as "Independent", the bishop of the diocese ordered the establishment of a Roman Catholic parish nearby. As an example, an "Independent" parish was established in Thorp. This provoked Bishop Schwebach to also establish the Parish of St. Hedwig Roman Catholic Church. A similar example involves the little town of Lublin which also built two churches. The Roman Catholic Church and the National Church were built and established as two parishes, the Polish National and the Roman Catholic. In addition, in Lublin the Parish of the Orthodox Church was also established.[498]

Polish Orthodox Church

As stated above, in the small town of Lublin in the Diocese of La Crosse, we can also find a Polish Orthodox Church. Its origin dates back to the 19th century. Immigrants began to arrive from the southeastern part of Galicia. After settling, they quickly organized their own parish. The founders and organizers of the parish were Daniel Majkowicz, Theodore and Simeon Dubiak, Stefan Lencz, Harry Kucynda, Elias Koruc, Wasyl Kowalkiewicz, Timko Hnat, Stefan Knahan, Timko Kon, Sylvester Pogar, Ambrose Peleschak, Andrew Bahur, Josafat Sweda, and Theodore Polonczak. They erected a small chapel on two acres of land which was donated by Marion Durski. The chapel was built and dedicated to St. Dimitros and was completed in 1908. Each of the parishioners tried to help either through financial support or by providing physical assistance. Over the next five years, the chapel became too small because a very large group of Orthodox immigrants had arrived and settled in this area. To accommodate all the faithful, it was necessary to make this church at least two times larger. Between 1908 and 1917, the church was under the care of a priest from Minneapolis who traveled back and forth on a temporary basis. In 1918, the parish received a permanent priest who also served in the parish church of St. John in Huron. Many

---
498   www.rootsweb.com/Lublin History (September 18, 2008), p. 8

vestments and religious items of the church used for the liturgy were imported from Russia.[499] The parish also built a school. In the 1920s and 1930s, the parish priest taught reading, writing, and singing in Russian. However, over time, this language was replaced by English.

Polish Independent National Church

In early 1872, one of the first Polish Independent parishes in America was established in Ellis, Wisconsin. The parish was also called "The Red Church"[500], because of its red roof. This congregation was located three miles from Polonia. The church had two towers resembling bony arms reaching toward heaven.[501] A rectory was constructed next to the church. These buildings were not very impressive. This small community located near Stevens Point was called "Polish Corner" because of the Polish immigrants who had settled there. This uproar occurred at "Polish Corner" between a few, unhappy inhabitants of Polish and German origin. Into this complicated situation, Rev. J. Frydrychowicz was welcomed with open arms. He had arrived from Texas where one year before, he had been excommunicated from the Polish-Czech mission in Mulberry, Texas.

The cause of the uproar was the reluctance of Bishop John Melcher of the Diocese of Green Bay and local priests to understand the problem faced in this community. The Polish settlers felt insulted and could not accept the situation of bars and stores being open on Sundays. They felt that customers after spending considerable time in the establishments were unable or unwilling to leave. They forgot about church, family, and visiting friends and were spending hard-earned money on alcohol. The situation between the bar and store owners and Bishop Melcher and Rev. Dąbrowski was tense. The owners of the businesses went to court accusing the church of conspiracy and financial damage to their businesses. The owners lost their case, and only envy and hatred remained.[502]

To resolve this problem, the suspended priest Rev. J. Frydrychowicz

---

499   www.rootsweb.com/Lublin History (September 18, 2008)
500   www.pchswi.org/archives/polish_heritage/soroka_pages_52_59.html
501   W. Kruszka, *A History of the Poles. Part 4*, p. 15
502   www.pchswi.org/archives/communities/polonia.html (July 16, 2008)

along with a group of unhappy parishioners decided to build a church and rectory. The construction of the church and rectory was completed quickly. A portion of the rectory was used for a school.

On May 9, 1874, the founder of this church, Rev. Frydrychowicz died during choir practice. In retrospect, a few priests who knew him felt that something bad had occurred which changed him. During his journey from Texas to Wisconsin, Rev. Frydrychowicz stopped in Chicago and visited Rev. Bakanowski. Rev. Bakanowski described his friend as one who lost his soul and had probably done something wrong.

After the death of Rev. J. Frydrychowicz, Rev. Funken from the Church of St. Agatha in Canada on May 9, 1874, wrote a letter to General Peter Semenenko of the Order of Resurrection. He wrote, "Rev. Frydrychowicz, who died, administered at the parish in Wisconsin without permission and the blessings of the bishop. During choir practice, he collapsed and died without reconciliation with God. After his death, his face became black and he was buried not far from this church."[503] His successor was another suspended priest Rev. Hulewic whose life was scandalized. Because of this situation, many of the ardent parish supporters left the church and returned to the Sacred Heart Parish in Polonia. Only six families decided to stay with the Independent Church which did not have much influence on the settlers in this area. This church functioned until 1894. The abandoned buildings remained until 1918 when the decision was made to use the wood in building the school at St. Stanislaus Parish in Stevens Point.

---

503 W. Kruszka, *A History of the Poles. Part 4*, p. 16

SUMMARY

Pope John Paul II said, "A nation that forgets its history is doomed." In interpreting the words of the Holy Father, we can say that everything that brings us closer to understanding our existence of who we are and where we should go – that is to discover our identity as individuals and as a nation – all this is worth the effort. Any work connected with this, and any search is never a waste of time. Each nation should honor and respect its past and see to it that the memory of her be continued. A nation should care about the culture, the richness of its language, art, science, faith, and traditions – all that constitutes its identity and what should be passed on to the next generation to continue that identity.

In this book, the story is told about specific people who built and created Polish parishes in the Diocese of La Crosse in Wisconsin in the period from 1868 to 2000. It shows how people were forced because of various factors to leave their homeland in search of a better future for themselves and their families. Once they made up their minds to find their place in the new land, their journey was accompanied by difficulties and adversities, joys and sorrows. One of the primary goals of Polish immigrants was related to preserving their future with faith. Many difficulties were encountered in building new temples and in trying to make this part of their heritage and identity.

Motives for Immigration

Poland was divided by three invaders: Prussia, Austria, and Russia and had a very diverse political situation. Occupants more or less continuously pursued a policy of denaturalization. That was the most important factor causing the emigration of Poles to the United States of America. Poles fighting to preserve their identity were often forced to leave their homeland. Another factor that prompted immigration was the difficult economic situation at home. To maintain their family and provide for a better future, many Poles were forced to leave the country.

Life in Immigration

The life of Polish immigrants was characterized by dependency and deep attachment to religious values. A community of Polish immigrants settling in the state of Wisconsin would be characterized by:

- Perseverance and cooperation in settling in and creating new communities.
- Support for each other materially and spiritually.
- Deep faith and devotion to the Catholic Church.
- Building their own temple and then requesting the local bishop assign a pastor.
- A high level of moral life. This was manifested by respect for families, the elderly, and with other co-inhabitants.
- Attachment to the traditions of their fathers and respect for the earth. The land was "family nursing" something for which you should care and have concern. In their homes, the immigrants cultivated and maintained the religious, wedding, and holiday traditions brought from their native country.
- Profound patriotism. Their lives were entwined with their faith, their homeland, and family they left in Poland. Poles sought printed Polish newspapers and books in which they found information about their home country. Special patriotic ceremonies and presentations were organized for various historic Polish anniversaries.

Poles and Changes

The adaption of Polish immigrants to the frequently changing territorial limits of American Dioceses was sometimes very difficult. Boundaries of the dioceses were redistributed several times. For example, the boundaries of the Diocese of La Crosse were changed twice after its founding in 1868. In the year 1905 and 1946, Polish immigrants who had settled in Wisconsin passed from the jurisdiction of one diocese to another. This situation very often introduced chaos and contributed to the breakdown of Polish immigrant communities.

Clergy

The Polish clergy working among the Polish immigrants in the Diocese of La Crosse met with many problems. The Polish clergy who came to this new land could not always find their way in this new environment due to the different styles of pastoral ministry operating in America. Secondly, the lack of knowledge of the English language often meant that Polish clergy were discriminated against or treated as inferior within the diocesan structure.

Female Religious Congregations

The role of female congregations in the Polish communities in the Diocese of La Crosse was very significant. The nuns came to America to assist immigrants and to help organize the parish school system. The interest of female congregations was education. The nuns became teachers and educators. Nuns made a remarkable contribution in the development of American education. They lived in parishes and later created small religious communities.

Polish Religious Traditional Customs

In America, cultivating Polish religious and folk customs was very important to everyday life. One of many practices common only among Polish immigrants was the erecting of crosses and small roadside shrines. At various times during the calendar year and the liturgical calendar of the Church, nearby residents would gather in common prayer at the shrines. Roadside crosses reminded people of the presence of God and inclined individuals to meditate when passing them in a very special way. Polish immigrants celebrated religious events in their families at Christmas, Lent, Easter, and Corpus Christi. Celebrations were held for various saints and patrons of the church. Customs such as the decorating of churches, shrines, and houses at Christmas and Easter; the singing of carols; and participating in Lenten Stations of the Cross while singing "Gorzkie żale" (Bitter Laments) were observed.

Ethnics Antagonisms

Disagreements with other ethnic nationalities were a daily occurrence. Many problems emerged especially in relations with Germans. The Polish immigrants did not like groups of Germans and had a lot of misunderstandings with them. These misunderstandings were brought from Poland. Separation and isolation between the two was obvious. The same situation appeared between the Poles and Irish with one difference: the antagonisms came from positions which were taken by Irish people. The Irish had a great advantage because of their knowledge of English.

Schools

Schools played a huge role in the life of the parish and parish community. They were often built next to the parish church as a result of contributions and the generosity of parishioners. The school became a place of learning but was also a place where traditions were nurtured, native language was supported, and good manners were emphasized. In school, students were taught religion, history, geography, mathematics, and the Polish language. A little later, they began to learn the elements of the English language. The school building was also used for social functions and various meetings. The schools were used by organizations to raise money for a variety of purposes and for meetings of various associations and groups that were active in the church.

Parish Groups, Associations, and Societies

An important role in Polish parishes was filled by societies and parish organizations. There were strict religious groups as a liturgical service, servers, as well as secular organizations such as scouting. For the youth, there were different associations for sporting activities. Adults could join societies that were devoted to prayer and charity. The main goal of these societies was to promote morality in the families that belonged to the parish.

Polish Press

In the life of Polish immigrants, the Polish Press played a very significant role. It informed them about the situation in Poland as well as current issues in the environment in which they now lived.

Schism

The uprising in the Polish community caused the creation of the Polish National Catholic Church and had wide repercussions across America. The uprising was due to the reluctance of the United States representatives of the Church to have constructive dialogue with the Polish community. In the early 19th century, the National Church wanted their faithful to be able to pray in their own native language. At that time, the idea was condemned by the hierarchy of the American Church. Later, it was developed by the Second Vatican Council and adopted worldwide by the Catholic Church.

In the history of Wisconsin, Poles were known as a solid people who were deeply religious and hardworking. Their hard work, deep faith, and tolerance earned the respect and esteem of others. The Poles showed that you can live anywhere and remain faithful to God, your homeland, and yourself.

Finally, I would like to quote the poem "To the Young" written by Adam Asnyk and published in 1880. Here are some verses that in my opinion deserve attention because they perfectly reflect the Polish immigration.

( ) Every era has its own objectives
It forgets yesterday's dreams…
So bear the torch of knowledge at the fore front
And participate in a new share eras' lore,
Futures' raise large building!
But do not trample past the altar,

*Even though you would think you can build a perfect one,
On them the sacred fire glows,
And love the human standing there on guard,
And you owe them the honor!
With the world which already occurs in the dark
With the whole rainbow in perfect dreams,
May the true wisdom reconcile them
And your stars, a winner of the young,
In the darkness they die out again.*

APPENDIX (1)

DIRECTORY OF CLERGY IN THE DIOCESE OF LA CROSSE IN THE YEARS 1868-1968[504] AND TO 2000[505]

1903
John L Brudermans

1914
Francis Brzostowicz
Stanislaus Lapinski
John J. Rolbiecki

1915
Willibald Hackner

1916
Hilary Leuther

1918
Edmund Cramer
Leo J. Lang
William Muehlenkamp
Paul Pitzenberger
Aloys Zinthefer

1919
Charles W. Gille
S. A. Krakowiecki
Stephan Mieczkowski
Rudolph Raschke

1920
Joseph Eisenmann

1921
Thomas E. O'Shaughnessy

1922
Herbert Hoffman
J. J. Sheridan

1923
Joseph B. Cysewski
L. Paschal Hirt
Paul Monarski
Alphonse N. Schuh

1924
Victor Plecity

---

504 G. E. Fisher, *Dusk is my Dawn*, p. 204-207

505 G. E. Fisher, *257 Things You Should Know About the Diocese of La Crosse 1868-1993*, Stevens Point, Wisconsin 1993

1926
Owen Mitchell John Pinion

1927
Arthur Cramer
Oscar Cramer
John Pittz

1928
William Daniels
Gerald Schuh
Francis Wallaca

1929
Urban J. Baer
Alvin J. Daul
Anthony W. Fischer
Nicholas E. Kreibich
Joseph F. Kundinger
Francis Mulligan
Vincent J. Peters
Leonard G. Stieber

1930
J. Francis Brady
Bernard Duffy
George R. Hardy

1931
Le Roy B. Keegan
John T. Murphy
John J. Pritzl

1932
Hugh J. Deeny
Roman Kirin

Louis J. Paquette
Peter F. Rombalski
Edward J. Roskosz

1933
Nicholas B. Beschta
Charles D. Brady
Hugo J. Diers
Francis S. Disher
Norbert E. King
Edwin L. Knauf
Philip T. Weller
Peter Zic

1934
Edmund G. Bettinger
Francis (Frank) C. Brickl [506]
Clarence P. Dais
James D. Geyer
Francis Knopp
Vincent E. Schwartz
Anthony J. Thuecks
La Vern H. Timmerman
Joseph Udulutch

1935
Paul A. Dockendorff
Hugo C. Koehler
Thomas E. Mullen
Robert J. Oberwinder
Joseph J. Schulist
Rudolph Urbic

---

506 Gerald E. Fisher, Rev., *257 Things You Should Know About the Diocese of La Crosse 1868-1993*, Stevens Point, Wisconsin 1993. The name in parentheses differs from the name listed in the *Dusk is my Dawn* book.

1936
John J. Agnew
Stephen Anderl
Stanislaus A. Andrzejewski (Andrzewjewski)[507]
Francis J. Brockman
Louis J. Clarke
Robert E. McCarthy
Francis A. Piekarski

1937
Aloysius F. Baumann
Walter J. Brey
Angelo J. Comoretto
George P. Mathieu
William L. Mooney
Raymond B. Schulz

1938
Ralph J. Geissler
Emil Hodnik
Garlan J. Muller
John F. Nowak
Albin P. Schreier

1939
John J. Cullinan
Phillip L. Daul
Joseph J. Gavin
Leander A. Koopman
Philip Leinfelder
Joseph W. Tetzlaff
Charles P. Wolf
Anthony Zvinklys

1940
Charles A. Blecha
Hubert L. Crubel
Thomas J. Halloran
Robert H. Hansen
Bernard F. Henry
John J. Krasowski
Daniel J. O'Reilly
Roman J. Papiernik
Thaddeus P. Szczerbicki
Chester A. Zieliński
Francis W. Zoll

1941
Raymond H. Bornbach
Joseph L. Brake
Jacob J. Burggraf
Walter J. Dillenburg
Thomas F. Hayden
Ernest J. Kaim
Bernard T. Kelly
Edward A. Masalewicz
Albert P. Roemer

1942
Clair P. Cooney
Paul N. Flad
Lloyd F. Geissler
Alfred F. Herbert
Jerome J. Kamla
Sigismund R. Lengowski
Francis I. Przybylski
Donald J. Theisen
Joseph M. Wagner

---

507   Ibid.

1943
Robert E. Agnew
Robert K. Cosgrove (J. Kelly Cosgrove)[508]
Dominic P. Eichman
Henry R. Hoerburgar
Edwin B. Klimasiewski (Klimaszewski)[509]
Pater J. Leketas
Francis M. Lestinsky
George M. Nelson
John J. Paul
Raymond H. Rucki
Hilary F. Simmons
Carl A. Wohlmuth

1944
Cletus L. Abts
Francis J. Grassl
Richard J. Hermann
John Patrick Trant

1945
Joseph N. Bach
Andrew H. Bofenkamp
Peter J. Butz
Eugene A. Comiskey (Cominskey)[510]
Robert V. Connolly
Norbert P. Dall

Carl J. Dockendorff
Joseph B. Ferron
Edward F. Hartung
Alfred Hemmersbach
Charles H. Herbers
Michael G. Mertens
Oswald W. Schulte
Edward J. Sobczyk
Augustine J. Sulik

1946
Anton L. Lecheter (Lecheler)[511]

1947
Donald M. Berg
Stanley J. Chilicki
Peter A. Eiden
James P. Finucan
Patrick J. Hollern
Joseph B. Marx
Chester B. Moczarny
Raymond W. Peters
Richard O. Rossiter
Bernard G. Schreiber
Anthony P. Wagener

1948
James Floyd Dwyer
Stanislaus Krupa
Francis V. McCaffrey
William V. Nikolai
Charles P. Schumacher
Alois D. Sherfinski

---

508 Gerald E. Fisher, Rev., *257 Things You Should Know About the Diocese of La Crosse 1868-1993*, Stevens Point, Wisconsin 1993. The name in parentheses differs from the name listed in the *Dusk is my Dawn* book.
509 Ibid.
510 Ibid.

511 Ibid.

1949
Donald J. Boyarski
Bernard O. McGarty
Matthew J. Molinaro
Chester P. Osowski
Robert D. Platt
Paul B. Schmitt
Norbert J. Wilder (Wilger)[512]

1950
John E. Brey
Constant E. Chilicki
James E. Ennis
Jerome G. Gerum
Joseph A. Grassl
John N. Manet (Mauel)[513]
Eugene P. Smith
Albert I. Thomas
Joseph A. Walijewski
Carroll Walljepcer (Walljasper)[514]

1951
Gerald E. Fisher
John I. Nilles
Thomas J. Reardon
Edwin J. Stanek
George A. Stashek
Edwin J. Thome
Herbert P. Zoromski

1952
Eugene P. Brennan
Henry J. Cassidy
Francis A. Heindl
Joseph N. Henseler
Thomas J. Mannion
James F. Murphy
Bernard J. Nowak
James F. O'Connell
Bernard J. Quint
Arnold F. Reuter
Francis P. Rushman
Richard S. Tomsyck
Raymond J. Wagner
Raymond A. Wozniak (Aloysius)

1953
George A. Becker
James E. Coke
George W. Hinger
Edmund J. Klimek
Jemes G. Landy
Jemes R. Lane
John E. Malik
William T. Rorke
John D. Rossiter
Francis Wavra

1954
William J. Buchman
John H. Hodges
Andrew K. Karoblis
Henry H. Lee
James C. McDonald
Myron J. Meinen
Robert F. Perkins

---
512 Ibid.
513 Ibid.
514 Ibid.

1955

Jeremiah Cashman
Thomas F. Dempsey
Emmeff N. Faber
James J. Falcone (Falconer)[515]
J. Thomas Finucan
Thomas F. Garthwaits (Garthwaite)[516]
Francis E. Hillesheim
John J. Lemke
John W. Puerner
Arthur S. Redmond
Norman R. Senski
Mark A. Wailjasper (Walljasper)[517]
Frederic W. Wirts

1956

James A. Barney
James Bertrand
James P. Binkowski
Thomas F. Crowley
Robert S. Hegenbarth
Daniel J. Kelly
Thomas E. Langer
James E. Lovejoy
Robert H. McKillip
Thomas E. McNamara
Patrick J. O'Lenny
Raymond J. Pedretti

Edward J. Penchi
Joseph J. Rafacz
Albert W. Sonnberger
Leonard C. Stashek
Richard A. Wisnewiki (Wisnewski)[518]

1957

John B. Curtiss
Robert W. Greatorex
Robert B. Houston
Joseph R. Keating
Thomas J. McInnis
George C. Passehl
Albert A. Raschke
Robert J. Wagner
Donald F. Wilger
John A. Wisneski (Wineski)[519]

1958

Eugene F. Berthiaume
Mark A. Doyle
James J. Hagmann
Leonard G. Kaiser (Roman F. Kaiser[520])
Richard F. Keegan
Charles E. Leisle
Delbert J. Malin
Bernard L. Raschke
Hilary F. Seubert
Leon R. Tice

---

515 Gerald E. Fisher, Rev., *257 Things You Should Know About the Diocese of La Crosse 1868-1993*, Stevens Point, Wisconsin 1993. The name in parentheses differs from the name listed in the *Dusk is my Dawn* book.
516 Ibid.
517 Ibid.
518 Ibid.
519 Ibid.
520 Ibid.

1959
William J. Blazewicz
James P. Eron
Thomas James Etten
Ambrose J. Follmar
Frederick A. Kulovits
James J. Lodzinski
James J. Logan
Paul L. Sankooriakal
Dennis P. Stanchik
James F. Stauber

1960
John Kipp
Joseph M. Martinson
Roy L. Mish
Lyle L. Schulte
Thomas J. Smith
Joseph R. Sullivan
David A. Ziegelmaier

1961
Steven Boehrer
Michael Charles Braun
Patrick T. Devine
Robert Peter Hundt
William J. Jablonske
Michael T. McKenna
John Allan Melloh
Robert Matthew Monti
Thomas John Rudolph
James Francis Schaefer
Terrance M. Schelble

1962
Robert T. Altmann
Ambrose J. Blenker
Norman J. Boneck
Vaughn W. Brockman
David Gilles
Charles J. Hiebl
Paul Servais

1963
Edmund J. Doerre
David J. Dresen
Jerome G. Hoeser
Jerome Kirsling
Donald Klauke
Eugene A. Klink
William Matzek
Donald J. Walczak
Eugene J. Wolf

1964
William N. Grevatch
Paul Kaiser
James J. Lesczynski
Robert F. Pedretti
Daniel Ritter
Lawrence Zawadski

1965
Robert J. Cook
John L. Heagle
Robert J. Kampine
Charles H. Major
John A. Schultz

1966
Thomas J. Abraham
Lawrence B. Berger

Joseph J. Bilgrien
Robert A. Brezinski
Richard L. Fliss
Stephen F. Gross
Dennis W. Rader
John A. Schultz

1967
Joseph M. Irvin
Patrick G. Kelley
James E. Mason
William G. Menzel
William P. Neis
John E. Olson
Rex A. Zimmerman

1968
Thomas J. Donaldson
Jerrol J. Leitner
Dennis J. Lynch
Richard J. Malak
James H. Miller

1969
John V. Cassidy
Robert A. Streveler

1970
R. John Swing

1971
James W. Genovesi
Michael J. Lynch
Leon A. Powell

1972
Daniel E. Kozlowski

1973
John P. Hogan
Wayne R. Kidd
James P. McNamee
Allan L. Slowiak

1974
John W. Beckfelt
Donald L. Przybylski
John W. Steiner

1975
Raymond L. Burke
Allen F. Jakubowski

1977
Robert W. Nelson

1978
Bruce E. Ball
Joseph Diermeier
Lawrence G. Dunklee
Thomas M. Oneill
John L. Parr
George R. Szews

1979
Varkey V. Velickakathu

1980
Michael J. Gorman
Raymond J. Kaluzny
David C. Kunz

Christopher W. Pratt
Charles D. Stoetzel
Patrick A. Umberger

1981
William P. Felix
Mark R. Pierce

1982
Steven J. Brice
Robert H. Flock
Joseph R. Konopacky

1983
Steven H. Baures
Leo J. Schneider

1984
Donald J. Meuret
Roger J. Scheckel

1985
Frank Corradi
Thomas J. Steinert

1986
Alan T. Burkhardt
Daniel B. DuChez
Joseph W. Hirsch
John S. La Porte

1987
Robert A. Schaller

1989
Kevin C. Louis

1990
Randy E. Olson
Edward J. Shuttleworth

1991
Daniel J. Kiedinger
G. Richard Roberts

1992
Thomas J. Krieg

1993
Richard C. Dickman
Paul R. Gitter
John T. McHugh

1994
Richard W. Gilles

1995
Steven J. Kachel
Thomas F. Lindner
Woodrow F. Pace

1996
Eric R. Berns
Douglas C. Robertson
James F. Trempe
Anthony J. Wolf

1998
Scott A. Bauer
Jeffrey D. Burrill
Daniel H. Farley
Brian D. Konopa
Todd A. Mlsna

David P. Olson

1999

Keith B. Apfelbeck
Kurt J. Apfelbeck
James T. Benzmiller
Brian J. Jazdzewski
Sebastian J. Kolodziejczyk
Samuel A. Martin
John A. Potaczek
Robert C. Thorn

2000

Michael E. Klos
Eric G. Linzmaier

APPENDIX (2)

INTERVIEW WITH REV. JOSEPH RAFACZ, PASTOR OF ST. AGNES PARISH, WESTON, WISCONSIN, CONDUCTED ON DECEMBER 24, 2008

Q. When did you begin your career as a professor at the seminary in the Diocese of La Crosse, and how long did you teach in the seminary?

A. I was ordained in 1956, and soon afterwards I began teaching at the seminary. I taught there until the seminary was closed in 1968.

Q. What were the subjects that you taught?

A. I taught English, Latin, and Greek.

Q. How many students did you teach and how many of them were in the seminary?

A. There were about 300 students. They were two years on the level of high school and two years on the level of college.

Q. How many priests have taught in the seminary?

A. There were eighteen teachers, and together we created a very good group of professors.

Q. How many professors taught in the seminary that were of Polish origin?

A. There were a few of Polish origin, perhaps two or three, and several who had Polish roots. The names of these priests I do not remember.

Q. Could you tell the difference between students from different backgrounds with different roots of origin?

A. There were differences, but we all tried to create a community.

Q. How many hours did you teach per day?
A. We taught three hours per day.

Q. What was the agenda in the seminary?
A. Morning Mass, breakfast followed by prayers, classes began at 8:30 in the morning.

Q. Did they wear cassocks in the seminary?
A. Yes, until the Second Vatican Council.

Q. How many years did the seminarians have to study to be ordained to the priesthood?
A. Two years of high school, two years of college, and two years of theology, usually in Milwaukee.

Q. How many students continued until ordination?
A. I would say half reached the priesthood.

Q. What amount of vacation did the seminarians have and of that time how much had to be spent at the parish practicing?
A. Summer which was between early June and September generally was free of studying for seminarians. At this time, retreats were organized for the priests and seminarians, and the seminarians served.

Q. When was the seminary closed and what was the reason?
A. The seminary was closed in 1968 due to the small number of vocations.

APPENDIX (3)

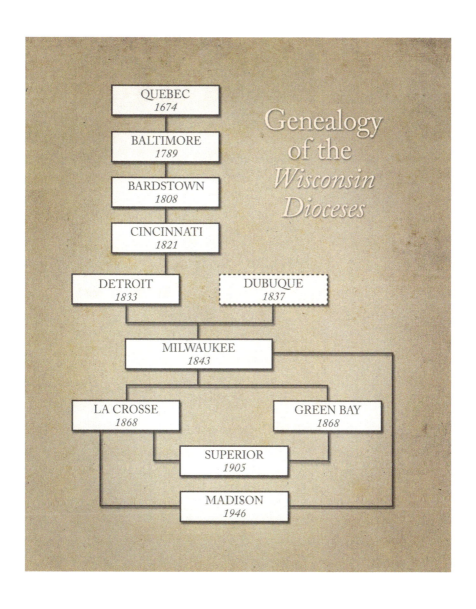

APPENDIX (4)

APPENDIX (5)

APPENDIX (6)

APPENDIX (7)

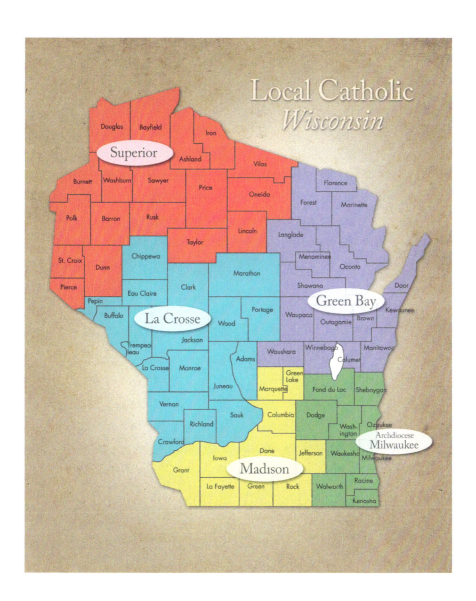

BIBLIOGRAPHY

A Standard History of Portage County Wisconsin, Chicago 1919

Allen, M. L., "A Polish Pioneer's Story," *Wisconsin Magazine of History*, Vol. 6:1923

Aubert, R. P., Grunican, E., Ellis, J, T., *Historia Kościoła 1848 do czasów współczesnych*, Vol. 5, Warszawa, 1985

Aubert, R. P., Grunican E., Ellis, J. T., "Katolicyzm w świecie anglosaskim," in Rogier, L. J., Aubert R., Knowles, M.D., *Historia Kościoła 1848 do czasów współczesnych*, Vol. 5, Warszawa 1985

Balack, E. G., *Our Slavic Fellow Citizens,* New York 1928

"Beautiful new $50,000 Church is community center for Poles," *The Superior News Tribune,* April 29, 1917

Bluma, F. D. OFM, *A History of the Province of the Assumption of the Blessed Virgin* Bonusiak, A., *Szkolnictwo Polskie w Stanach Zjednoczonych Ameryki w latach 1984-2003. Analiza funkcjonalno-instytucjonalna*, Rzeszów 2004

Borum, T., *The History of the Milwaukeeans of Polish Descent and a Record of Their Contributions to the Greatness of Milwaukee*, Milwaukee 1946

Brozek, A., *Polonia amerykańska 1854-1939*, Warszawa 1977

Buczek, D., "Polish Americans and the Roman Catholic Church," *The Polish Americans*, Vol. 21:1976, No. 3, New York

Bukowczyk, J. J., *And my children did not know me; a history of the Polish-Americans*, Bloomington 1987

Bukowczyk, J. J., *Polish Americans and their History*, Pittsburgh 1996

Cirilli, A., *Diamond Jubilee 1961 of St. Mary's Church Wisconsin*, 1961

Cirilli, A., "St. Mary History, long, colorful – with long tenured priests," *The centennial Jubilee 1886-1986 St. Mary of the Seven Dolores Catholic Parish Hurley,* Wisconsin 1986

Crane, F., *The Catholic History of La Crosse*, La Crosse 1904

Curtiss-Wedge, F., *History of Trempealeau County, Wisconsin*, Chicago and Winona 1917

"Dictionary of Peoples," Report of United States Immigration Commission Senate Document, No. 662, 747, 338

Diocese of Superior, *Our Journey through Faith. A History of the Diocese of Superior*, Ireland 2005

Doman, M. T., "Mother Mary Angela Truszkowska, Foundress of the Felician Sisters," *Polish-American Studies*, Vol. 10:1953

Dotts, F. J., Paul, B., *The Badger State a Documentary History of Wisconsin*, Grand Rapids, Michigan 1979

Dusza, Edward, *Kalendarz polonijny 2010*, Stevens Point 2010

Endecavage, M. Ch., *The Chicago Felicians*, Chicago 1999

Federal Manuscript Census, Population Schedule 1870 and 1880, in Manuscript Collection, State Historical Society, Madison-Wisconsin

Fichter, J. H., *Priest and People*, New York 1965

Fisher, G. E., *257 Things You Should Know About The Diocese of La Crosse 1868-1993*, Stevens Point 1993

Fisher, G. E., *Dusk is my Dawn*, La Crosse 1969

Fox, P., *The Poles in America*, New York 1970

Geschichte Katholishen Kirche in Wisconsin, Milwaukee 1899

Goc, M. J., *From Past to Present: The History of Adams County*, Adams County 1999

Goc, M. J., *Native Realm*, Stevens Point 1992

Golembiewski, T. E., *Study of obituaries as a source for Polish genealogical research*, Chicago 1984

Greene, V., *For God and country: the rise of Polish and Lithuanian ethnic consciousness in America 1860-1910*, Madison 1975

Haiman, M., *Polish past in America, 1608-1865*, Chicago 1974

Hauck, J. L., "Catholic Church in Trempealeau County," in Curtiss-Wedge, Franklyn, *History of Trempealeau County Wisconsin 1917*, Chicago and Winona 1917

Heaming, H. H., *History of the Catholic Church in Wisconsin*, Milwaukee 1895

Herberman, Ch. G., Pace, E. A., Pallen, C. B., Shahan, T. J., Wynne, J. J., *The Catholic Encyclopedia*, New York 1911

Hetzel, G. A., "The Sacred in the City; Polonian Street Processions as Countercultural Practice," in *Polish-American Studies*, Vol. 60, No. 2 autumn 2003, Stevens Point

"History of Rusk County Wisconsin," *Rusk County Historical Society*, 1983

"History of St. Stanislaus BM Church Lublin," *Archives of Diocese of Superior* – parish catalog of St. Stanislaus Church in Lublin, Superior 1910

Hollnagel, G., "Polish Tradition adds to Arcadia Christmas," *La Crosse Tribune*, December 7, 1985

Jeremiah, S. M. CDF., "Rev. Dąbrowski and the Felicians," *Polish-American Studies*, Vol. 16:1959

Jones, G. O., *History of Wood County Wisconsin*, Minneapolis 1923

Jubilee 2000 Christ yesterday today and forever, Diocese of Superior, Olan Mills 2000

Kleban, E., Gromada, T. V., "The Polish Americans," *The Polish Review*, Vol. 21:1976, No. 3

Kolinski, D. L., "Shrines and Crosses in rural central Wisconsin," *Polish-American Studies*, Vol. 51:1994, No. 2, Stevens Point

Kolinski, D. L., "The Origin and early development of Polish Settlements in Central Wisconsin," *Polish-American Studies*, Vol. 51:1994, No. 1, Stevens Point

Kruszka, W., *A History of the Poles in America to 1908. Part 1-4*, Washington 1993

Kruszka, W., *Historja polska w Ameryce. Od czasów najdawniejszych aż do najnowszych*, Vol. 1, Milwaukee, Wisconsin 1937

Kumor, B., *The History of Polish roman-catholic St. Joseph church in Norwich, Conn. 1904-1970*, Norwich 1980

Kuznicki, E. M., CSSF, "The Polish American Parochial Schools," in F. Mocha, *Poles in America*, Stevens Point 1978

Kuzniewski, A.J., *Faith and fatherland*, Indiana 1980

Le Page, N. J., "Hands Foundation gives gift to Thorp Museum," *Marshfield News-Herald*, January 31, 2009

Libera, P., "Polish settlers in Winona," *Polish-American Studies*, Vol. 15:1958

Marchetti, L., *History of Marathon County Wisconsin and Representative Citizens*, Chicago 1913

Marthaler, B. L., Dorr, C. C., *Catholic Daughters of the Americas*, Rockville, MD 2003

McGlachlin, E. A., *Standard History of Portage County Wisconsin*, Chicago & New York 1919

Millenium of Christianity in Poland, Stevens Point 1966

Miller, F. H., *The Polanders in Wisconsin*, Milwaukee 1896

Morison, S. E., *The European Discovery of America Northern Voyages 500-1600*, Oxford 1971

"New St. Stanislaus Church to be dedicated May 16," *The Arcadia News-Leader*, May 13, 1948

Nowacki, L. S., "St. Stanislaus Congregation Superior," *Catholic Herald Citizen*, September 5, 1953

Nuesse, C. J., *The Social Thought of American Catholics 1634-182*, Maryland 1945

Orchard Lake Good News, No. 70:2002

Parish Book, *The Blue Hills Catholic Cluster, St. Mary – Bruce, SS. Peter & Paul – Weyerhauser, Assumption of the Virgin Mary – Strickland*, Wisconsin 1993

Parish Book, *Holy Family Church Poniatowski Wisconsin*, 1977

Parish Book, *History of St. Ladislaus Bevent Wisconsin*, 1971

Parish Book, *St. Lawrence Wisconsin Rapids Wisconsin*, 2004

Parish Book, *Holy Family Parish Ashland Wisconsin*, 1954

Parish Book, *Księga pamiątkowa złotego jubileuszu parafii świętego Piotra w Stevens Point, Wisconsin*, Stevens Point 1926

Parish Book, *Sacred Heart Congregation Polonia Wisconsin*, Stevens Point 1964

Parish Book, *Saint Boniface Chetek*, Chicago 1984

Parish Book, *Saint John the Baptist*, Wisconsin 1991

Parish Book, *Saint Peter Parish in Stevens Point, Wisconsin*, Stevens Point 1976

Parish Book, *SS. Peter & Paul Church Independence 1875-1975*, Wisconsin 1975

Parish Book, *St. Florian's Parish Hatley, WI 1885-1985*, Wisconsin 1985

Parish Book, *St. Hedwig's Church Congregation Wisconsin*, 1966

Parish Book, *St. John Cantius – 1887 Centennial 1987*, Wisconsin 1987

Parish Book, *St. John the Baptist in Peplin Wisconsin*, Wisconsin 1991

Parish Book, *St. Ladislaus, Bevent 1886-1986*, Wisconsin 1985

Parish Book, *Church of St. Michael Wausau, Wisconsin 1887-1977*, Wausau 1977

Parish Book, *St. Michael's 1887-1987*, Irick Studio

Parish Book, *St. Michael Catholic Parish Wausau Wisconsin*, 2000

Parish Book, *St. Michael's Church Junction City Wisconsin*, 1958

Parish Book, *St. Michael's Catholic Church Junction City, Wisconsin 125 Year Anniversary 1883-2008*, Wisconsin 2008

Parish Book, *St. Stanislaus Catholic Church*, Stevens Point 1992

Parish Book, *St. Stanislaw Parish Stevens Point, Wisconsin*, 1961

Parish Book, *St. Mary of Czestochowa Catholic Church,* Wisconsin 1983

Parish Book, *The History of Saint Bronislava,* Wisconsin 1996

Parish Book, *St. Bronislava a Centennial History 1896-1996*, Wisconsin 1996

Parish Book, *100th Anniversary of Sacred Heart Congregation*, Polonia, Wisconsin 1964

Parish Book, *Celebrating 100 years St. Adalbert Catholic Parish Rosholt Wisconsin*, Wisconsin 1998

Parish Book, *Parish of St. Michael the Archangel North Creek Wisconsin*, Wisconsin 1988

Parish Book, *Our Stewardship Program Holy Cross Parish La Crosse*, 1956

Parish Book, *Sacred Heart of Jesus Cassel Wisconsin*, 1986

Parish Book, *St. Casimir Catholic Church Stevens Point*, 1997

Parish Book, *Saint Casimir Parish 100th Anniversary, Town of Hull Portage County*, Wisconsin 1971

Parish Book, *Sto Lat Wiary 1881-1981*, Holy Rosary, Sigel, 1981

"Parish remembers 1880 Disaster," *Stevens Point Daily Journal*, July 26, 1972

Pastusiak, L., *Kościuszko, Pułaski i inni*, Toruń 2003

Peszkowski, Zdzisław J., *Ojciec Seminarium Polskiego w USA: ks. Józef Dąbrowski*, Warszawa 1942

Piątkowska, D., *Polish Parishes in New York,* New York-Opole 2002

Pienkos, A. T., *Ethnic politics in urban America, the Polish experience in four cities*, Chicago 1978

Polzin, T., *The Polish Americans Whence and Whither,* Pulaski, Wisconsin 1973

Potaczala, G., *Polacy na Trójcowie. History of the Holy Trinity Church in Chicago*, bmw (2006)

Praszałowicz, D., *Amerykańska etniczna szkoła parafialna. Studium porównawcze trzech wybranych odmian instytucji,* Wrocław 1986

Pula, J. S., *Polish Americans: an ethnic community*, New York 1995

Rajski, A., *100 years of Polonia in Windsor 1908-2008,* Windsor 2008

Record Herald Newspaper, Wausau, Wisconsin March 26, 1954

Record Herald Newspaper, Wausau, Wisconsin January 1, 1967

Renkiewicz, F., *Poles in America, 1608-1972: a chronology & fact book*, Dobbs Ferry, New York 1973

Renkiewicz, F., *The Polish Presence in Canada and America*, Toronto 1982

Rosholt, M., *A photo album of Marathon County 1850-1925*, Wisconsin 1978

Rosholt, M., *Our County, Our Story Portage County*, Wisconsin 1959

Rummel, L., *History of the Catholic Church in Wisconsin*, Madison, Wisconsin 1976

Sandberg, N. C., *Ethnic Identity and Assimilation: Polish-American Community*, New York 1974

Sanford, A. H., "Polish People of Portage County," *Polish Genealogical Society Newsletter*, Stevens Point, Wisconsin Spring 1989

Schaefer J., *The Wisconsin Lead Region*, Madison 1932

Siekaniec, L. J., "The Poles of Ashland, Wisconsin, 1884-1888," *Polish American Studies,* Orchard Lake, Michigan January-June 1949

Silverman, D. A., *Polish-American Folklore*, Illinois Press 2000

Słabczyński, W., *Polscy podróżnicy i odkrywcy*, Warszawa 1988

Smith, A., *The History of Wisconsin*, Madison 1973

Smith, C. J., Callahan J., *The making of Wisconsin*, Eau Claire, Wisconsin 1927

Stratford Centennial Book 1891-1991, Stratford, Wisconsin

Straub, A. G. assisted by Szymanski, Joe, *The History of Marathon, Wis. 1857-1957*, Marathon, Wisconsin 1957

Syski, Aleksander, *Ks. Józef Dąbrowski*, Orchard Lake, Michigan 1942

Taras, P., "The contribution of Polonia into the Development of the Roman-Catholic Church in the United States," *Biblioteka Polonijna*, Wrocław-Warszawa-Kraków-Gdańsk 1979, Vol. 4:1979

Targosz, S., *Polonia katolicka w Stanach Zjednoczonych w przekroju,* Detroit, Michigan 1943

The Staff of La Crosse Register, Holy Cross Seminary, La Crosse, Wisconsin 1951

Tindall, G.B., Shi, D.E., *Historia Stanów Zjednoczonych*, Poznań 2002

Thorp Courier, Thorp County Wisconsin, August 19, 1906

Times Review, La Crosse Diocesan Newspaper, September 17, 1970

Walaszek, A., *Polish Americans,* Western Reserve Historical Society, Cleveland 2002

Walkusz, J., *Polonia i parafia Matki Boskiej Częstochowskiej in London, Ontario*, Lublin-Pelplin 2007

Watrous, J.A., *Memoirs of Milwaukee*, Madison 1909

Wayne, A.G., *History and memories Portage County Belmont Township*, La Crosse, Wisconsin 1968

Wisconsin History Records Survey (Series 1953) 1936-42 Inventory of Church Records by County Box 226 Folder 11 County of Ashland

Wisconsin History Records Survey (Series 1953) 1936-42 Inventory of Church Records by County Box 229 Folder 12 County of Clark

Wisconsin History Records Survey (Series 1953) 1936-42 Inventory of Church Records by County Box 252 Folder 20 County of Taylor

Wytrwal, J. A., *Americans Polish Heritage*, Detroit 1961

Wytrwal, J. A., *Poles in America*, Minneapolis 1969

Zawistowski, T. L., "The Polish National Catholic Church: an acceptable alternative," in Mocha, Frank, *Poles in America*, Stevens Point 1978

Znaniecka Lopata, H., *Polish Americans*, New Jersey 1976

WEBSITES

http://holyfam.com/St.%20Stanislaus%20History.hmt

http://home.att.net/~Local_Catholic/CatholicUS-MilwaukeeWI.htm

http://www.ratzingerbendettoxvi.com/clementeX.htm

http://www.rootsweb.ancestry.com/~wibarron/communities/chetekhist.htm

www.ampoleagle.com/default.asp?sourceid=&smenu

www.catholic.org

www.CatholicOnline

www.DioceseoflaCrosse.com

www.holyfam.com/St.%20Stanislaus%20 History

www.holyrosarysigel.com

www.ipgs.us/parishhistories/ststaislaussuperiorwi.html

www.knights.com

www.Marathoncountyhistory.org/PlacesDetails.php

www.mcmillanlibrary.org/history/shorthistory.html

www.pannamariatexas.com,

www.pchswi.org/achives/church/st_bart. Html

www.pchswi.org/archives/church/religionPC.htm

www.pchswi.org/archives/church/st_stans

www.pchswi.org/archives/church/stmary_torun

www.pchswi.org/archives/communities/polonia.htlml

www.pchswi.org/archives/polish_heritage/soroka/soroka

www.pcswi.org/archives/st_bart.html

www.polishroots.org/history/PAHA/lenten_customs

www.polishroots.org/history/PAHA/polish_folkways

www.polishroots.org/history/PAHA/superior_wisc.htm

www.rc.net/superior/mjpps/stanshistory.html

www.rootsweb.ancestry.com/wispags/ch-stmary.html

www.rootsweb.com,Lublin History

www.rootsweb.com/-witaylor/histories/lublinhistory

www.scls.lib.wi.us/mcm/taylor/album_pt3.html

www.scouting.org/cubscouts/aboutcubscouts/history.aspx

www.stbrons.com/history.htm

www.stjosephstratford.org/church-history.html

www.stmaryshurley.org/history.htm

www.usgennet.org/usa/wi/county/clark/webbs/records

www.usgennet.org/usa/wi/county/webbbs/records/index

www.usgennet.org/usa/wi/county/webbbs/records/index.cgi